T0384106

Competing *for* and *with* Human Capital

It Is Not Just for HR Anymore

Competing *for* and *with* Human Capital

It Is Not Just for HR Anymore

By
J. Stewart Black

Routledge
Taylor & Francis Group

A PRODUCTIVITY PRESS BOOK

First edition published in 2019
by Routledge/Productivity Press
52 Vanderbilt Avenue, 11th Floor New York, NY 10017
2 Park Square, Milton Park, Abingdon, Oxon OX14 4RN, UK

© 2019 by J. Stewart Black
Routledge/Productivity Press is an imprint of Taylor & Francis Group, an Informa business

No claim to original U.S. Government works

Printed on acid-free paper

International Standard Book Number-13: 978-0-367-24719-5 (Hardback)
International Standard Book Number-13: 978-0-429-28409-0 (eBook)

This book contains information obtained from authentic and highly regarded sources. Reasonable efforts have been made to publish reliable data and information, but the author and publisher cannot assume responsibility for the validity of all materials or the consequences of their use. The authors and publishers have attempted to trace the copyright holders of all material reproduced in this publication and apologize to copyright holders if permission to publish in this form has not been obtained. If any copyright material has not been acknowledged please write and let us know so we may rectify in any future reprint.

Except as permitted under U.S. Copyright Law, no part of this book may be reprinted, reproduced, transmitted, or utilized in any form by any electronic, mechanical, or other means, now known or hereafter invented, including photocopying, microfilming, and recording, or in any information storage or retrieval system, without written permission from the publishers.

For permission to photocopy or use material electronically from this work, please access www.copyright.com (http://www.copyright.com/) or contact the Copyright Clearance Center, Inc. (CCC), 222 Rosewood Drive, Danvers, MA 01923, 978-750-8400. CCC is a not-for-profit organization that provides licenses and registration for a variety of users. For organizations that have been granted a photocopy license by the CCC, a separate system of payment has been arranged.

Trademark Notice: Product or corporate names may be trademarks or registered trademarks, and are used only for identification and explanation without intent to infringe.

Library of Congress Cataloging-in-Publication Data

Names: Black, J. Stewart, 1959- author.
Title: Competing for and with human capital : it is not just for HR anymore/J. Stewart Black.
Description: 1 Edition. | New York : Taylor & Francis, [2019] | Includes bibliographical references and index.
Identifiers: LCCN 2019005331 (print) | LCCN 2019006514 (ebook) | ISBN 9780429284090 (e-Book) | ISBN 9780367247195 (hardback : alk. paper) Subjects: LCSH: Human capital. | Competition. | Business planning. Classification: LCC HD4904.7 (ebook) | LCC HD4904.7 .B533 2019 (print) | DDC 331—dc23
LC record available at https://lccn.loc.gov/2019005331

Visit the Taylor & Francis Web site at
http://www.taylorandfrancis.com

Contents

SECTION III   COMPETING *WITH* HUMAN CAPITAL

Author

J. Stewart Black, Ph.D., is Professor of Management Practice in Global Leadership and Strategy at Institut Européen d'Administration des Affaires/European Institute of Business Administration (INSEAD). He specializes in strategy, organizational transformations, leading change in turbulent times, and stakeholder engagement.

Across his career Dr. Black has lived and worked in Europe, Asia, and North America. During that time he has worked with over 200 organizations and 10,000 executives. Much of this work has been with senior teams as they determine strategic direction, identify needed culture shifts, define required leadership capabilities to implement their strategies, and align systems, technology, and processes to support the organizational transformation. In addition, he is frequently a keynote speaker at conferences and events on the topics of leading change, organizational culture, global leadership, innovation, and strategy.

He is the author or co-author of over 100 articles and cases. His research has been published in the most respected academic journals, such as *Academy of Management Review, Academy of Management Journal, Journal of International Business Studies*, as well as in practitioner-oriented journals such as *Harvard Business Review, Sloan Management Review,* and *Human Resource Management Journal*, and he has published articles in and had his work featured in a variety of newspapers and magazines such as *Financial Times, The Wall Street Journal*, and *BusinessWeek*. He is frequently sought out by and has appeared in both print and live media.

He is also the author or co-author of 18 books, including best-selling textbooks, *Management: Meeting New Challenges, Organizational Behavior,* and *International Business Environments: Text and Cases*, as well as books written for practicing executives, such as *Failure to Globally Launch*, *It Starts with One: Changing Individuals Changes Organizations*, *The Global Leadership Challenge*, and *International Assignments: An Integration of Research and Practice*.

Dr. Black received his undergraduate degree in emphasizing psychology and English from Brigham Young University, where he graduated with honors. He earned his master's degree from the business school at Brigham Young University, where he was on the dean's list and graduated with distinction. After graduation, he worked for a Japanese consulting firm, where he eventually held the position of managing director. Dr. Black returned to the U.S. and received his Ph.D. in Business Administration from the University of California, Irvine.

Dr. Black started his career on the faculty at the Amos Tuck School of Business Administration, Dartmouth College, later becoming a professor of business administration at the University of Michigan and Executive Director of the school's Asia Pacific Human Resource Partnership. Prior to joining INSEAD, Dr. Black was Professor of Global Leadership and Strategy at IMD in Switzerland. At INSEAD Dr. Black served for four years as Associate Dean of Executive Development Programs for the Americas, as the founder and program director of Learning to Lead and Leading for Results, and as the program director for a variety of company-specific programs including Astra Zeneca, Ciba, Ernst & Young, Lexmark, HSBC, IFF, Jones Lang LaSalle, Manpower, National Commercial Bank of Saudi Arabia, Nissan, NYSE, Rio Tinto, Siam Cement, Shell, Takeda Pharmaceutical, Toshiba, and Western Union among many others.

Introduction: Straight to the Point

Let me get straight to the point. If you want to know if this book is worth your time, take just 20 seconds and answer the seven questions below:

1. Are *people* your firm's most important asset?	Yes	No
2. Does your company seek to be the *employer of choice* in its industry?	Yes	No
3. Is it harder these days than in the past to attract and retain the best talent?	Yes	No
4. Does the quality of talent make a difference to your company's performance?	Yes	No
5. Does your firm have a clear strategy for becoming the employer of choice?	Yes	No
6. Does your firm have good metrics for determining how you're doing as an employer of choice?	Yes	No
7. Do you hold managers and executives accountable for their successes and failures in waging and winning the war for top talent?	Yes	No

My guess is that for questions 1–4 you answered "Yes." If so, you're in the same boat as 92.7 percent of the 5,000-plus executives I've surveyed over the last several years—executives from more than 500 companies across 100 countries. How did you answer the next three questions? My guess is that for questions 5–7 you answered "No." Am I right again? If so, you're with 84.3 percent of the executives I've surveyed. In particular, if you answered "No" for question #7, then you share the company of 96.3 percent of the executives I have surveyed. In total, my survey results show that most executives believe that human capital is critical to business performance but that this belief is not supported by the needed strategies, metrics, and accountabilities. Consequently, when it comes to human capital, most executives and their firms exhibit what I call the human capital "say-do gap." In other words, executives and companies are talking the talk, but are not walking the walk.

This gap would be no big deal, if the talk—"people are our most important asset"—were mistaken. If people were *not* that critical to sustained competitive advantage and if sustained competitive advantage was *not* key to superior performance, not walking the talk about people being a firm's most important asset would not matter much. However, my research, and that of other scholars, demonstrates that today people *are* in fact a firm's most important asset and *are* key to sustained competitive advantage. Not only are they now, but increasingly as they go forward. Hence, this human capital say-do gap *is* a very big deal.

My research also demonstrates that part of the reason the human capital say-do gap exists is because many executives don't really understand *why* this oft-cited platitude about people is true. This point is worth repeating. In interviews with over 200 executives, almost all had an intuitive sense or believed that human capital was their most important asset but did not understand why or could not really articulate why that was the case. Ironically, it turns out to be more true than most executives even realize. In fact, it is so true that in this book I argue that the final competitive frontier lies in a firm's ability to compete *for* and *with* human capital. If this is the final competitive frontier, it is important to recognize that logically you have to win the battle *for* human capital before you can compete effectively *with* human capital. I stress this because unfortunately many executives don't see the coming battle "for" human capital or if they see it, they vastly underestimate its intensity and challenge.

I say many, but not all, fail to see or underestimate the coming challenge. In fact, recently, after a presentation I made in Europe on this topic, a CEO who had been in the audience came up to me and articulated my main point better than I put it myself. He said, "If *people* are the source of competitive advantage in the future and if it is only going to get harder to attract, retain, and engage them, then it seems to me that my company has *no choice* but to become the *employer of choice.*" Like I said, I couldn't have put it better myself.

Unfortunately, not all executives I speak with are so quick to get the point. In these cases, I try to shine a spotlight on the issue by asking a somewhat provocative question. That question is:

Help me understand why the people *you* want would want *you?*

In the nicest way possible, I put this question to you. "Why would the people you want to join or stay with or work hard for your company, your unit, or your team—why would they want you?"

Of course, if the people you want and need are rather mediocre, run of the mill, solidly average, firmly among the "also-rans," then the alarm bells I've sounded are irrelevant. After all, it is not that hard to attract and retain average talent. However, very few executives tell me that their mission or ambition is to be solidly among the large set of "also-rans." In fact, nearly all say the exact opposite. Their ambition is to be "the leading supplier," "the developer of choice," "the preferred partner," and so on. As a consequence, almost all executives need a great answer to the question, "Why would the people you want, want you?" However, having a great answer to this question is not the end, it is just the beginning. In addition, most executives need a clear strategy, a set of consistent metrics and measures, and a plan for how to hold managers accountable for putting the answers to my provocative question into practice. Without a strategy, metrics, and accountability, top executives will continue to talk the talk but not walk the walk—a failing that while only profoundly problematic at present will become a fatal flaw in the future.

At this point, you may asking yourself, "Why is he making such a big deal of competing for and with talent? Surely there are tangible assets like plant, equipment, real estate, etc. and financial capital that also determine the competitiveness of a business?" They do, but as I will demonstrate with data in subsequent chapters, the days when plant, equipment, real estate, and other tangible assets were the core sources of competitive advantage and when financial capital was the chief enabler are going, going, and nearly gone. Increasingly, competitive advantages come from intangible assets, like innovation, customer insight, and agility, rather than from tangible assets. To the extent that intangible assets become the source of competitive advantage, then human capital becomes the key enabler rather than financial capital.

To appreciate why intangible assets are so critical to competitive success and why human capital is the chief enabler, indulge me just for a moment.

First, think of an intangible asset that might be a competitive advantage for your firm. Perhaps it is innovation, friendly service, deep customer relationships, or something else. Whatever it is, imagine it being unavailable to you as source of competitive advantage. How competitive would you be? Or put differently, how competitive would you be if all you had as sources of competitive advantage were tangible assets such as plant, equipment, real estate, and the like? Nearly every executive I've ever put this question to has had the same answer. Without the possibility of having intangible assets (i.e., culture, innovation, customer intimacy, etc.) as sources of competitive advantage, virtually all executives feel they would be at a competitive *dis*advantage. This helps reinforce the importance of intangible assets in today's competitive landscape.

If you will humor me for a few more lines, I will illustrate why human capital rather than financial capital is the chief enabler of intangible assets as sources of competitive advantage. Again think of any intangible asset that could be or is a competitive advantage in your firm—innovation, customer insight, customer service, speed, etc. For example, let's suppose that your firm's culture of productivity gives your firm a competitive advantage because it helps keep your costs on a unit basis low. Now imagine taking people out of your culture of productivity, what would you have left? Or let's suppose that innovation is a competitive advantage for you. Imagine taking people out of innovation, what remains? Or imagine that your competitive advantage is customer service. Suppose you take people out of customer service, what do you have left? I'm willing to bet that the answer in every case is *"not much."* This is because in most cases, people are the sum and substance of intangible assets. While I am not saying that financial capital is irrelevant, I am saying that if you can't attract, retain, and motivate the right people, you can't just buy your way to the level of innovation, customer service, agility or whatever other intangible asset on which you hope to differentiate yourself. It doesn't matter how much cash you have on your balance sheet or can access in the capital markets, intangible sources of competitive advantage cannot just be bought. They have to be developed, and in virtually every case, the core of that development lies in attracting, retaining, and engaging the right people.

However, at this point don't just take my word for it; read on and I will supply a fair bit of empirical evidence to support these three key points:

1. Increasingly intangible assets are the source of competitive advantage.
2. People are the source of intangible assets.
3. Attracting, engaging, and retaining talent is going to get ever more difficult.

If all three of these statements are true, then creating competitive advantage via intangible assets is going to get more difficult in the future. While this may sound a bit over the top, trust me, the unvarnished reality is even more dramatic.

But don't despair. There are very concrete things you can do to win both the competition *for* and *with* human capital. (Otherwise, there is no need for me to write this book or for you to read it.) To get at what you can do to win both the competition *for* and *with* human capital, I have organized this book into three accessible sections or parts.

Part 1 lays out *why* competing *for* and *with* human capital is the final frontier for competition in the 21st century. Specifically, it reveals with data—data that some find quite startling—why tangible assets and financial capital used to rule the competitive advantage landscape and why that is no longer the case. Part 1 explains why there has been a shift from tangible assets to intangible assets and from financial capital to human capital as the basis for competitive advantage. This first section further explains why this will continue to be the case going forward. It also explains why it is getting and will continue to get ever more difficult to attract, retain, and motivate the people you need in order to create and sustain competitive advantages you need. Importantly, I demonstrate that this increased human capital challenge is NOT just related to the new generations of employees, such as Millennials, but applies to all the generations, including the Baby Boomers.

While *Part 1* lays out *why* competing *for* and *with* human capital are growing and critical challenges, Parts 2 and 3 lay out *how* to meet these two challenges.

Part 2 solves the challenge of competing *for* human capital. It does so by detailing *how* to create a superior value proposition that will enable you to get the people you want to want you—in other words, it outlines how to be able to attract, retain, and motivate the talent you need.

Part 3 solves the challenge of competing *with* human capital. This section explains *how* to create sustainable competitive advantage through people. It also examines how you can deeply imbed your human capital-based competitive advantages into your organization so that they become part of your firm's DNA. This helps you avoid the risk that your efforts will otherwise be viewed as just another "*flavor-of-the-month fad*"—soon to be forgotten.

Across all three sections of this book, I take a bit of a novel approach. Unlike some books, this one is not a collection of war stories loosely attached to an untested framework nor is it a theoretical model buttressed by academic studies with no practical application. Instead, I coordinate my research, and that of other scholars, to show how various concepts and tools that have been scientifically tested have been—and can be—applied in the real world to deliver real impact. Over the past three decades, the business executives I have worked with have found this rigorous but relevant approach quite helpful. I hope you find that to be the case here as well.

WHY ARE COMPETING *FOR* AND *WITH* HUMAN CAPITAL THE FINAL FRONTIERS?

1

As I mentioned, the vast majority of executives claim that people are their most important asset, but they don't walk the talk. What's behind this disconnect? Why do so many executives fail to link reality to their rhetoric?

In general, the human capital "say-do gap" ("talking the talk, but not walking the walk") is a function of the same force that causes us to say we should exercise more or eat better but then don't. The culprit? In a word—superficiality. This may seem like a flippant or overly simplistic answer, but it is neither. Allow me to explain.

Often we espouse things like "exercise is good for you" but we don't walk the talk because the truth is we often have a rather superficial understanding of why the statement is true. To illustrate this, let's take the example of the widely espoused platitude that "exercise is good for you." Stopping at the surface or simply accepting the platitude superficially contributes to not following through and not walking the talk in at least three ways. First, stopping at the surface keeps us from seeing fully what it takes to achieve the desired outcomes. It creates an artificially inflated balloon of positive expectations that burst the first time we encounter one of the hard realities of exercise (like getting up at 6 AM each day to go to the gym), and as a consequence we talk the talk but we don't walk the walk. Second, stopping at the surface of a truth keeps us from seeing the full value of the benefits (like a stronger immune system in the case of exercise). When we underestimate the benefits, it takes smaller negative consequences or surprises to make us feel like it's just not worth it and we talk the talk but fail to walk the walk. Third, stopping at the surface then causes us to miscalculate the ROI (return on investment). For example, for many getting up at 6 AM is a big price to pay just to lose a couple of pounds but may *not* be a big investment relative to having 20% more energy and 15% less days that you are sick.[1] A superficial understanding of exercise leaves us with a rather shallow belief and conviction that exercise is good for us. We say it, but we don't deeply mean it. As a consequence, when the alarm goes off at 6 AM, we hit the snooze button, turn over, and go back to sleep. We talk the talk but we don't walk the walk.

The dynamics of superficiality regarding human capital are no different. Like a thin puddle of water that quickly dries up under a hot, noon-day sun, our superficial understanding and resulting shallow belief in the importance of human capital quickly evaporates in the heat of having to actually formulate an effective human capital strategy, put in place metrics and measures, and hold executives accountable for human capital successes and shortfalls. Simplified: superficial understanding leads to shallow beliefs, which produce weak convictions, which in turn lead to poor or no follow through on what we espouse, and *voilà* we have the human capital "say-do gap."

Suppose the case I've just made makes sense to you. If so, I can imagine that you might be saying to yourself, "You know, he's right. I can see that a superficial understanding would lead to a weak conviction and that a weak conviction would result in a lack of aligned actual actions." Even if you are thinking this, you might want even deeper insights. In this case, you might naturally ask the question: "If a superficial understanding is the starting point for this chain reaction that leaves us talking the talk but not walking the walk, then what accounts for not diving deep enough into the issue in the first place? Why do so many of us stop at a superficial level of understanding? Why don't we dig deeper?" While this is a great question to ask, you may not like the answer. The main reason we don't dig deep enough to get the depth of understanding and strength of conviction to bridge the human capital say-do gap (or any other say-do gap for that matter) is because we allow ourselves to be a bit lazy—not physically but mentally lazy. But before you get too upset, give me a chance to explain.

I think you would agree that platitudes like "exercise is good for you" or "people are our most important asset" are inherently appealing. The problem is that it only takes a little bit of mental laziness before we unconsciously assume that our simple mental acceptance will be enough to lead to a strong conviction and real action. Yet, if we are honest, we know in the back of our minds that shallow beliefs, whatever they are about, generally do not generate the strength of conviction needed for us to walk the talk. In other words, deep down we know there is no free lunch, but we allow ourselves to be mentally lazy enough to assume that we can get something for nothing, that we can get the required strategies, metrics, and accountabilities for making people our most important asset with just a superficial understanding of *why* it should be the case.

To more fully illustrate this dynamic, let's return to the issue of exercise. We all know that in order to get up at 6 AM every morning and go to the gym we need a strong conviction that exercise is the right thing to do. A superficial belief that "exercise is good for you" just won't cut it. We also know that strong convictions do not miraculously appear out of thin air. Strong convictions require deep understanding. Deep understanding of why exercise is good for us takes some time, effort, and investment. However, if we are just a little bit lazy in our minds, we can avoid all these needed investments and inconvenient truths, look away, and fool ourselves (at least for a while) into assuming that if we just accept the platitude at the surface we will not only talk the talk but we will walk the walk.

In order to appreciate the pervasiveness of this human frailty, you only have to think about the billions of dollars companies make off it each year. For example, how many billions of dollars have companies made telling us that we can just "eat anything we want and still lose weight" or that we can "tone our abs while watching TV"? Deep down we know these "promises" are too good to be true. But they are appealing enough that *if* we just don't think about them too deeply, *if* we don't confront them too closely, *if* we are just a bit mentally lazy, we can maintain the wishful mirage that there is a free lunch.

Likewise, deep down we know that a shallow belief about people being our most important asset will not miraculously generate the necessary energy and investment required to ensure we have the needed strategies, metrics, and accountabilities to back up the platitude. Deep down we know the truth, but we allow ourselves to be just lazy enough to look the other way and avoid a direct confrontation with the fact that there is no free lunch. As a consequence, we simply don't dig deep enough to understand why people are our most important asset, and as a consequence, we fail to close the say-do gap and fail to walk the talk.

So at this point, let me offer a fair warning. Getting to the point that you can win the battle for human capital by putting in place the strategies, metrics, and accountabilities is *not* free. It requires some investment. I hate to break it to you, but there is no free lunch whether we are talking about exercise or human capital. Getting to the point where you can bridge the human capital "say-do" gap in your firm will require some investment on your part. That's the bad news. The good news is that my goal is to help make the necessary investment to bridge the say-do gap as interesting, engaging, and efficient for you as possible.

But before we get too deep into this, I keep using the term "say-do" gap as though it were unidimensional, but in fact it has two important forms or types. Highlighting the two different forms is important because the consequences of each are rather different.

I have already illustrated the first form of the say-do gap or what I will refer to as Type 1. Type 1 of the say-do gap is where we say something but then our actions fall short of living up to what we espouse. We may honestly intend for our actions to be aligned with our words but in the end they fall short. We say exercise is important and so we set the alarm, but then at 6 AM when it goes off, we hit the snooze button.

In the context of the human capital Type 1 say-do gap, we say people are the most important asset, but then we don't put into place the strategies, metrics, and accountabilities required to back up the claim; or we put all three in place, but they are inconsistent, weak, and otherwise insufficient. If we are guilty of the first form of the say-do gap (i.e., our actions are headed in the right direction but come up short), people typically perceive us as having good intentions but just not having sufficient discipline, motivation, or conviction to follow through.

In saying this, I am not suggesting that there are no negative consequences to this first form of the say-do gap. There are. Clearly, if we say people are our most important asset and then we fall short of aligned actions, the next time we state that people are our most important asset, employees will be a bit more skeptical about whether we mean it; they will doubt that we will walk the talk. They will think, "Hey, last time he didn't really follow through on what he said. I wonder if this time will be any different?" As a consequence, if we are guilty of the first form of the say-do gap, the next time we address the issue we start from a "credibility deficit."

Type 2 of the say-do gap is much more serious. In this second form, we don't just fall short of aligned actions, we are perceived as doing the opposite of what we espouse. In the case of human capital, we say people are our most important asset but then we treat them the opposite. For example, we say people are our most important asset but then when times are tough, the first thing we do is cut people. We say people are our most important asset, but when financial results fall short, we ditch training, we cancel development programs, we suspend mentoring initiatives, and the like. In this case, people quite often interpret the contradiction between our words and actions as hypocrisy. People may go so far as to interpret this second form as evidence that we purposefully lied, deceived, or misled them from the outset; we never really meant what we said.

The consequences of Type 2 say-do gap are usually rather serious. When our actions do not just fall short of our words but are perceived as misaligned with and opposite of what we espouse, the next time we espouse something, we don't just start from a credibility deficit, we start from "credibility bankruptcy." As with financial bankruptcy, getting out of credibility bankruptcy takes an enormous amount of effort and exponentially more time, effort, and energy than it took to fall into it.

Here, I realize that I am not telling you anything you didn't already know. The reason I stress both Type 1 and Type 2 say-do gaps is *not* because you don't know they exist (of course you do), but because it is easier than we think to stumble into the pits of both types of gaps. To put a spotlight on how easy it is to stumble into the gap, just ask yourself the following question:

■ During past economic downturns (such as happened in 1991, 1997, 2001, and 2009), did your firm increase or decrease its spending on human capital? Specifically, during any one of these downturns did your firm spend more or did it spend less on recruitment, hiring, training, and development?

If your firm is like 82 percent of the nearly 300 companies I have surveyed specifically on this issue, during economic downturns, your firm did not increase investments in human capital; it cut them, and typically cut them by more than it cut spending on most other items.

Cutting human capital expenses during economic downturns may seem like an innocent act or even a prudent one, but seen from the perspective of current or prospective employees, executives proclaiming that "people are our most important asset" and then cutting investments in human capital when times are tough can be, and often is, interpreted *not* as a prudent action but as a *hypocritical* move (i.e., a Type 2 say-do gap). With that interpretation comes all the more severe negative consequences. To illustrate this, let me share with you a recent experience.

Not long ago, I had the opportunity to listen to a CEO present to his troops at a "town hall meeting." During his speech, he repeated to his employees, more than once, the famous line, "*you* are *our* most important asset." Later, when the CEO and I were chatting in a fairly casual setting, I had an inconspicuous opportunity to ask him why he made such a point about saying that people were the firm's most important asset in his speech. "Because it's true," he replied with a bit of a skeptical look thrown my way for good measure. Given that we had known each other for some time, I pressed a bit further. "Yes, I know it's true but why? Why is it true? Why do you believe it? And why is it more the case today than 20 years ago?" He quickly replied, "Because," but then paused and stumbled to articulate any coherent or compelling reasons. Finally, he said a bit indignantly, "Because, without them, we wouldn't have a business." I wanted to ask why this was more true today than in the past. After all, the firm had human capital 10–15 years ago, but back then he hadn't made a big deal of it nor put forward the argument that without the proper talent they wouldn't have a business. I wanted to press this further but just at that moment several others joined our conversation and the opportunity to press the issue passed.

In relating this part of the incident, I'm not saying the CEO didn't believe what he said about people being the most important asset. Rather, I am saying that his belief was rather shallow because he didn't have a deep understanding of why it was true. As a consequence, you might not be surprised to learn that his firm had no strategy for how to attract and retain top talent, it utilized no metrics for measuring progress, and it did not hold executives accountable for performance regarding human capital.

If this first form of the say-do gap had only been observed by me and had gone unnoticed by his employees, it might not be any big deal. But the lack of strategy, metrics, and accountability was very much noticed by employees. His employees were plenty bright enough to spot this Type 1 say-do gap. Not only did they notice it, but the gap had a negative impact on the firm's recruiting results, turnover, absenteeism, and employee engagement levels, all of which were worse than its peers.

Sadly, insult was added to injury when, during the economic downturn in 2012 in Europe, the firm cut its investment in people development by 16 percent—a much bigger cut than for almost all its other activities or assets—despite the CEO's proclamation that people were the firm's most important asset. Again, this Type 2 say-do gap might not have had a big negative impact if I had been the only one who noticed, but I wasn't. The company's employees were not only bright enough to notice the Type 1 say-do gap but also this subsequent Type 2 gap as well. As one employee said to me, "If we are the most important asset, then why are we cutting our recruiting, training, and development costs more than our other expenses? It's a bit hypocritical. At the end of the day, it's not what our leaders say but what they do that tells us what really matters to them and what doesn't. You know we're not blind nor stupid." It should come as no surprise after committing this Type 2 "say-do gap" that employee satisfaction and engagement scores declined further and employees' assessment of top management's credibility plummeted.

However, don't get me wrong. I'm not trying to pick on this CEO or to imply that he was a bad leader. Not at all. I am simply using this case to illustrate what I see quite frequently. Many executives say people are their firm's most important asset but they don't have a deep enough understanding of why it is the case to drive a sufficiently strong conviction to cause them to not just talk the talk but also to walk the walk, especially when the going gets tough.

But surely every CEO knows, as does any experienced manager, that *actions speak louder than words*. In addition, surely every CEO knows that when reality doesn't follow rhetoric, the next wave of rhetoric starts from a credibility deficit. Of course they know this, and yet, the vast majority of leaders (and not just those at the top of the organization) suffer from a "say-do gap" when it comes to human capital. All this speaks volumes regarding how strong this human tendency is to superficially grab on to appealing platitudes or promises without putting in the required effort to reach a level of understanding sufficient to drive conviction and aligned action.

So the bad news is that we all have this frailty; to one degree or another we all allow ourselves to believe in the mirage that aligned action will follow from superficial understanding. The sad fact is that it doesn't and it won't. If we want a conviction strong enough to drive subsequent aligned action, we have to acquire it the old-fashioned way; *we have to earn it.*

The good news is that once earned, our deep understanding and the subsequent conviction can bridge the "say-do gap" and can cause us to not just talk the talk but to walk the walk. To test this principle, just think about how many pulmonologists you know who smoke? I'll wager it's not many if any. Pulmonologists have a deep understanding of the relationship between smoking and lung disease and so they personally follow the advice they give to their patients. But the depth of understanding they have did not come quick or cheap. Most pulmonologists spent 12 years in college and specialized training at a cost of over $200,000 to reach that depth of understanding. However, with that depth of understanding comes a sufficiently strong conviction for them to walk the talk.

But before you panic, I am not saying that you have to spend 12 years of study and $200,000 in order to reach a sufficient level of understanding and conviction of belief to walk the talk relative to people being your firm's most important asset. I'm only suggesting that a superficial understanding and a shallow belief will not bridge the current and pervasive human capital say-do gap. Although there are nearly 12 years of research behind this book, I don't think it will take you that long to read it. I also promise that it will not cost you $200,000 to reach a deep enough understanding to bridge the gap. With that in mind, let me briefly describe what each chapter in this section is designed to do for you.

Chapter 1 explains what has changed that has caused the change in the role of human capital relative to a firm's competitive advantages. Specifically, Chapter 1 examines the shift from *tangible assets* (such as plant and equipment) as the principal basis of competitive advantage and *financial capital* as its chief enabler *to intangible assets* (such as innovation, corporate culture, leadership, or brand) as the principal basis for competitive advantage and to *human capital* as its chief enabler. The major takeaway from Chapter 1 is that, although people have been part of organizations for a very long time, shifts in the nature of competitive advantage have moved human capital from "backstage to center stage," from "supporting cast to leading role."

Chapter 2 dives deeper into this shift and explains how and why competition in general and globalization in particular drove the diminishing impact of tangible assets as the source of competitive advantage and financial capital as its chief enabler. In Chapter 2, I go backstage and expose the role of six factors that accelerated competition and globalization, which in turn sped up the diminishing impact of tangible assets and financial capital.

Chapter 3 examines why, when firms started to reach the diminishing returns of tangible assets and financial capital, they began to look to intangible assets and human capital as alternative sources of competitive advantage. Chapter 3 also begins to explore how this seemingly innocent shift in source of competitive advantage had a much more intriguing impact on the balance of power between employers and employees. Specifically, I pull back the curtain and reveal that this shift in source of competitive advantage shifted power away from employ*ers* and toward employ*ees*. I then highlight how and why this shift in power has and will continue to make it more difficult for firms to attract, retain, and motivate the employees they want and need going forward.

Chapter 4 continues the examination of the shift in balance of power and its implications by unveiling four additional forces that have and continue to accentuate and accelerate this shift in power between employers and employees. Chapter 4 concludes by showing how the shift in competitive advantage and in balance of power makes a firm's ability to compete *for* and compete *with* human capital the final competitive frontier.

In summary, these first four chapters lay out plainly and at some depth why intangible rather than tangible assets are key to future competitive advantage and why you need people to secure both those intangible assets and competitive advantage. It also lays out why it is getting and will continue to get more challenging to attract, retain, and motivate the talent you need in order to secure the intangible assets competitive advantage that is required for sustained, profitable growth. With that overview, let's get started.

Note

1. Warburton, Darren E.R., and Crystal Whitney Nicol. "Darren E.R. Warburton." *Canadian Medical Association Journal.* N.p., 14 Mar. 2006. Web. 26 Apr. 2017.

Chapter 1

The Shift in Sources of Competitive Advantage

Wave of Change

Here's the frustrating thing about major shifts: by the time you can prove they are happening, it's too late to get out in front of them. Like the surf along the Southern California beaches where I grew up, you'll never catch a wave if you wait to see it rise up and crest. You have to start paddling long before the peak of the wave arrives; otherwise, you will miss it and be left behind.

Unlike the relatively tame surf of Southern California where I grew up, however, the sea change that is affecting competitive advantage and human capital is more like a tsunami (or what sometimes is incorrectly called a *tidal* wave). In order to appreciate the tsunami analogy, allow me a few lines to describe some key causes, characteristics, and consequences of tsunami waves.

Most severe tsunami waves are created not at the ocean's surface, as the term "tidal wave" conjures up in your mind, but at its floor. For example, one of the most devastating tsunamis in modern history occurred on March 11, 2011 off the eastern coast of Japan. It was caused when a portion of the Earth's crust, known as the Pacific Plate, slid under the section called the Honshu Plate—a process called subduction. However, subduction is rarely a smooth process. As the two plates grind against each other while trying to move in opposite directions, friction and pressure build up until literally the "slipping point."

When the slipping point was reached in 2011, it produced a 20- to 27-foot upthrust of the Honshu Plate along a 108-mile long seabed about 36 miles off the Japanese coast. This upthrust displaced trillions and trillions of gallons of seawater, causing the tsunami. As you likely recall, the results were catastrophic. According to the U.S. Geological Survey (USGS), the slippage created a 9.0 magnitude earthquake with a total energy release equivalent to 9,320 gigatons of TNT (600 million times the destructive force of the atom bomb dropped on Hiroshima in 1945).[1]

Because the displacement happened miles below the sea's surface, along the ocean's floor, the earthquake and upthrust caused only small ripples on the surface directly above. From the epicenter extending out hundreds of miles, the tsunami waves were so small that they barely rocked tiny fishing boats, even though the waves were traveling faster than a 747 jetliner. It was only when the tsunami waves entered shallow water near the shore that their might became evident. At that point, the waves rose to more than 132 feet at their highest and traveled more than six miles inland. Tragically, 15,891 people lost their lives in Japan (including 2,584 still listed as missing), and more than one million were displaced from their homes of which nearly 250,000 did not return.[2]

Major shifts in business have some scary similarities. Like a tsunami, by the time you can prove a major shift is occurring, it's too late to get in front of it. Although the results of being in the wrong place relative to a business shift may not be as fatal as being in the wrong place relative to a tsunami, the negative impact can still be devastating. My research suggests that many leaders and firms are poorly positioned for the coming shifts in competition and, worse, too many don't even *see* the coming tsunami.

I can't predict when this wave will crest, but the warning signs are clear, and the chance that this wave of change in competitive advantage will miraculously recede and reverse itself is just about zero. Therefore, the odds that unprepared firms will suffer significant negative consequences are about 100 percent.

Defining Competitive Advantage

To understand the change in competitive advantage and the new role of human capital, we need to step back and establish a sound but practical understanding of what a competitive advantage is and how to recognize one when you have it (and when you don't). In general, there are three major criteria for competitive advantage (see Exhibit 1.1).

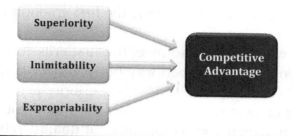

Exhibit 1.1   Factors of competitive advantage.

Superiority

The first necessary (though not sufficient) criterion for competitive advantage is superiority. In other words, you must be better than your competitors at whatever you believe is your advantage—be that economies of scale, geographic coverage, asset size, and so forth. However, you can't just be slightly better, you need to be *distinctively* better than your *competitors*. I stress both "distinctiveness" and comparison to "competitors" because as obvious as both might seem, too often when I talk to executives, their point of comparison is misdirected and their degree of superiority is miscalibrated.

Let me address the issue of comparison first. Although it may seem obvious that you have to compare yourself to your competitors and be better than they are, too often when I ask executives to tell me their firm's competitive advantages, their reference point is an internal one rather than an external one. For example, when asked recently, one executive commented, "We do many things well, but we are probably best at operational excellence." As you can see, she was not really comparing her firm's level of operational excellence to her competitors' level but rather to the various things internally her firm did well. In other words, she was offering up a *comparative advantage* rather than a *competitive advantage*.

As a simple parallel, if I asked you, "Can you throw a ball faster right-handed or left-handed?" you would likely have a very quick answer. Most people have a relative advantage with one hand or the other. If you answered that you can throw faster with your left hand, then you have a *comparative* advantage with your left hand. But having a *comparative* advantage does not necessarily mean that you have a *competitive* advantage. The first test of *competitive* advantage is *not* whether you can throw faster with one hand compared to the other but whether you throw faster than all the other people out there throwing the ball—regardless of whether you, or they, throw right-handed or left-handed. If you throw faster than all the others, you are on your way to satisfying the first criterion of competitive advantage (i.e., superiority).

I say "on your way" because to meet the first criterion you need to have not merely *any* level of superiority but you need a *distinctive* level. To understand why a distinctive level of superiority is required, we just need to take the perspective of a customer for a moment. While you may be fractionally better than your competitors at quality, reliability, innovation, etc., and while achieving that small difference may have been very difficult, these small differences are typically not so interesting to customers as they are to you. Why? Because trying to verify whether the small superiority you claim really amounts to anything or not is *not* free to customers. If your advantage is not distinctive, customers incur *transaction costs* in assessing and verifying your superiority. This transaction cost *you cause* (by not being distinctively superior) is added to the sticker price *you charge* and the result is an effectively higher price to *your customers*. The only way to avoid this higher effective price is to have *distinctive* superiority.

If we go back to my analogy of throwing a ball, the test of "distinctive superiority" is when you throw so much faster than your rivals that just by sight of the ball whizzing by or by the sound of the ball when it hits the catcher's glove someone could quickly tell that your throws were faster than the others. If someone has to get out a radar gun and measure speeds out 3 decimal places to see if your throws are faster, you don't have a distinctive superiority.

In summary, to pass the first test of competitive advantage, you have to be *distinctively superior.* Although the first criterion is the easiest to understand, in practice it is often misunderstood as relative rather than absolute superiority and miscalibrated as any degree of superiority rather than a distinctive degree.

Inimitability

Let's assume for the moment that your firm's economies of scale, geographic coverage, innovation, customer intimacy, or whatever is distinctively superior. In other words, you've passed the first test of competitive advantage. Now you have to pass the second test. Your distinctive superiority must be hard to copy; it must be *inimitable.* I say hard to copy not impossible because with enough time, money, effort, etc. virtually nothing is impossible to copy.

To illustrate this, let's again go back to my simple analogy of throwing a ball. Let's assume that you can throw the ball distinctively faster than others. The question now is: "How hard will it be for others to copy you and throw just as fast?"

Is your distinctively superior speed due to the ball you use? If so, it seems likely that others could go out and buy the same ball and soon close the gap on you.

Perhaps your superior speed is due to building up arm strength since you were five years old when you started throwing rocks at tin cans on a log. For argument's sake, let's assume over the years you spent more than 10,000 hours throwing rocks and balls at things to build up your arm strength. Someone could also spend that amount of time throwing and as a consequence potentially catch up to you. But they could not catch up to you in a day, a month or even a year; there simply aren't enough hours in that time frame to catch you. With a head start of 10,000 hours, it would likely take your rivals 5–10 years before they could close the gap on you.

Or let's suppose that you throw a ball faster than others because you have a naturally faster throwing motion due to an inherited high concentration of fast twitching muscle cells in your arm. In this case, others may never catch up to you because they simply don't have the same natural endowment. Or to compensate for their lower level of natural gift, they may have to come up with a combination of compensatory actions to close the gap with you. For example, they may have to innovate a new and superior throwing motion, come up with new arm strengthening technique, and then practice for hours, days, and months on end to close the gap and throw as fast as you naturally do.

In summary, in addition to distinctive superiority, for something to truly qualify as a competitive advantage it must be hard to copy. If your advantage is not hard to copy, then even if you have a distinctive superiority today, soon others will catch up; your advantage will be commoditized away; and it will soon yield no differential competitive benefit.

Expropriability

Finally, even if your firm is distinctively superior at something and even if that advantage is hard to copy, it doesn't qualify as a competitive advantage unless it (a) directly delivers value for customers *or* (b) *in*directly delivers value by enabling something else that directly delivers value for customers. It is only if your distinctive and inimitable advantage directly or indirectly creates value for customers can you *expropriate* some of that value from the market. "Expropriate" is a fancy word for the simple but important notion of being able to capture value from the market. You can't have superior results unless you can differentially expropriate value from the market. For example, you may be taller than everyone else and your height advantage may be very hard for others to copy. (After all rivals cannot just think and grow tall.) However, for your hard-to-copy, distinctive height advantage to pass the final test of competitive advantage, you must be able to extract value for it from the market? If the market is gymnastics, then your *inimitable* and distinctive *height superiority* may not enable you to capture much value. In contrast, if the market is basketball, your *inimitable* and distinctive *height superiority* may indeed allow you to expropriate value.

But what does "expropriating value" really mean or in concrete terms what does it look like in real life? In the vast majority of situations, you expropriate value in one of two fundamental ways: price premium or volume premium.

Price premium is the one we think of most often. If you have a hard-to-copy superiority that customers value, often they will pay you more for it. This is great, and, as long as you don't squander that price premium away with equally large cost premiums, your profit margin should be higher and you should make more money—you should be able to *expropriate* value.

However, in many cases, even though your customers value your hard-to-copy distinctive superiority, they will not give you a price premium; they will only give you a volume premium—meaning that at a competitive price, they will give you more of their business. While a volume premium may not seem as valuable as a price premium, it easily can be. We only need to do some simple math to see why.

Assume you have a net profit margin of 10 percent on a product that sells for an industry average price of $100. That yields a $10 profit per unit sold. Assume further that the average number of units sold per customer is 100. This means that you would make $1,000 profit per customer. Now assume that at a market standard price of $100 per unit, your firm's competitive advantage (e.g., speed, reliability, geographic coverage, etc.) causes customers to give you a 50 percent volume premium but no price premium. In this case you make $1,500 profit per customer or an additional $500 per customer (i.e., $10 profit per unit × 50 extra units). Not bad. And if you have any economies of scale, the higher volume might actually lower your unit costs and enhance your profit per unit from $10 to $11, in which case you make $1,650 per customer versus the industry average of $1,000. Even better.

So at the end of the day, expropriating value is a key criterion for competitive advantage. That expropriation is typically either through a price or volume premium. However, one type of premium is not inherently more valuable than the other. It just depends on the situation.

As a final note, if customers value your hard-to-copy superiority so much that they will give you *both* a price premium *and* a volume premium, please call me, because I would love to buy stock in your company. To appreciate how valuable a price premium combined with a volume premium can be, we only need to take a quick look at Apple.

First, let's briefly examine Apple's iPod—arguably the company's first non-computer breakthrough product. From the iPod's launch in 2001 until this book went to press, Apple has held roughly a 70 percent market share in portable music players. In general, market share is not a bad proxy for, or measurement of, volume premium. Also across the history of the iPod, Apple charged about 15–25 percent more for its product compared to its rivals. Effectively, Apple expropriated both a volume and a price premium. Even though iPods sales peaked in 2008 and declined significantly thereafter, since its launch, Apple iPods brought in $81 billion in revenue and made an estimated $28 billion in profits across all its different models. That means it brought in about $7.4 billion a year in revenue and over $2.5 billion a year in profits (about a 33% profit margin) just from this small device. While Apple no longer breaks out iPod sales because they have declined so much and smartphones have largely substituted for portable music players, an $81 billion revenue run and a $28 billion profit capture over 15 years is not bad—or some would argue is amazing. Had the iPod been a stand-alone company during this period, its price and volume premiums would have put it among the top 25 most profitable *firms* in the *Fortune 100* list.

Now let's look at Apple's iPhone. Since late 2007 when the first iPhone was launched, Apple has seen its market share (measured by sales) in the smartphone industry go from next to nothing to number one in 2017 at about 42 percent. The price for an iPhone during this period averaged more than 100 percent higher than its rivals. As evidence that Apple did not squander its price premium with an equal cost premium, Apple's share of profits in smartphones in 2017 was more than 90 percent. In other words, its profit share was 100 percent higher than its market share (measured by sales). Its market share measured by units shipped was only about 20 percent. To put this in perspective, Apple made 9 times more money in 2017 on its smartphones than all smartphone competitors (including Samsung) did *combined*!

These two examples are all the more remarkable when you view them within the context of the growth in Apple's stock price. Just consider that if you had invested $10,000 in Apple stock on October 23, 2001 when the first iPod was launched and invested another $10,000 on June 29, 2007 when the first iPhone was launched, that $20,000 investment would have become over $2.2 million as of late 2018! Now you see why if you have a competitive advantage that delivers *both* a price and volume premium I'd like you to let me know so I can buy stock in your company.

Competitive Advantage Summary

As I mentioned earlier, many executives espouse people as their most important asset and a source of competitive advantage. However, without a sound but practical definition of competitive advantage, it would be difficult to intelligently argue for or against the notions that people are the most important asset or that they are more important now than in the past. But now that we have established that a competitive advantage requires superiority, inimitability, and expropriability, we can take up this discussion. Specifically, we can trace key changes in the sources of competitive advantage over time without losing our bearings. This is critical because while the sources of competitive advantage have changed, the three criteria I just presented have not. Whether we are talking about competitive advantage 10 centuries ago, 10 decades ago, or 10 days ago, the three criteria I've outlined remain constant—like the North Star.

This foundation regarding competitive advantage will also facilitate our deep dive into understanding why people are and will increasingly be the source of competitive advantage. I stress this because if executives are to close the human capital "say-do gap," forging a deeper understanding of *why* competing *for* and *with* human capital is the final frontier of competition is a prerequisite.

Three Million Years of History of Competitive Advantage

As stated, even though the definition and essence of competitive advantage have not changed over the eons, the sources of competitive advantage have changed. In order to understand the current shift in the basis of competitive advantage, however, we first need to peer backward in time. But don't worry; this will be a very quick trip through history. I divide over 3 million

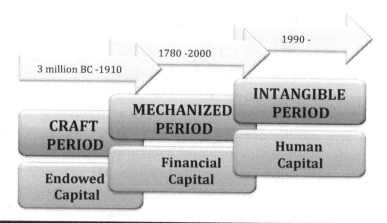

Exhibit 1.2   Three periods of history and capital.

years into just three somewhat overlapping historic periods: the Craft Period, the Mechanized Period, and the Intangible Period (see Exhibit 1.2).

The Craft Period of Competitive Advantage

What I call the Craft Period lasted from the Stone Age to the beginning of the 1900s (more than 3 million years). During this time, competitive advantage largely rested in hands—physical hands. If your hands could craft a better stone hammer, fashion a sharper spear, weave a higher quality fabric or cultivate more abundant crops, you had the beginnings of a competitive advantage. If your hammer, spear, fabric, or crops were hard for others to copy, you were even further up the path toward achieving competitive advantage. If others also wanted your superior and hard-to-copy hammer, spear, fabric, or crops, and you could expropriate value from the market, you arrived at the promised land of competitive advantage.

However, during this period you could only leverage your competitive advantage so far. Communication by runner, transportation by horse, and the lack of large-scale production (meaning no economies of scale) restricted how far and wide you could ply your competitive advantage.

These limitations also meant that neither financial capital nor human capital were critical to success (they were helpful, but not critical). For example, even if you had lots of money, you couldn't buy greater craftsmanship or purchase machines to replicate your craftsmanship. Likewise, access to human capital didn't help you much either. Even if lots of people were available to employ, it took a long apprenticeship for them to learn and master the craft from you and you could personally train only a few apprentices at a time even if thousands were available. As a consequence, neither financial nor human capital was that helpful during the Craft Period. Instead what I call "endowed capital" was key—in other words, the talents and capabilities with which you were endowed or blessed were key.

Endowed capital, coupled with some hard work, helped you become a better maker of stone hammers, fashioner of spears, weaver of cloth, or farmer of crops. The greater your endowed capital and the harder you worked, the more likely that your superiority was hard for others to copy. With superior and hard-to-copy stone hammers, spears, cloth, or whatever, you simply needed someone to value it and expropriate that value.

However, during the Craft Period virtually all value expropriation was through price rather than volume premiums. This was for the simple reason that the inability to mass-produce your products meant that volume premiums were simply unattractive to you. With no real economies of scale, you had no incentive to expropriate value through volume premiums; you only had incentive to expropriate value through price premiums. Rather than getting more volume, what you cared about was how many extra eggs or how fat of a hog you could get in payment for your hand-crafted products.

The Mechanized Period of Competitive Advantage

As the sun set on the Craft Period and rose on the Industrial Revolution, it ushered in what I call the "Mechanized Period of Competitive Advantage." And although the three fundamental criteria of competitive advantage did not change, the source did.

During the Mechanized Period, machines replaced hands, and economies of scale replaced craftsmanship as the basis for competitive advantage. In addition, financial capital replaced endowed capital as the chief enabler. Like a tsunami, however, the initial waves of this sea change produced barely noticeable ripples on the surface of commerce during the first 50 to 80 years of the Mechanized Period (roughly 1780 to 1860), which is why the Craft Period and Mechanized Period overlapped and co-existed for quite a while. Nevertheless, from 1860 to 1900, the ripples grew. Still, it wasn't until we entered the 20th century that the biggest waves of mechanization rose up and crashed down onto the shores of craftsmanship. For example, although James Watt patented the steam engine in 1781, it wasn't widely used for travel or to power factories for another 75 years. Likewise, although Thomas

Edison invented the first commercially practical incandescent light in 1879, it took another 50 years (1929) before 90 percent of Americans had electric lights in their homes.

Like a tsunami, the first 120 years of the Mechanized Period created only small ripples that largely went unnoticed, especially by those who were deeply embedded in the Craft Period competitive advantages. Then just as the waves of the tsunami in Japan seemed to rise out of nowhere as they reached shallow waters near the shores, so too did the Mechanized Period seem to rise up and appear out of nowhere around the turn of the 20th century. Over the next 30 years, what were before small ripples of change in competitive advantage turned into giant tsunami waves, which when they crashed down wiped out millions of craftsmen across the world. The economy-of-scale limitations of hands simply couldn't compete with the higher volumes, greater reliability, and lower costs generated by machines. As a consequence, when the small ripples of conflict that had been rolling in for arguably 120 years turned into giant waves of destruction, it was too late for most craftsmen. As the waves crashed down over the next 20 or so years, the impact was broad and deep. Literally whole cottage industries were leveled. Craftsmen such as barkers, blacksmiths, chandlers, coopers, cutlers, dyers, fletchers, furriers, glassblowers, hatters, joiners, potters, sawyers, skinners, tanners, thatchers, weavers, and wheelwrights were swept away. As a consequence, the battle between industrialist and craftsman was largely over by 1940. As these battles between craftsmen and industrialists died out, the conflicts between *industrialist* and *industrialist* surged.

As industrialists turned their attention to each other, a new competitive frontline emerged in which industrial rivals engaged in an arms race to overwhelm each other with ever greater economies of scale. This in turn required ever greater financial capital because new and better machines and factories were not free. Essentially the winning industrialists were those who with more financial capital could buy and build bigger and better machines to manufacture a better hammer, fabricate a higher quality shirt, or harvest a bigger crop more economically than their mechanized rivals. This shift in competitive advantage from hands to machines put tangible assets—property, plant, equipment, tools, etc.—at center stage. Quite simply, the size and quality of the machines and related property, tools, and other tangible assets largely determined the economies of scale that could be achieved and the competitive advantage that could be leveraged. In addition, because it took money to acquire, maintain and improve these tangible assets, greater access to financial capital, not endowed capital, separated winners from losers.

This sounds well and good but is there empirical evidence to support the claim of the importance of tangible assets during this time? Is there a way to show how much the markets valued tangible assets relative to the total value of a firm? For public companies, there is a fairly straightforward way to get at this. You simply look at the relationship between market value and net asset value of a company. The net asset value is commonly referred to as the "market-to-book" or "price-to-book" value. Despite its fancy name, this ratio is fairly easy to understand. To get the book value of a company, you go to the firm's balance sheet and essentially subtract liabilities from assets to get the net worth or "book" value of the company. You then take that value and divide it by the total number of shares the firm has outstanding. That gives you the book value per share. You then compare that book value per share to the market value of the company per share (i.e., the open market price per share).

A share price-to-book value ratio of 1 to 1 means that the market is paying $1 for every $1 of book value (i.e., net worth). A ratio of 2 to 1 means that the market is paying $2 for every $1 of net value on the balance sheet. Or a different way to view it is that the market is paying $1 for every $1 of net value on the balance sheet and then paying an additional $1 for value the market sees but is not reflected on the firm's balance sheet.

If we look at the market value of publicly traded firms in the U.S. from 1930–1980, we find that most of it was composed of their net tangible assets (i.e., assets minus liabilities on the balance sheet). Specifically, the price-to-book ratio during this period fluctuated a little but averaged about 1.40. This meant that on average for every $1.40 in firm market value, $1.00 was represented on the balance sheet via the firm's net assets. Thus, during these 50 years, on average about 71 percent of a firm's market value was tied to its net tangible assets—its plant, equipment, tools, land, inventory, etc.

To understand why this was so, we only need to think about a typical firm during this period. Consider Ford, for example. In the early 20th century, Ford's output was directly linked to the size and scope of its property, factories, equipment, tools, and other tangible assets. The storyline for Ford and other firms in this competitive drama was a simple one, as illustrated in Exhibit 1.3.

- Access to financial capital allowed Ford to buy bigger and better equipment.
- Bigger and better equipment allowed Ford to produce more and better cars.
- Producing more cars allowed Ford to capture economies of scale that in turn lowered unit costs.

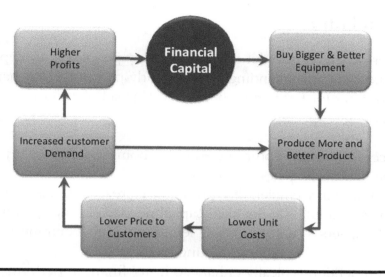

Exhibit 1.3   The virtuous cycle of financial capital and tangible assets.

- Producing at lower unit costs allowed Ford to push prices down to levels that stimulated demand while maintaining good profit margins.
- Stimulating more demand meant that Ford could produce more cars to sell, which again helped them produce more at lower unit costs.
- Producing more cars to meet increased demand at lower unit costs generated absolute higher profits for Ford.
- Higher profits produced both greater internal access to financial capital (via cash flow) and external access to financial capital (via debt or equity markets).
- Greater access to financial capital enabled Ford to maintain and improve existing equipment or purchase new equipment and a virtuous cycle was born; growing stronger with every turn of the wheel.

This basic storyline is not a new one, and several scholars have examined it in much greater detail than I can here,[3] but the key points are clear. Once the tsunami of the Mechanized Period of competitive advantage had crashed down on the shores of the Craft Period, the battle was one of simply getting into the virtuous cycle captured in Exhibit 1.3 and working hard to crank this flywheel harder and faster than competitors. While this was the basic story, it had two complementary subplots:

1. Barriers to Entry
2. Vertical Integration

Barriers to Entry

The "barriers to entry" subplot is one that many people fail to appreciate, but it is critical for understanding how the early part of the Mechanized Period played out for Ford and other firms. This subplot in the story had five main components:

- As successful firms captured greater economies of scale, they increased the minimally efficient level of entry.
- As the minimally efficient level of entry increased, it raised the entry barriers (including the financial capital needed) for new competitors.
- Higher barriers to entry typically led to fewer new entrants and less intense competition among existing rivals.
- Less competition typically enhanced firms' financial performance because they did not compete away profits.
- Enhanced size and performance generated both greater internal sources of financial capital and access to external sources.

All of this simply worked to sustain the original competitive advantage in tangible assets and the critical role of financial capital. As a consequence, it is easy to see how the subplot of higher barriers to entry reinforced the main storyline of tangible assets as the key source of competitive advantage and financial capital as its chief enabler.

Vertical Integration

The "vertical integration" subplot was also important and, to some extent, it complemented higher entry barriers. The vertical integration subplot had four keys:

- Greater throughput and economies of scale were not only influenced by the amount of physical assets available for processing, but also by the size, reliability, and quality of inputs.
- Lack of sophisticated information and communication technology in the first half of the 20th century made the transaction costs between firms along the value chain high, creating a natural incentive for vertical integration (i.e., an incentive for firms to own key inputs into their production process).

- Through vertical integration, firms could better control their inputs and, as a result, could better enhance their throughputs and better capture their targeted economies of scale.
- The subsequent increase in scale and size associated with vertical integration reinforced higher entry barriers and elevated further the importance of access to financial capital.

Entry barriers and vertical integration both served to reinforce the virtuous cycle of tangible assets and financial capital. These dynamics are what allowed Ford to turn the automobile around the turn of the century from a curiosity that only the very rich could afford ($50,000 in today's prices) into something that millions of middle-class families could afford. As evidence, consider that by 1920 after 11 years of perfecting the economies of scale in Ford factories, the price of a Model T had fallen 60% and cost only $395 or about $5,161 in 2018 dollars.

These reinforcing dynamics are captured in Exhibit 1.4 and are what enabled Ford to capture 50 percent of the U.S. auto market by the 1930s. As it illustrates, physical, tangible assets were central to these competitive dynamics. Therefore, it is not surprising that tangible assets represented a lion's share of what the market used to determine a firm's value.

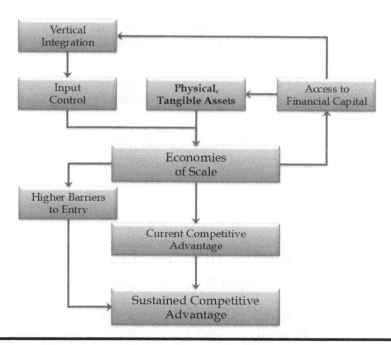

Exhibit 1.4   Tangible assets and competitive advantage.

In stressing the important role of tangible assets in determining firm value, I do not mean to suggest that Ford (or any other company at the time) did not have *intangible* assets, or that those intangible assets didn't have value. Nor do I mean to suggest that only financial capital mattered. Even in its early days, clearly Ford had intangible assets, such as its brand, and those intangible assets had value. Ford also had human capital and the people it employed mattered as well. However, the price-to-book ratio of Ford (and virtually any other company of the time) illustrates that tangible assets and financial capital ruled the day. For example, when Ford was first publicly listed in 1956, 70 percent of its value was tied to its net tangible assets. From then until 1998, tangible assets on average explained more than 80 percent of Ford's value, and in fact, through 1997 explained over 90 percent of Ford's value.

To further understand why tangible rather than intangible assets played such a strong role in the value of firms during the early and middle of the Mechanized Period of Competitive Advantage, we should also keep in mind the large role that manufacturing played in the overall economy of the U.S. (as well as other developed countries) during the early 20th century.

At the turn of the 20th century, manufacturing comprised about 70 percent of the U.S. economy. This emphasis on manufacturing vs. services is easy to see in the composition of the workforce. As an example, Dr. Leonard Nakamura examined the prevalence of what he termed "creative workers" (architects, artists, engineers, entertainers, etc.) as a percentage of the total workforce at the turn of the 20th century.[4] He noted that in 1900 the number of "professional creative workers" was only 200,000 or just 0.7 percent of all employment. By 2000, however, creative workers numbered 7,600,000, which represented an eightfold increase as a percentage of the workforce.

Even though intangible assets existed, and human capital played a role in competitive advantage during the early and middle Mechanized Period, tangible physical assets and financial capital played *the starring role*. Intangible assets and human capital were more like obscure stagehands or invisible understudies.

The Decline of Economies of Scale, Tangible Assets, and Financial Capital

What happened to change this picture? What happened to diminish the role of tangible assets and financial capital? Just as most things experience birth, adolescence, and a prime, they also experience decline. The same holds true for the role of economies of scale, tangible assets, and financial capital in the history of competitive advantage. Economies of scale, which were at the heart of competitive advantage via tangible assets during the early to middle Mechanized Period, were gradually commoditized as the sun set on the 20th century. They were commoditized because they had reached their natural limits. After all, economies of scale do not thrive indefinitely. At some point, they produce diminishing levels of returns following along an "S-curve." Exhibit 1.5 offers three different snapshots of firms (the dots) moving along the lifecycle of economies of scale during the Mechanized Period.

In the early days of the Mechanized Period (roughly 1870–1920), only a few firms had climbed very far along the economies-of-scale curve. Those early movers enjoyed important advantages. As they moved up the curve and got bigger and had greater internal and external access to financial capital, they gained more advantage for their growing economies of scale.

Seeing the advantage of economies of scale, rivals had little choice but to jump on the curve and try to work their way up it as fast as they could. However, by the 1930s to 1950s, the first movers were well into what is often called the "fat" part of the curve. It is during this period that "first mover advantages" can really show up. In fact, during this period the differential between the early winners and the latecomers can be so great that governments often break up, enact anti-trust legislation, or otherwise limit the power of early movers. Governments often take anti-trust actions at this stage out of fear that the virtuous cycle for the biggest players is so strong that the smaller players have no hope of effectively catching up and competing; they simply cannot get their economies of scale high enough to get their unit costs low enough to challenge the "big boys." Governments at that point often fear that if nothing is done to aid the small players or limit the large players, the virtuous cycle for the largest early movers will only

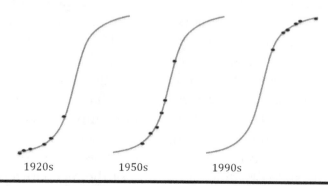

1920s   1950s   1990s

Exhibit 1.5   Diminishing returns over time of economies of scale.

grow stronger with every crank of the flywheel until they have a virtual monopoly. This is part of what was behind the break up of companies such as Standard Oil and AT&T in the U.S.

However, barring the emergence of a monopoly, as the earliest movers move ever higher on the curve, they get closer and closer to the point of diminishing returns. At this point on the curve, building a factory 50 percent larger than the previous one doesn't yield the same decrease in costs as before. Ironically, as the earlier movers hit the diminishing return portion of the curve in the 1960s and 1970s, the second and third movers entered the fat part of the curve. As a consequence, it didn't take long before the relative distance between the early movers and later arrivals started to shrink. In the 1980s and 1990s as enough firms reached the top of the curve, economies of scale and tangible assets became commoditized and declined or even disappeared as a means of differentiation. At this point, firms increasingly were forced to compete on price. When whole industries are pushed into price wars because they are so far up the economies-of-scale curve, typically the entire industry suffers. We witnessed this dynamic play out in a variety of industries such as steel, paper, home appliances, desktop computers, and commercial airlines in the last third of the 21st century.

Think of it this way. If you have a basketball team composed of players who are all 6 feet 11 inches tall and are playing against teams whose players are 5 feet 11 inches tall, your difference in height is a real advantage. However, suppose after a period of time that your team height increased but more slowly and now your players average 7 feet 1 inch. In contrast, your opponents grew much faster, and although they started out years ago averaging 5 feet 11 inches, they now average 6 feet 11 inches. Your team and your competitors are now very tall, but now height no longer makes as much of a difference in determining who will win the game.

Likewise, when you have the majority of firms bunched up at the diminishing return portion of the economies-of-scale curve for tangible assets, tangible assets no longer make *the* difference. However, I want to be clear that it is *not* the case that firms do *not* have tangible assets or that those assets and access to financial capital do *not* matter; they do. Just as height still matters in basketball. Rather, it *is* the case that these assets and access to financial capital have less of a differentiating impact. Just as height determines less of the outcome of the game when players on Team A average 7 feet 1 inch and players on Team B average 6 feet 11 inches. For many firms, this was the state of affairs at the end of the Mechanized Period of

Competitive Advantage and the close of the 20th century and the dawn of the 21st century.

Notes

1. http://www.bosai.go.jp/e/pdf/Preliminary_report110328.pdf
2. "Damage Situation and Police Countermeasures Associated with the Tohoku District – off the Pacific Ocean – Earthquake." National Police Agency. http://www.npa.go.jp/archive/keibi/biki/higaijokyo_e.pdf
3. Baruch Lev, 2001. *Intangibles: Management, Measurement and Reporting*, The Brookings Institution, Washington, D.C.
4. Leonard Nakamura, 2000. "Economics and the New Economy: The Invisible Hand Meets Creative Destruction," Federal Reserve Bank of Philadelphia *Business Review*, July/August, pp. 15–30.

Chapter 2

The Accelerant Roles of Competition and Globalization

Even if you accept this illustration of what happened to the power of economies of scale, to the value of tangible assets, and to the role of financial capital, it still begs the question, "What factors drove the speed of this change?" After all, the Craft Period lasted many millennia. Why did the Mechanized Period last just two centuries?

If you wanted to point just one finger and single out one culprit that pushed firms up the economy-of-scale curve and commoditized tangible assets and access to financial capital, you would point the finger at *competition*. How this happened is as simple as it is powerful, which I will illustrate in the next few paragraphs.

As it became clear that a craftsman's hand simply could not compete against industrialist's machines, early industrialists pushed up the economy-of-scale curve. As one industrialist gained a cost or quality advantages with a new or better machine and larger and more productive plant, others industrialists had little choice but to respond. As they did, the gap between them would shrink, and the first mover would have no choice but to move higher on the curve. The laggards would in turn have no option but to respond again or get left far behind. However, as they all ascended the curve, tussling back and forth as they climbed, the differential impact of each move to improve tangible assets diminished. But as firms were keeping their eye on their rivals behind them or on their left or right and trying to increase their own competitive pace of ascent, many failed to look ahead and see that they were only accelerating their arrival at the flatland of diminishing returns.

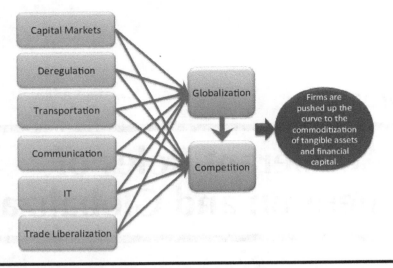

Exhibit 2.1   Drivers of the commoditization of tangible assets and financial capital.

Like a logger who as he swings his axe faster and harder to stay ahead of the competition only accelerates the rate at which the axe blade dulls. As an ironic consequence, the faster the logger swings his axe only serves to accelerate the diminishing impact of each chop of the axe. The diminished impact is the same as it is for firms pushing themselves closer and closer to the diminishing returns portion of the tangible asset S-curve.

But even if competition is the headline culprit in this tale of diminishing returns, the full story lies in the subplot of one co-conspirator and at least six henchmen.[1] The co-conspirator was globalization and the six henchmen were capital markets, deregulation, transportation, communication, IT, and trade liberalization (see Exhibit 2.1).

While it is well beyond the scope or intent of this book to describe these key trends in any detail, it is helpful to highlight them enough to demonstrate their role in driving firms high enough on the tangible asset and financial capital curve to the point that the diminishing returns left them with virtually no alternative but to jump to a new curve.

Capital Market Improvements

As I already described, during the Mechanized Period, financial capital was a critical resource as firms raced to buy and build bigger and better machines, plants, and factories in order to capture economies of scale faster than competitors. Responding to this growing demand for capital, financial firms in particular and financial markets in general increased their ability to provide both debt and equity capital in order to satisfy this growing demand from corporations. Over time, the increased effectiveness and efficiency of capital markets were such that they could supply capital not just to the largest firms but to mid-sized and small firms as well.

As one way to grasp how size came to matter less and less in accessing financial capital, consider the growth of IPO (initial public offering) funding for new companies. Specifically, as the U.S. entered the 20th century, IPO proceeds as a percentage of GDP in the U.S. rose from 0.15 percent in 1890 to 1.4 percent by 1927—an 833 percent increase.[2] Thus, while small firms had less access to capital than large firms, over this period they gained more than an eight-fold increase in access.

We can get a broader view of the increase in capital markets by going beyond IPOs and looking at the general market. In the U.S. arguably the best proxy for this change is the New York Stock Exchange (NYSE). The NYSE began in 1792 and adopted its formal constitution 25 years later in 1817. At the beginning of 1900 (after being in existence for more than 100 years), the NYSE had only 123 stocks listed with a total value of $2.86 billion. The top 10 companies accounted for about 40 percent of the total value.[3] One hundred years later in 2000, it had over 3,000 companies listed, which were worth $12.37 trillion![4] By then the top 10 companies accounted for only 10 percent of the total.

As financial capital in various forms and from a wide variety of institutions became more available, an organization's size became less of an advantage in accessing financial capital. As this became the case, firm size became less important in securing tangible assets needed to acquire and maintain competitive advantage. Barriers to entry thus came down. As barriers to enter came down, more firms entered. As more firms entered, the race intensified and the increased competition pushed more firms onto the economy-of-scale curve and pushed them all ever higher up the curve to its point of diminishing returns.

Deregulation

Deregulation also played an important role in increasing competition and driving firms up the economy-of-scale curve to the point of diminishing returns. Specifically, deregulation of industries such as transportation, airlines, financial services, electricity, and power, especially from the 1960s through the 1980s, made it harder (or in some cases impossible) for one firm to dominate an industry. As more and more firms populated an industry, competition intensified. This in turn put more firms on the curve and pushed them higher up the curve and closer toward the natural limits of economies of scale.

Transportation Improvements

The massive changes in transportation that occurred during the Mechanized Period are too numerous to mention. Here I provide a few illustrative examples:

- The completion of the transcontinental railroad in the U.S. in 1869 allowed freight and people to go from New York to San Francisco in six days instead of the 60 days to six months previously required when traveling by ship or by wagon—and far fewer people lost their lives along the way, as well.
- With the enactment of the Federal-Aid Highway Act of 1956, a total of 47,714 miles of freeways were constructed connecting all 48 "lower" states. The project cost $426 billion in 2006 dollars (when the system celebrated its 50th anniversary). It is estimated that the U.S. economy gained $6 in benefit for every $1 invested in the project, and trucking transportation costs were reduced by an average of 17 percent.[5]
- The implementation of containerization in the late 1960s lowered the cost of shipping many goods to the point where they could be shipped to new and distant destinations and still remain competitively priced. In addition, containerization shortened total shipping time by increasing port productivity by 20,000 percent.[6]

These and other advances in transportation meant that more firms (not just the few and the large) could economically secure raw materials, as well as ship their finished goods, all around the world, driving both globalization and competition.

Communication Improvements

As with transportation, improvements and advancements in communication are too numerous to cite a comprehensive list. That said, some examples of the increased speed and scope and decreased costs of communication illustrate how these improvements fueled both competition and globalization:

- A three-minute call from New York to London in 1930 cost $300 (in 2010 prices). By 2010, the same call, using Skype or other Internet-based options, cost about $0.03—a 99.99 percent cost reduction.
- The cost of transmitting a trillion bits of data in 1970 was $150,000. By 2010, the cost was about $0.10—a 99.99993 percent decrease.

As with transportation advancements, communication innovations, and improvements lowered entry barriers and enhanced firms' ability to expand abroad and still keep their far-flung operations organized. As firms expanded geographically, the pace of competition quickened and firms worked even harder to leverage their tangible assets. In addition, the various communication advances lowered transaction costs between firms, and with this, the previous incentives for, and the power of, vertical integration fell. The lowering of the need for vertical integration in turn made firm size less of a barrier to entry. This in turn provided opportunities for new companies to enter the fray and for competition to escalate.

IT Improvements

Separating IT improvements from communication improvements isn't easy, but even if we focus only on computing power and price, the changes are phenomenal and their effects on how quickly companies (big and small) could capture economies of scale are staggering.

- In 1975, computing power and price was such that it cost approximately $1 per instruction per second. By 1995, that had dropped to $0.01 per instruction per second—a 99 percent cost reduction.
- In 1970, it cost $1,000 to send 45 kilobytes a second one kilometer. By 2000, it cost $0.10 to send 45 gigabytes a second one kilometer—a million times more information could be sent a distance of one kilometer at a 99.99 percent reduction in cost.
- In 1956, IBM introduced the first hard disk drive with 50, 24-inch disks and a memory capacity of five megabytes. In 1980, the company introduced a refrigerator size IBM 380 that cost over $100,000 and had a storage capacity of 2.5 gigabytes. By 2010, you could buy a personal

computer with a hard disc drive of two terabytes for around $2,000. Or in other words, in the space of 30 years you could get nearly a thousand times as much memory for 98% less money.

As the cost of computing power dropped and actual power skyrocketed, even small firms were able to afford computing power that 15 years before only the largest and richest firms were able to buy. With this, firm size and financial capital mattered less and less, the scope of the competitive landscape increased, and the intensity of competition soared.

Liberalization of Trade

All of these changes made it theoretically possible to source, ship, manufacture, and sell globally. In addition, the political environment also changed in ways that allowed this theoretical potential to achieve commercial reality. Specifically import duties and rates were lowered significantly between 1956 and 1973. The GATT (General Agreement on Tariffs and Trade) Geneva II, Dillon, Kennedy, and Tokyo rounds during this period reduced tariffs by approximately $350 billion, and reduced tariff rates by an average of 30 percent. These early but important liberalizations significantly increased exports as a percentage of world GDP and accelerated globalization, which in turn elevated competition.

Globalization Tipping Point

The result of these major changes (and others beyond the scope of this book) was that competition intensified dramatically both directly and through the great facilitator of globalization. Toward the close of the 20th century, more than ever before, these changes in what we might label the "big six" meant that you could venture out from home to win new customers in new markets more than ever before. However, in the process of venturing into foreign lands, you were also likely to encounter and provoke new rivals and their competitive responses. At the same time, foreign rivals, many of which you had never heard of before, could come from literally anywhere in the world to your home turf and steal your customers away and provoke you. As a consequence, it is easy to understand how globalization intensified competition. With greater competition, firms had little choice but to push farther up the economy-of-scale curve and try to squeeze out of their tangible assets every last ounce of competitive advantage. However, as they pushed farther up the curve, they pushed themselves closer and closer to diminishing returns. Put differently, they pressed harder and harder on the gas pedal but at some point the pedal was all the way to the floor and the car just couldn't go any faster and increasingly there wasn't a lot of difference in speed among the racers.

Although these dynamics were active for several decades, it was only in the 1990s, the last decade of the 20th century, that global competition in particular had built up enough momentum to have wide impact. To some readers this may sound strange because firms such as Coca-Cola or Nestlé went global long before 1990. However, as you will see from the empirical data in a moment, these iconic firms were the exception rather than the rule. The reason is because it simply took a while for the political and technological factors I highlighted earlier to gain full traction and drive globalization across most industries and firms. When this finally happened, though, globalization surged ahead and dramatically intensified competition.

The first wave of this increase in globalization can be seen in exports—an issue referred to earlier in this chapter. Although firms have been shipping goods around the world for literally hundreds of years, Exhibit 2.2 shows the dramatic increase that advances in trade liberalization, transportation, communication, and the like had on global exports as they surged

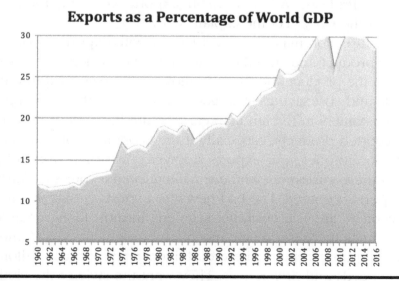

Exhibit 2.2 Global exports as a percentage of world GDP.

Sources: World Investment Report 2015; UNCTAD; World Bank.

forward in the mid-1970s. Specifically Exhibit 2.2 shows that exports as a percentage of world GDP was about 10 percent until the Kennedy and Tokyo rounds of GATT and the full implementation of containerization boosted it by nearly 50 percent. For the next 30 years, that percentage fluctuated somewhat, but averaged about 15 percent.

However, once communication, IT, and other innovations were widely disseminated by the mid-1990s, exports gained increased traction and surged again. As a consequence, over the next decade-and-a-half, exports shot up 75 percent, with the notable pullback relative to the financial crisis of 2008 and global recession of 2009 but subsequent recovery and stabilization at just under 30 percent.

However, exports were a double-edge sword. On the one hand, as an exporter, they gave you access to a greater set of customers and increased revenues. On the other hand, greater ease of exports enabled foreign competitors to send products into your home market and potentially take customers and revenue away from you. In both cases, the result was increased competition. This increase forced you, your domestic competitors, and your foreign rivals to all move ever farther up the economy-of-scale curve, pushing you ever closer to the point of diminishing returns.

If exports were the only aspect of globalization, we might be able to relax because it seems that as a percentage of world GDP exports may have leveled off; however, as I have documented in a separate book with a long-time colleague, Professor Allen Morrison, exports were only the beginning not the end of the story.[7] Let me explain why.

By their nature, you make the most money with exports if you can standardize your product and ship the same thing everywhere in the world. Standardizing the product and process allows the greatest capture of economies of scale and cost savings. The good news is that there are a good number of customers in foreign markets who are happy to buy your standardized exported products, especially if the economies of scale you captured allow you to offer your exports at lower prices than "locally" produced goods. I call these customers who are willing to take your standardized exports "export accepters." The bad news for exports is that as important as "export accepters" are as a customer segment, in most foreign markets and for most products there is a much, much larger segment of customers who are not easy export accepters; these customers want products tailored to their unique needs and preferences. They want the style of the clothes, the taste of the food, function of the refrigerator, the size of the box of laundry soap, and so on customized to what they need and locally prefer.

When firms discover that in order to meet these needs and penetrate this larger segment of customers they have to modify their products, they see that incorporating all these adjustments "at home" and then exporting the different product variations to the different markets around the world just doesn't make as much economic sense as making these customized products closer to their end destination. As a consequence, they start to make direct investments into foreign markets (FDI). They make capital investments in various tangible assets, such as plant, equipment, warehouses, land, offices, etc. As they do this, these "foreign invaders" typically provoke a competitive response in the local players. The local players usually do not just roll over and allow the foreign invaders to take market share without a fight. Rather, the local firms in response typically move up the curve to capture additional economies of scale or risk having too few tangible assets of sufficient scale to compete.

But where is the empirical evidence to back up this description and explanation that globalization moved beyond exports? In Exhibit 2.3, we see an explosion in foreign direct investment assets as a percentage of world GDP beginning in the late 1990s. Keep in mind that this is after the first surge in exports in the 1970s and even after the second surge in exports in the early 1990s. While there was a major pullback in FDI with the financial crisis of 2008 and the "Great Recession" of 2009, FDI reaccelerated afterward.

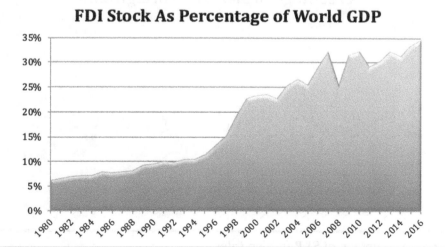

Exhibit 2.3   Foreign direct investment stock as a percentage of world GDP.

Source: World Investment Report 2017; UNCTAD.

In combination, these data illustrate the dramatic rise in globalization via exports and subsequently FDI, especially since the mid-1990s. As a consequence, we can see that while indeed there have been firms that have been global for a long time, the broad and sweeping effects of globalization are much, much more recent. This wave of globalization has in turn served to drive greater competition—at home and abroad.

But if it is the case that globalization has surged across more firms since the mid- to late-1990s, we should see that reflected in the percentage of revenue coming from outside a firm's home market. One of the best databases to track this over time is the Standard and Poor's 500. Exhibit 2.4 reveals a dramatic rise in international sales as a percentage of companies' total revenue beginning in the late 1990s, just as one would expect with the rise of both exports and FDI.

In summary, the data show that the first important spurt of globalization happened in the mid-1970s and was largely due to increases in exports. Then as the innovations discussed earlier in this chapter took hold and as firms saw the limits of exports, a new burst of globalization via FDI was launched in the mid-1990s and carried into the first decade of the 21st century. The direct impact of the various changes on competition and their indirect impact via globalization, pushed firms farther up the economies of scale and tangible asset curve. However, with every move up they made,

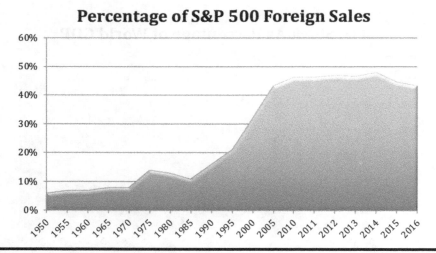

Percentage of S&P 500 Foreign Sales

Exhibit 2.4   Percentage of S&P foreign sales.

Source: S&P 500 2016: Global Sales in Review; www.spindicies.com accessed 09/09/2017.

the benefits they sought got smaller and smaller as they hit the diminishing return portion of the curve. By the late 20th century and early 21st century, the sun was setting on the Mechanized Period of competitive advantage. In the words of economics Professor Baruch Lev, "Once economies of scale in production have essentially been exhausted, production activities, intensive in physical assets, became commoditized and failed to provide a sustained competitive advantage and growth."[8]

The market recognized the diminishing returns and over time ascribed a smaller and smaller portion of a firm's value to its book value even as total tangible assets increased dramatically as illustrated in Exhibit 2.5 for the S&P 500.

Specifically, Exhibit 2.5 shows that the total value of firms' tangible assets increased nearly 2,200 percent in absolute terms across this entire timespan, while their relative impact on firm value decreased. In other words, even though the total value of firms' assets was growing dramatically, their share of firms' overall value was shrinking. Thus, even though tangible assets were going up in absolute value, firms were already so far up the economy-of-scale curve that the differential competitive advantage and financial performance gained through increased tangible assets were diminishing. They diminished to such a point that by the dawn of the 21st century, net tangible assets accounted for only 20 percent of a firm's value, whereas just 30 years prior they had accounted for more than 80 percent.

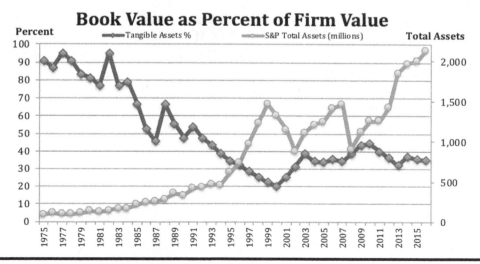

Exhibit 2.5   Declining value of tangible assets.

Source: YCharts.com accessed 24/10/2016.

Summary

In this chapter I have illustrated that competition pushed firms up the economy-of-scale curve to the point of diminishing returns. This push was amplified by globalization, which in turn was accelerated by improvements in capital markets, increased deregulation, advancements in transportation, communication, and IT, and by the lowering of trade barriers. Despite a significant increase in tangible assets over this period, the market recognized the diminishing distinctive competitive advantage that tangible assets could provide and as a consequence decreased the portion of firm value ascribed to tangible assets from an average of about 85% from 1975–1985 to about 35% from 2004–2016.

Notes

1. Anant K. Sundaram and J. Stewart Black, 1995. *International Business Environments: Text and Cases*, Englewood Cliffs, NJ: Prentice-Hall.
2. Thomas Philippon, 2011. "The Size of the U.S. Finance Industry." newyorkfed. org accessed November 10, 2014.
3. Elroy Dimson, Paul Marsh, and Mike Staunton, 2002. *Triumph of the Optimists: 101 Year of Global Investment Returns*, Princeton University Press, Princeton, NJ.
4. NYXdata.com accessed May 12, 2015.
5. Wendall Cox and Jean Love, 1996. "Forty Years of the U.S. Interstate Highway System." Publicpurpose.com accessed September 20, 2014.
6. Wayne K. Talley, 2009. "Container Port Efficiency and Output Measures." http://www.trforum.org/forum/downloads/2009_31_ContainerPortEfficiency_paper.pdf
7. Allen J. Morrison and J. Stewart Black, 2014. *The Failure to Launch Globally*, Global Leadership Press.
8. Baruch Lev, 2001. *Intangibles: Management, Measurement and Reporting*, The Brookings Institution, Washington, D.C.

Chapter 3

The Rise of Intangible Assets and Human Capital

As mentioned at the end of Chapter 2, even though powerful forces led to the decline of tangible assets as the source of competitive advantage and financial capital as the chief enabler, it doesn't automatically follow that intangible assets and human capital would take their place. How and why this happened is the focus of this chapter. However, it is helpful to start off with a visual overview of dynamics discussed in Chapter 2 (see Exhibit 3.1).

The Nature, Appeal, and Rise of Intangible Assets

Even if we understand the dynamics described earlier and accept the declining role in competitive advantage of tangible assets, economies of scale, and financial capital, we are still left with a critical question: "What makes intangible assets and human capital attractive replacements?" The answer is two-fold. First, unlike tangible assets, most intangible assets offer increasing rather than diminishing returns to scale. Second, compared to tangible assets, intangible assets are much more difficult to imitate, which as you recall was a critical criterion for competitive advantage.

Increasing Returns to Scale of Intangible Assets

As discussed in Chapter 2, at some point tangible assets have diminishing returns to scale as illustrated in an "S-shaped" curve. In contrast, intangible

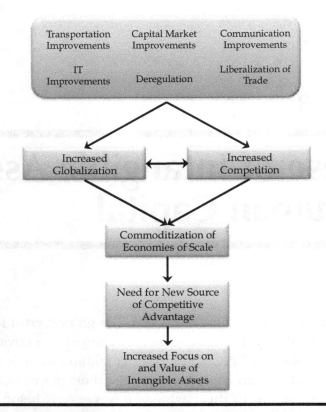

Exhibit 3.1   Decline of tangible assets and the rise of intangible assets.

assets in general have increasing returns to scale. Instead of an "S-shaped" curve, intangible assets generate an upward-sloping, hockey stick, or exponential curve (see Exhibit 3.2).

What explains the difference in the shape of the curves and what difference does this difference make? The principal explanation of the difference in the shape of the curve can be found in the fundamental nature of tangible and intangible assets. Tangible by definition means "perceptible by touch." Therefore, tangible assets are those that have a physical nature that you can physically verify. This has several important implications.

First, the physical nature of tangible assets is such that they cannot be in two places at once. As a consequence, once a tangible asset is fully utilized, you need to add another one to increase output. For example, once your building is fully occupied, you need to add another if you want more space; once a plane has all its seats filled with passengers, you have to add another plane if you want to fly more passengers. Thus, as the occupancy of a building or a plane increases, both its output and efficiency improves, but then tops out once it is fully utilized.

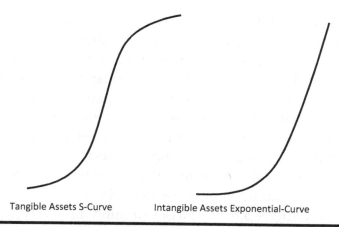

Tangible Assets S-Curve   Intangible Assets Exponential-Curve

Exhibit 3.2   Tangible and intangible asset curves.

Second, the physical nature of tangible assets means that the more you use these assets, the more you must spend to maintain and repair them in order to keep them running. For example, from your own experience, you know that the more you drive your car, over time the more you have to spend on maintenance and repairs in order to keep it running. While you are repairing or maintaining the asset, it is either not in use or not in optimal use. For example, it is hard to repair a tire as you drive down the road. As a consequence, over time, as maintenance and repairs increase, the effectiveness and efficiency of the asset flattens out and you reach the top of the "S" curve.

Third, and somewhat ironically, the more you spend to keep tangible assets in use and the more you use them, the faster you move toward the end of the assets' useful life. Again, just think of the case with your own car. Suppose you drive your car 50,000 miles per year. To keep it running you would have to spend some money on maintenance (such as an oil change every 7,000 miles) and likely before too many years you would have to spend some money on repairs, not just on maintenance. Driving 50,000 miles a year even assuming an adequate spend on maintenance and repairs will result in reaching the end of the car's useful life in fewer years than if you drove it only 12,000 miles a year.

Fourth and finally, once you get to the end of a tangible asset's useful life, if you still desire the benefit it provided, you then have to replace the "used up" asset with a new one. With a car, even if you do a good job keeping your car maintained and repaired, at some point it simply makes more economic sense to retire the old car and replace it with a new one. At that point, you are starting over on a new "S-curve" for the new car, building, plane, or whatever other tangible asset is involved.

Hopefully, at this point it is clear why tangible assets have "S-shaped" curves and you can see even more clearly how the shape of the curve affects the asset's economies. At the beginning of the curve when the asset is just beginning to be utilized, its effectiveness and efficiency is low. As you increase the asset's utilization, its effectiveness and efficiency increases. As the asset gets fully utilized, its effectiveness and efficiency improvements decline and the curve flattens out. As the asset ages and requires maintenance and repairs just to keep it running, its effectiveness and efficiency flattens even further and its economies decline to the point where you reach the end of the curve and the end of the tangible asset's useful life. At that point, it costs more to keep the old asset running than to replace it with a new one, so you retire, decommission, shut down, dispose of, or otherwise get rid of the old tangible asset and replace it with a new one.

In contrast, the nature and character of intangible assets are almost the exact opposite. As a consequence, both the shape of the curve and the nature of intangible assets' economies are markedly different from tangible assets.

First, the non-physical nature of intangible assets allows them to be in two places at once. For example, some firms consider their brand to be an intangible asset. There is nothing that prevents the brand from being utilized by two different salespeople at two different places at the same time. Thus, while the inability of tangible assets to be in two different places at the same time restricts and flattens their curve, the lack of this restriction is in part what contributes to intangible assets having exponential rather than "S-curves."

Second, the non-physical nature also means that in most cases the more you use an intangible asset, the lower, rather than higher, its maintenance and repair costs. For example, the more your brand is promoted, the more self-reinforcing it becomes and the less you have to actually spend to maintain it. Obviously, this enhances both the effectiveness and efficiency of the intangible asset and contributes to its exponential curve.

Third, and perhaps most strangely of all, the more you use an intangible asset, in most cases, the more you actually prolong or push out, rather than shorten or pull forward, its useful life. Again, in the case of a brand, the more you utilize and reinforce a brand, the stronger it becomes and the longer it is likely to last. This does not mean that if you ignore and do nothing to maintain intangible assets, such as brand, that they will not eventually atrophy and die; they will. But it does mean that that the greater use of intangible assets such as brand or culture tends to make them stronger and thus prolongs rather than shortens their useful life. This obviously contributes to an exponential rather than "S-shaped" curve.

Fourth, many intangible assets have network effects—meaning that the greater the use of the network, the more value the network creates. Think Facebook. The more people who use Facebook, the more value Facebook has for you as a user and the more likely you are to use it. This in turn serves to reinforce the network's value. This also contributes to an increasing slope to the curve rather than a flattening of the curve as in the case of tangible assets.

All this combines to yield the exponentially increasing curve that I illustrated previously in Exhibit 3.2. It also contributes to many intangible assets having increasing effectiveness and efficiency and improving rather than diminishing economies over time as compared to tangible assets.

Inimitability of Intangible Assets

The reality is that the non-physical nature of intangible assets also makes them generally harder to copy. For example, it is much more difficult to reverse engineer a friendly culture and copy it than a piece of machinery. Although you can get your hands on a tangible piece of equipment that your competitor might use, how do you get your hands on your rival's customer service culture? While you can reasonably determine if you have all the pieces of equipment needed to operate a particular plant similar to your competitor's, how can you determine if you have all aspects of your competitor's customer service culture in hand? Although you can see the real estate on which a rival's plant sits, how can you see the recruiting, onboarding, performance management, development, and other relevant foundations on which its service culture is built? Whether an intangible asset takes the form of culture, leadership, brand, customer knowledge, JV management expertise, M&A capabilities, or whatever, intangibles are by their non-physical nature harder to reverse engineer, understand, and copy.

While this is the good news, as I will present in Part 3 of this book, the bad news is that putting intangible assets in place so well that they become competitive advantages is much easier said than done. Although the non-physical nature of intangibles make them hard to copy, this same non-physical nature means that there is no guarantee that you will achieve distinctive superiority or be able to expropriate value from the market with intangible assets, both of which you need in order to turn a hard to copy intangible asset into a competitive advantage.

In summary, intangible assets are an appealing alternative to tangible assets as a source of competitive advantage because they have increasing rather than diminishing utility curves and because they are much harder to copy. However, all this being the case, for an intangible asset to be a competitive advantage, it still must meet all three of the required criterion of superiority, inimitability, and expropriability.

The Rise of Human Capital

If we accept the decline of tangible assets as differentiators as the 20th century drew to a close, and if we agree as to why intangible assets were an appealing replacement, the next question is, "Why has human capital replaced financial capital as the chief enabler?" Why couldn't financial capital be used to purchase intangible assets today and in the future as it had purchased tangible assets in the past? Why did human capital become the chief enabler? As briefly discussed at the outset of this book, the answer is fairly straightforward. If you think about intangible assets such as culture, leadership, service innovation, etc., people either are the sum and substance of most intangible assets or they are the principal driver. You likely recall the simple mental exercise I asked you to do in Chapter 1: Take people out of any intangible asset you could think of and see what you have left. Whether the focus of your company's intangible assets is customer service, cross-unit collaboration, product or service innovation, speed, or whatever, if you take people out of the equation, you typically have not much left.

Intangible Assets, Human Capital, and Expropriating Value

Up to this point, I have presented the case for why once tangible assets reached diminishing returns firms viewed intangible assets as attractive alternatives and why human capital (versus financial capital) would be intangible assets' chief enabler. However, unless intangible assets can yield expropriation opportunities, they would not be a source of new competitive advantage. As a consequence, even if people were naturally the chief enabler of intangible assets, human capital would not become more important than financial capital if firms were not able to expropriate value via intangible assets. Perhaps the best way to get at this issue of expropriation is to look at it from ground level by examining a couple of specific company examples.

Southwest Airlines

Southwest Airlines is a company most readers know and can easily understand. Arguably Southwest invented the low-cost airline business model when it was founded more than 40 years ago. Without going into great detail regarding its strategy, everyone knows that it keeps its costs lower than its competitors so that it can keep its prices lower, stimulate demand, and still make money. This has been and remains its basic strategy. If we dive a bit deeper, we can look at exactly how it keeps its costs lower than competitors and what keeps customers coming back and driving revenue up for the company. In the process, we can examine the role of both tangible and intangible assets in Southwest's competitive advantages.

In terms of its lower costs, it is important to point out that over the last decade, Southwest has been able to keep its costs approximately 20 percent lower than the major U.S. airlines (i.e., United, Delta, and American). Most executives would agree that costs that are 20 percent lower than your competitors constitute a distinctive level of advantage. One way Southwest keeps its costs lower than competitors is through higher tangible asset utilization. As you might guess for an airline, Southwest's key tangible assets are its planes. The fundamental metric used to measure effective plane utilization is hours per day it is in the air flying passengers. Each Southwest plane is in the air about 15 percent more hours per day than the other major U.S. airlines. Most airline executives would also agree that 15 percent higher plane utilization constitutes distinctively superior efficiency. Southwest's high plane utilization is in part due to the fact that it uses only Boeing 737s. Using only one type of plane means that cleaning crews and others can turn the plane faster at the gate and maintenance crews can get the plane in and out of the maintenance and repair shop faster as well. Obviously, the less time the plane spends on the ground or in the repair shop, the more time it can spend in the air earning money. Having one model of plane also means that if for some reason one plane has to be swapped out for another due to a major mechanical problem, it can be done very quickly. However, no matter this efficiency, a single plane cannot be in the air flying passengers and on the ground getting maintained at the same time. Similarly, a given plane cannot fly two separate routes at once. If Southwest wants to fly two different routes at the same time, it needs two separate planes.

However, as any given plane flies more hours, it requires more time in the shop for maintenance and repairs. For example, the maintenance and repair costs per hour of flight double after the first five years of flying the plane.

Between its fifth and tenth year of service, the maintenance and repair costs per hour of flight increase another 50 percent. Even though using only one type of plane lowers Southwest's cost and increases plane utilization, using only one model of plane cannot defy the laws of physics. As a consequence, the more hours Southwest puts on a given plane, the more time it is unavailable to fly because it must go to the shop for maintenance and repairs. Once you pass 30 years of daily passenger service, you approach the useful life limits of the plane. Thus, while Southwest has consistently been able to move its planes farther up the curve than its rivals, its planes still have an "S-shaped" tangible asset curve.

In making this point, I in no way want to diminish Southwest's superior ability to leverage its key tangible asset. Nonetheless, no matter how efficient the company is at using its tangible assets, it cannot defy the laws of physics. It can't simultaneously fly the same plane on two different routes or have it in the air and in the repair shop at the same time. It cannot fly its planes more and spend less on maintenance and repairs as the plane ages. Also, it cannot extend the life of the plane by flying it more.

But Southwest's *intangible* assets are different. Let's take for example an intangible asset that Southwest believes is a competitive advantage and plays an important role in delivering superior financial results—its friendly culture and customer service.[1] Southwest claims, and independent surveys seem to confirm, that its employees are friendlier and treat customers better than the employees of most other airlines. Specifically, from 2005 through 2016 Southwest averaged more than a 15 percent higher customer satisfaction rating than its main rivals (e.g., American, Delta, and United).[2] Most executives I have spoken with, regardless of industry, would consider a 15 percent higher customer satisfaction rating as distinctively superior. Friendlier service leads to a more enjoyable travel experience, which increases the likelihood that customers will choose to fly with Southwest again in the future and recommend it to others. However, if one employee in one location is leveraging the Southwest culture to give a customer a great experience, this in no way prevents another employee in another location from simultaneously leveraging the culture to deliver the same great experience to another customer. In fact, the more employees in different places that leverage the friendly culture of Southwest, the stronger the culture actually becomes.

Similarly, the more employees Southwest has in different places living the culture of friendly service, the *less* (not more) it costs Southwest to keep that culture flying. In fact, the more culturally consistent the actions of employees, the more self-reinforcing the culture becomes. The intangible asset of Southwest's friendly culture can create a virtuous cycle that gets stronger with every turn of the crank:

- Southwest employees in different places use the same culture to concurrently deliver a friendly flying experience to customers.
- This friendly service makes customers happy.
- These happier customers come back to fly Southwest again and recommend it to family and friends.
- This repeat business and word of mouth business makes Southwest more money.
- More money means more job security for employees and given Southwest's incentive and reward system reinforces Southwest's friendly culture.

Southwest's culture also enjoys a network effect. The greater the network of employees providing friendly service to customers, the greater the social reinforcement to employees of that behavior.[3] Similarly, as the culture becomes more widespread and deeply ingrained in all Southwest employees, the more value it creates for customers. Specifically, the more widespread and deeply ingrained the culture is among all Southwest employees, the greater customers' confidence that, no matter what plane or route they fly, they will enjoy a friendly experience with Southwest. Thus, the intangible asset and competitive advantage of friendlier service results in an exponential curve, not an "S-curve."

Thus far, the example of Southwest illustrates the "S-curve" of Southwest's tangible assets (specifically planes) and its exponential curve of its intangible assets (specifically its friendly culture). It also illustrates that it was able to meet the first criterion of competitive advantage (i.e., distinctive superiority) relative to both its tangible asset of planes and its intangible asset of friendly service.

But what about the inimitability of its planes versus its culture? Southwest's fleet strategy was identified and "reverse engineered" long ago, and it was *not* hard to copy. Anyone could buy only 737s from Boeing (or only A320s from Airbus). Southwest had no patent protection for this practice. In fact, over the last 43 years, more than 100 companies have been formed and have copied this aspect of Southwest's strategy. However, 97% of these new start-ups failed to survive. Why? Southwest executives believe that their rivals were unable to copy its intangible assets, in particular the productivity of its employees in keeping its planes in the air and their employees' friendly service that keep customers coming back.[4] The fact that Southwest has sustained both its higher plane utilization through quicker turnarounds at the gate and higher customer satisfaction through friendlier service for so long is testimony to the inimitability of its human capital.

However, even if Southwest's productivity and friendly service driven by its human capital are superior and hard to copy, they don't constitute a competitive advantage unless they enable Southwest to expropriate value from the market. While I noted that Southwest executives believe that their intangible asset of culture driven by their people has helped them expropriate more value than their tangible assets over time, just because Southwest executives believe it doesn't make it so. They could be mistaken or even delusional in their beliefs. As a consequence, we don't want to just take their word for it; we want to look at empirical evidence relative to the expropriation of value via tangible or intangible assets.

Although Southwest was founded in 1971, it wasn't considered a "major airline" until the end of 1989. This was simply due to the fact that the U.S. Department of Transportation defined a major airline as having $1 billion or more in annual revenue. Southwest crossed that mark at the end of 1989, so we will begin our expropriation analysis from that point in time. Specifically what we want to know is, "In 1989 how much of Southwest's value did the market assign to its tangible assets versus its intangible assets and has that changed over time?" As I explained before, a firm's price-to-book ratio is arguably a very reasonable measure to get at this question. You will recall from Chapter 1 that the price-to-book ratio tells us the relationship between the market price per share and the book value per share. A ratio of 1:1 means that the market price per share is equal to the value per share of the net assets on the firm's balance sheet. At the end of 1989, Southwest's price-to-book ratio was 1.02 to 1, meaning that 98 percent of its value was attributable to its net tangible assets and only 2 percent was attributed to intangible assets. Thus, early in its history, the market felt that Southwest's value and competitive advantage was coming almost exclusively from its use of its tangible assets, such as planes. It is worth noting that at the time, Southwest's market cap was $600 million.

Over the next two-and-a-half decades, Southwest worked hard to build up its intangible assets, especially its culture of friendly service. The key question for us is whether Southwest was able to expropriate value from the market and how much of that expropriation was due to its tangible versus intangible assets.

During this 25-year period when Southwest was classified as a major airline, its revenue exploded from $1.01 billion to $18.5 billion—a 1,732 percent increase. In the airline industry, revenue increases come from two primary sources: charging more per seat and selling more seats. In Southwest's case, only about 40 percent of its revenue increase came from charging more per seat (i.e., price increases). On this point it is worthwhile to point out that Southwest's price increases were about the same as the industry overall. These price increases were largely driven by increases in jet fuel prices. The other 60 percent of Southwest's revenue increase came from selling more seats (i.e., flying more passengers). Specifically, passengers flying Southwest increased from 18 million in 1989 to 125 million in 2016. To fly more passengers, Southwest needed to fly more planes. As a result, during this 25-year period its fleet increased from 94 aircraft to 723 planes.

This is all fine and good, but to get at the expropriation issue, we still need to know a few more things. First, we need to know if Southwest's growth was simply keeping pace with the growth of the market or whether its growth was faster than the market and thus allowing it to gain share. We also need to know what value the market was putting on Southwest's performance and what portion of that value was ascribed to its tangible versus intangible assets.

Answering the first question regarding Southwest's market share is fairly straightforward. In 1990, Southwest had about a 7 percent market share with six other airlines having larger shares. Over the next 25 years as Southwest recognized the competitive advantage limits of tangible assets and put focus on building up its intangible assets, Southwest nearly tripled its market share to 19.1 percent in 2016 and flew more passengers domestically than any other carrier. This increase in market share was despite all the consolidation in the U.S. airlines industry that transpired during this time period. Knowing that it increased its prices only at the market rate but grew its volume at a rate much higher than the market, we can reasonably deduce that during this 25-year period Southwest expropriated value from the market primarily through volume, rather than price, premiums.

This then begs the question, "Did the market recognize and reward Southwest for its ability to expropriate value and what proportion of this value did the market allocate to tangible versus intangible assets?" In terms of assessing the value the market was assigning to Southwest, one key metric is market capitalization or the total market worth of the company. Southwest's market cap shot up from $600 million at the end of 1989 to $35.3 billion by late of 2018; that is a 5,300 percent increase! It is worth noting that Southwest's market cap went up at twice the rate of its revenues and went up nearly six times more than the general market.

But what portion of Southwest's increase in value was ascribed to its tangible versus intangible assets? Interestingly, even though Southwest's tangible assets increased in absolute terms (increasing 1,670 percent), their portion of Southwest's market value decreased significantly. Specifically, Southwest's price-to-book ratio went from 1.02 to 4.15 in late 2017, meaning that the value ascribed to its tangible assets fell from 98 percent to 24 percent and the value ascribed to its intangible assets soared from a mere 2 percent to 76 percent, a 3,700 percent increase!

These are impressive numbers, but it is worth taking a minute to examine what Southwest would have been worth if the market saw the same relative value in Southwest's tangible and intangible assets in 2018 as it did in 1990. In other words, what if Southwest had not been able to build competitive advantage in its intangible assets and leverage its human capital enough for the market to recognize and reward it? As mentioned, in 2018 Southwest had a market cap of $35.3 billion and a price-to-book ratio of 4.15. If the market had seen no increase in Southwest's ability to build and leverage its intangible assets and its human capital and if it had maintained its 1989 price-to-book ratio of 1.02, the company would have been worth just $8.6 billion in 2018 instead of $35.3 billion. In other words, it was worth *four times* more than what it would have been had it not been able to expropriate value through its intangible assets.

In the process of expropriating value from the market, Southwest also created value for shareholders. In fact, if you had invested $10,000 in Southwest at the beginning of 1990, by late 2018 your $10,000 would have been worth $617,000. The same $10,000 investment in the overall stock market as proxied by the S&P 500 would have been worth only $86,150. In other words, you would have done more than *seven times* better investing in Southwest than the general market!

So what's the bottom line of this case example? First, Southwest had competitive advantages relative to both its tangible and intangible assets. In its earlier years, the market ascribed nearly all the value of its competitive advantage to its tangible assets. Over time, this shifted. Twenty-five years after it became a major airline, the market ascribed a majority (about 75 percent) of its value to competitive advantages via its *in*tangible assets generated largely by its human capital. To be clear, leveraging tangible assets and accessing financial capital at Southwest mattered in 2018 and it did a great job at leveraging both. However, creating competitive advantage through its intangible assets and human capital mattered more than *three times as much*.

Apple

Now let's take a look at another case in a totally different industry. I mentioned the case of Apple in Chapter 2 relative to expropriating value via both price and volume premiums. Here we want to return to this example, but examine it in more depth relative to the source and shift of its competitive advantages over time.

You may recall, Steve Jobs founded Apple in 1976 and then was fired in 1985. He returned to Apple in 1996, and was made CEO in 1997. Sadly, he tragically passed away on October 5, 2011. Nonetheless, during Job's second stint as CEO, Apple logged some impressive results. Revenues skyrocketed from $7 billion in 1997 to $108 billion in 2011—a 1,443 percent increase. During the same period, it went from losing money to making $26 billion, and Apple's market capitalization soared from about $2.3 billion to roughly $346 billion—a 14,943.5 percent increase.

It is impressive that under Jobs the value of Apple went up at ten times faster than the growth rate of its revenue. Trust me, if you could increase the value of your company at ten times the rate of revenue growth, you'd be a pretty happy camper; your career advancement would be secure; and your shareholders would be singing your praises. What explains Apple's rise in value?

As with Southwest, we want to first look at the market's assessment of Apple's value relative to its tangible and intangible assets. When Jobs returned to Apple in 1996, the market was paying $1.18 for every $1 of net worth on Apple's balance sheet. This meant that in 1996 tangible assets accounted for 84.8 percent of Apple's value, while intangible assets accounted for only 15.2 percent. When Jobs passed away, the price-to-book ratio was 4.9, meaning tangible assets declined from 84.8 percent of the firm's value to just 20 percent. Meanwhile, intangible assets soared from 15.2 percent of the firm's value to 80 percent. The role of intangible assets in determining Apple's competitive advantage and their value had increased more than five-fold.

What was the main intangible asset that shareholders came to value? Most would argue that it was innovation—Apple's ability to develop and introduce new products that consumers wanted.

But what drove the intangible asset of innovation? The plant and equipment Apple owned? The real estate it owned? The cash on its balance sheet? No. What drove innovation were the people (human capital), who, it is worth noting, Apple did not own.

To again highlight the role of human capital in an intangible asset such as innovation, do the same exercise I mentioned earlier. Think of Apple's innovations (iPod, iPhone, iTunes, etc.), and then in your mind remove the people from the process. What's left? The answer is obvious—not much.

With this in mind, Jobs personally was so closely associated with Apple's perceived ability to innovate that with Jobs' passing, the market had to decide how much of Apple's innovation was tied to one person (Steve Jobs) who was now gone versus how much was tied to the larger organization and people who were still there. Obviously, this sort of assessment is never easy. In addition, it is difficult to know exactly how the market made this determination or if its assessment was correct. Still, we can get a reasonable idea of the verdict by tracking changes in Apple's price-to-book ratio after Jobs' passing until the time this book went to press.

After Jobs' death, Apple's price-to-book ratio declined from 4.9 to 2.8 (June 26, 2013). This means that the value ascribed to Apple's *in*tangible assets *de*creased from 80 percent to 65 percent and the value ascribed to its tangible assets increased from 20 percent to 35 percent. You could argue that the initial decline in Apple's price-to-book ratio represented the market's worry that an important portion of the firm's innovation capacity was tied to a single entity of human capital—Steve Jobs. However, as the market saw evidence that innovation at Apple went beyond Jobs, within a year the company's price-to-book ratio rose from its low of 2.8 in mid-2013 back to where it was when Jobs passed away (i.e., 4.9), and continued to rocket upward until in November of 2014 it stood at 6.2. In October 2018, it averaged over 9.6. As a consequence, you could make the case that this recovery and further advancement of Apple's price-to-book ratio provided evidence of the market's judgment that the intangible asset of innovation went beyond one person and had been inculcated broadly into the organization.

As with Southwest, it is instructive to assess what the worth of Apple would have been had the market ascribed the same value to tangible and intangible assets in 2018 as it did in 1996. In short, instead of being worth $1.1 trillion, Apple would have been worth only $135 billion. That is a difference of over $965 billion in value! That is dramatic in anyone's book.

And like Southwest, through this process, Apple created value for its shareholders. Specifically, if you had invested $10,000 in Apple in 1997 when Jobs became CEO for the second time, it would have been worth $4.6 million in October of 2018! The same $10,000 invested in the S&P 500 would have been worth just $33,311. Think of that: $4.6 million vs. $33,000!

General Shift in Valuing Intangible Assets

The case studies of Southwest and Apple are interesting, and clearly demonstrate the shift from tangible assets to intangible assets. They also highlight the key role of human capital and illustrate the value that the shift in competitive advantage can make. Still, the question remains, "What do we see if we look across the full spectrum of companies and not just a couple of case studies?" Does the market increasingly recognize the declining value of tangible assets and the growing value of intangible assets? To be clear, the shift isn't an "either-or" choice, but a "figure-ground" relationship in which tangible assets and financial capital fade to the background and intangible assets and human capital move to the foreground.

In order to get a sense of the shift in the relative value of tangible and intangible assets, we need to look at the broader market over a long period of time. I touched on this earlier but now want to come back to it directly. As I mentioned in Chapter 1, the price-to-book ratio provides empirical insight into the extent to which the market is assigning value to a firm's tangible and intangible assets. Exhibits 3.3 and 3.4 show the percentage of firm value that came from tangible assets and intangible assets respectively for the S&P 500 from 1975–2015. The general trend line is also captured in the exhibits.

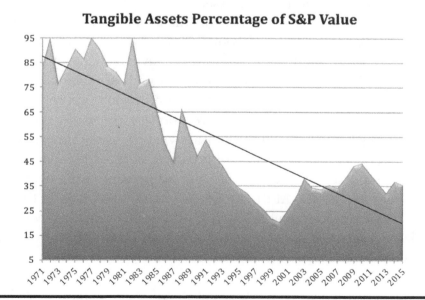

Tangible Assets Percentage of S&P Value

Exhibit 3.3 Tangible assets as a percentage of firm value.

Sources: YCharts.com accessed 11/11/2015; Baruch Lev, Intangibles: Management, Measurement and Reporting, *2001.*

Intangible Assets Percentage of S&P Value

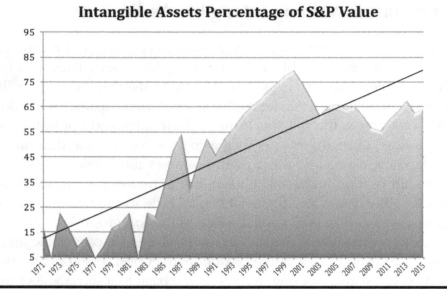

Exhibit 3.4 Intangible assets as a percentage of firm value.

Sources: YCharts.com accessed 11/11/2015; Baruch Lev, Intangibles: Management, Measurement and Reporting, *2001.*

As the exhibits illustrate, the real change began in the middle 1980s as the share of value attributed to tangible assets declined from 80 percent to a low of about 20 percent. Over the last decade, the average value from tangible assets seems to have stabilized at around 35 to 40 percent of firm value. In contrast, the value ascribed to intangible assets averaged about 15 percent through the middle 1980s and then soared to a high of 80 percent. Over the last decade, it seems to have stabilized to around 60–65 percent of firm value. A move from 15 percent to 65 percent over the last 45 years is significant.

While it is impossible to definitively say what these data mean, it seems reasonable to conclude that from the beginning of the 20th century up to about 1985 the market ascribed about 75 to 80 percent of the average firm's value to its tangible assets. At that point, the market recognized that even as firms were adding more tangible assets that the differentiating "value-add" of these additional tangible assets was diminishing. Thus, the sun was setting on the Mechanized Period of competitive advantage and rising on what I call the Intangible Period.

As a side-note it is worth pointing out that if markets had their choice, they would prefer to not ascribe *any* value to intangible assets and would rather put it all on tangible assets. The reason I say this is simple. With a tangible asset, you can hire someone to verify that the plant, equipment, property, land, etc. the firm claims to have actually exist; you can have someone independently confirm that they exist in the form, quantity, and quality the company stipulates. Additionally, you can also reasonably verify the value of those tangible assets by comparing the value carried on the firm's balance sheet and the price at which those assets are selling on the open market. In other words, you can literally "mark to market."

Intangible assets are a different story. How do you audit or verify intangible assets? How do you verify the service, quality, innovation, or continuous-improvement orientation of a firm's culture? How do you audit and verify the creativity of its people? How do you audit or verify the quality of a firm's ability to identify, develop, and deploy effective leaders? Because these things are not owned, they can't be sold on the open market. Because they can't be sold on the open market, how do you "mark them to the market"— even if you could verify their existence?

For all of these reasons, the market would rather not have to attach value to intangibles. Thus, you can make the case that this radical rise in the value of intangible assets relative to a firm's total value was one that was made reluctantly rather than enthusiastically by the market.

This reluctance may explain why we often see a lag between when a firm starts using human capital to build up intangible assets as competitive advantage (like friendly customer service in Southwest's case or innovation in Apple's case) and when the market recognizes and rewards these efforts. Exhibit 3.5 shows that Apple's market cap did not increase in a linear way. It took some time before the market was convinced that Apple possessed the

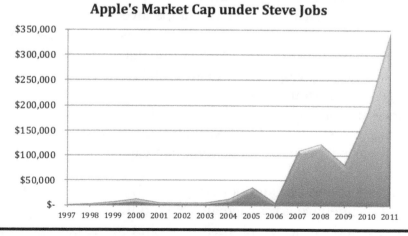

Exhibit 3.5   Apple's market cap under Steve Jobs.

Source: Yahoofinance.com accessed November 2, 2014.

intangible asset of innovation to such a degree that it would affect the firm's performance. However, once the market was convinced, it rewarded Apple in rather dramatic fashion.

Whether Apple's competitive advantage in innovation can continue is anyone's guess. But it seems safe to say that at the time of Jobs' passing and beyond, the market certainly has judged that Apple is distinctively superior at innovating and that this intangible asset has been hard for others to copy and that Apple has successfully expropriated value from the market via both price and volume premiums. While tangible assets and financial capital still mattered throughout this process, by 2018 they mattered only about a fifth as much as Apple's intangible assets—the most important of which was the intangible asset of innovation and the people who generated that innovation.

Having talked with many CEOs and top executives worldwide, it's clear to me that many firms have sought to secure competitive advantage via intangible assets and human capital before the last decade of the 20th century. As a consequence, as illustrated with Apple and the shape of its market cap curve, I would argue that a lag between when executives pursue competitive advantage through intangible assets and when this shift gets recognized and valued by the market is to be expected. Nonetheless, when the market recognizes and values the role of intangible assets, a swift and dramatic increase in value can also be expected.

In summary, as the sun set on the 20th century and dawned on the 21st century, tangible assets as *the* source of competitive advantage for most firms had reached the point of diminishing returns. The exponential-curve nature of intangible assets and their generally higher level of inimitability made them an attractive alternative source of competitive advantage—especially if you were well into the flat part of the tangible assets "S-curve." As companies moved away from tangible assets to intangible assets as sources of competitive advantage, people or human capital became more important than financial capital. Human capital, not financial capital, was the sum and substance and principal driver of intangible assets. Taken together, and as the specific case studies of Southwest and Apple illustrate, this brings into clearer focus why competing *with* human capital is the final frontier of competition.

However, as I will discuss in more depth in the next chapter, this shift in the source of competitive advantage also shifted the balance of power away from employers and toward employees. This shift in the balance of power turns out to be a major force behind why competing *for* human capital has been and will increasingly become more challenging. And as I have stressed before, it is hard to imagine how you can win the battle *with* human capital if you cannot win the contest *for* human capital.

Notes

1. Jody Hoffer Gittell, 2003. *The Southwest Airlines Way*, McGraw-Hill.
2. Jdpower.com accessed November 15, 2017.
3. Charles O'Reilly and Jeffery Pfeffer, 2000. *Hidden Value*, Harvard Business School Press.
4. Jody Hoffer Gittell, 2003. *The Southwest Airlines Way*, McGraw-Hill.

Chapter 4

The Decline of Employer and the Rise of Employee Power

Up to this point, I have highlighted the decline of tangible assets and the rise of intangible assets as sources of competitive advantage and the shift from financial capital to human capital as chief enabler. While these shifts are critical, there is an important backstory that is equally important to appreciate. It is the shift in the balance of power between firms and employees—a shift from employ*ers* having the balance of power largely in their favor to having the scales tip away from them toward employ*ees*. Some of this movement has been driven by the shift in the source of competitive advantage and some of it has been driven by other factors. Detailing all this and the implications it has for winning the contest *for* human capital is the subject of Chapter 4.

Ownership, Assets, Control, and Power

While it may seem obvious, it is important to highlight the fact that while companies own their tangible assets and their financial capital, they most often do not own their intangible assets and they certainly do not own the human capital that drives their intangible assets. Owning or not owning an asset or enabler turns out to be extraordinarily important in this final frontier of competitive advantage.

For the tangible assets a company owns, it is free to use or abuse its tangible assets and capital as it pleases. It can install, decommission, redeploy, sell, or trade its tangible assets as it wishes. It can horde, spend, save, invest, squander, loan, or otherwise use its financial capital as it wishes. Well, "as it wishes" is a bit of an overstatement. Obviously, there are governance structures for most publicly held companies that place parameters and processes around a company's discretion regarding the use of assets and financial capital. Nonetheless, ownership by its nature bequeaths a rather wide prerogative to firms regarding the discretionary actions they can take relative to the assets and financial capital they own.

In addition to bequeathing a rather wide latitude of action, ownership also bestows an important amount of control and power to the owner over the assets owned. This relationship between legal ownership and practical control and power understandably generates a certain mindset in the "owner" relative to what is "owned." This mindset is characterized by a simple notion that "what I own will obey what I decree." This ownership mindset was reinforced for 200 years during the Mechanized Period of competitive advantage when tangible assets, which companies owned, were at the center of competitive advantage. As a consequence, you can imagine how companies might get a fairly entrenched view of "I own; I control; I have the power" when it comes to tangible assets and financial capital and how that attitude might spill over to intangible assets and human capital as well. Allow me a few sentences to elaborate on this.

During the Mechanized Period, tangible assets and financial capital were at the center of competitive advantage. As I mentioned, ownership of tangible assets and financial capital engendered a mindset of power and control. When you couple this with abundant and cheap labor during this period, it was relatively easy for companies and their leaders to view human capital as not much more than cogs in the mechanical gears of competitive advantage—cogs that could easily be replaced if needed. If you search the annals of business history at the time, you will not find executives talking about "people as our most important asset" as is common today. In addition, you did not hear executives talk about talent management or use the term "human capital." You didn't even hear the term "human resources" during the first half of the 20th century. Rather, the function that was responsible for the human cogs in the machinery was typically referred to as "personnel administration."

However, to be clear, it was not just that employers thought they were more powerful than employees; they were more powerful. The central role of tangible assets and financial capital, which firms owned, made employees much more dependent on firms than firms were dependent upon employees. It was firms' wise use of tangible assets and capital that generated jobs upon which employees were dependent.

However, as discussed in the previous chapter, especially over the last half of the 20th century, tangible assets became increasingly commoditized and undifferentiated. As firms shifted from tangible to intangible assets as the source of competitive advantage, human capital rather than financial capital became the key enabler. The fact that firms had no ownership rights to their human capital and were increasingly dependent on them for competitive advantage via intangible assets shifted the balance of power away from employ*ers* toward employ*ees*. In contrast, employees, rather than employers, owned the capabilities, insights, knowledge, attitudes, behaviors, etc. on which firms were dependent. Because slavery had been outlawed many decades before, employees were free to walk out of the company with all the knowledge, skills, insights, capabilities, etc. that drove the firm's intangible assets and source of competitive advantage and to not walk back into the company with those capabilities the next day.

I know I am making a big deal of ownership, but it worth stressing it even a bit more. If you own a piece of equipment, you can deploy it in one plant and then move it to another as you like. You needn't care what the machine thinks of the move; it doesn't matter whether it is a nice or nasty new location. By contrast, you can *ask* employees (whom you don't own) to redeploy from one country to another, or from one position to another, but you can't force them to *accept* the moves. They can always refuse. You can even threaten to fire them if they refuse, but they can still say no. You cannot force them to make the move.

As another illustration, if you own a piece of real estate, you can sell it or trade it for another as you please. The land has no say in the matter. It doesn't matter if the new owner is nice or nasty. However, you cannot sell or trade employees. Even if you sell the unit to which certain employees belong, you can't force them to stay with the entity after the sale. You might draft a legal document that creates financial and other incentives to keep the employee with the new owner, but you cannot force the employees to sign the document. If they don't value the incentives highly enough, they can simply say "No."

If you own a piece of equipment, you can decommission it regardless of how much productive life is left in it, and you can even refuse to sell it after its decommission in order to keep it out of the hands of a rival. However, you can't force employees to remain idle with you and prevent them from applying their capabilities elsewhere. You cannot chain them to their workstation and prevent them from leaving. Even non-compete legal agreements have limitations that often do not extend beyond 12 months.

Unlike plant, equipment, real estate, or other tangible assets, which have no choice or volition in what happens to them, people have both choice and volition. Thus, as firms increasingly moved from tangible assets and financial capital (which they owned) as sources of competitive advantage to intangible assets and human capital as the chief enabler (which they did not own), the balance of power shifted away from firms and toward employees.

In combination, this shift in the source of competitive advantage and ownership created a profound implication. As human capital became increasingly the driver of competitive advantage through intangible assets, the risk increased that a portion of the firm's competitive advantage would walk out the door at night and not only not walk back in the next day but would walk through the door of a competitor—a risk that firms simply did not have with tangible assets. A piece of equipment, a building, a plot of land that you owned could not decide that it didn't like working for you and as a consequence walk out the door and go to work for your competitor. In contrast, employees could do just that. As a consequence, over time as this shift in the source of competitive advantage grew, employees were able to generate more risk *for* employers than they had to take *from* employers. Any time you have an *"asymmetric risk profile,"* the net "risk imposing" party has more power than the net "risk receiving" party.[1]

Thus, the shift in the source of competitive advantage from tangible assets to intangible assets and from financial capital to human capital pushed the balance of power away from employers and toward employees. However, the power-balance shift between employers and employees didn't stop here. In fact, it merely began here. This shift in power was, and continues to be, amplified by four additional forces.

The Four Amplifiers

The four amplifiers of the shift in the balance of power (as dramatized in Exhibit 4.1) are:

1. A shift in competitive scope
2. A shift in information asymmetry
3. A shift in firm-specific benefits
4. A shift in talent supply and demand

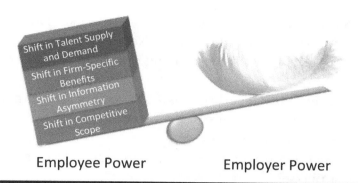

Employee Power   Employer Power

Exhibit 4.1   Shift in balance of power.

Shift in Competitive Scope

As discussed earlier, for most firms the competitive scope of business has shifted from primarily domestic to global in just the last generation. For example, a generation ago, the vast majority of revenue for the average S&P 500 firm came from its home market in the U.S. In the last few years, the amount of revenue derived from foreign markets has climbed to nearly 50 percent. As presented in Chapter 3, during this period, companies around the world, not just those in the U.S., have significantly increased their foreign direct investment, and consequently, FDI stock has grown from less than 10 percent of world GDP to about 30 percent. Greater geographic scope has produced greater opportunities, but also threats and uncertainties. When competition was mostly domestic, competitors were known; they lived "across the street." Today, competitors are often unknown and can come from anywhere on the planet.

How this change shifts power away from employers and toward employees, especially certain employee talent, is probably best explained with a concrete illustration—the mobile phone industry. If I asked you what company was number one in the world in 1991, who would you name? If you are like most people, you would probably name "Nokia." However, in 1991 that wasn't even close to the case. At the time, the company with the highest global market share by sales was Motorola—the company that made the very first commercial mobile phone in 1979. In 1991, Motorola enjoyed record sales of more than $11 billion and huge profits. It also introduced the smallest, lightest phone yet—the Motorola Microtac, which weighed a mere 88 grams.

With that in mind, imagine you are the CEO of Motorola in 1991. You are holding a retreat with your top executives to think about new customer trends, new technologies, new competitors, and the like. During the meeting, one of your leaders raises the issue of Nokia as a potential future threat. Being open minded, you ask some probing questions of your subordinate:

CEO: OK. I've never really heard of Nokia. We have a global market share of almost 40 percent. What's Nokia's share?

Subordinate: Less than thirteen percent.

CEO: Our new Microtac II weighs less than 88 grams. How small is their smallest phone?

Subordinate: Their smallest phone is called the Cityman; it weighs almost ten times more at over 800 grams.

CEO: We invented key mobile communications technology and built the first commercial mobile phone in 1979. What's their claim to fame?

Subordinate: Nokia was founded in 1865 as a pulp and paper manufacturer. Then in the 1960s it merged with Finish Rubber Works, which was founded in 1898, making them one of the largest makers of rubber fishing boots in the world. Subsequently, Nokia also merged with Finnish Cable Works, which was formed in 1912. As a consequence, it sells a lot of coaxial cable for fixed line phones.

CEO: We're anticipating sales of $13.3 billion in 1992 and profits of $453 million. What about them?

Subordinate: Nokia is likely to have sales of only $3.4 billion in 1992, which is down from $3.7 billion in 1991 and down from $6.1 billion in 1990. It is projected to lose, not make, money this year; it will likely lose $134 million in 1992.

CEO: We operate in the world's largest market for mobile phones—a market with a population of over 250 million. What about Nokia?

Subordinate: They're based in Finland with a total population of about 5 million, which is less than the city of Chicago (near our headquarters).

CEO: Remind me again why you're bringing these guys to my attention?

Subordinate: They have a new incoming CEO, Jorma Ollila, who's talking about pushing Nokia into mobile communication.

CEO: What's his background? What technology firms has he run before?

Subordinate: He's a former banker, not a technologist.

If you were the CEO of Motorola, how worried would you be? Hindsight is 20/20, but at the time, you might not be too worried about this company from frozen, far-off Finland.

Fast forward five years to 1996, and again you are still the CEO of Motorola. You've introduced the StarTAC—a "clam shell" design that flips open like the communicators on *Star Trek*. It is the smallest phone on the market and seems to be "*the* phone everyone wants to own." This analog phone becomes a huge hit and sells more than any phone in the history of the industry. You have sales of nearly $28 billion and profits over $1.2 billion. Nokia is less than one-third your size at $8.5 billion in sales. What's more, in 1996 Nokia earned only $707 million. Are you worried? (Probably not—even if you should be.)

Fast forward five more years to 2001. Nokia has sales of $27.7 billion, and you (Motorola) have sales of $30 billion. More importantly in that year, you lose $3.9 billion while Nokia makes $1.9 billion. Are you worried now? Absolutely, but now it may be too late.

One year later in 2002, Nokia earned $3.6 billion in profits, which, because of big losses for Motorola in 2002, 2001, and 1998, was more profit than Motorola made in the past ten years. That's right. Nokia made more money in one year than Motorola made in the previous ten years. In addition, Motorola's market share by 2002 had fallen by more than half to 19 percent.

In just over ten years, Nokia went from zero to hero. This little company from small, frozen, and faraway Finland had overtaken the number one company in the industry—a company that hailed from the largest mobile phone market in the world; a company that invented the first commercial mobile phone and once dominated the market.

Now fast forward just three years from 2002 to 2005 and switch gears from being CEO of Motorola to being the CEO of Nokia. You've surged past Motorola in terms of market share, but Motorola is unwilling to "go quietly into that good night." They come roaring back, introducing the Razr, a huge hit around the world. By mid-year 2006, the Razr has sold more than 50 million units and Motorola's revenues have soared from $35 billion in 2005 to $43 billion in 2006. At Nokia you are larger, at $54 billion in sales, but Motorola's profits of $5.5 billion are nearly the same as yours at $5.6 billion. If you're the CEO of Nokia, whom are you worried about? Motorola, of course.

Move forward just one year from 2006 to 2007. Motorola again falls from grace, watching revenues drop from $44 billion to $36.6 billion. It goes from making $5.5 billion to losing nearly $700 million. In the meantime, at Nokia you have surged ahead. Sales exploded from $54 billion to $75 billion in just one year, and profits nearly doubled from $5.6 billion to $10.5 billion.

As the CEO of Nokia, you are the number one player in the world with a global market share exceeding 40 percent and a global profit share of nearly 80 percent. That means that out of every 10 dollars, euro, or yen spent on mobile phones across the entire world, 4 of them are spent to buy your phones. At the same time, out of every 10 dollars, euro, or yen made in profits on mobile phones across the entire world, 8 of them are made by you! How are you feeling? Pretty confident no doubt.

Midway through 2007 some company in California (Apple) that was making music players and computers says, "We're going to start making mobile phones." As Nokia, you are four times bigger than Apple in total sales, and three times larger in profits. You understand the technology of "data packets," CDMA vs. GSM, and so on and have been in the industry for nearly two decades. What does Apple know about phones or wireless communication? Not much. Also, Apple announces it is only going to focus on smartphones. In 2007, smartphones represent just 11 percent of the total global market for mobile phones. Even though they plan to focus solely on this small segment, it's a segment you know well and have dominated; your market share for smartphones is 48 percent. This is largely because you made the first commercially successful smartphone over a decade ago (the Nokia 9000), which was part of the Nokia Communicator line. Apple also announces that its new iPhone will only have a touch screen interface. Would you be worried about this knowing that you launched a touch screen phone four years earlier in 2003? While hindsight is 20/20, it is easy to imagine that if you were the CEO of Nokia in 2007, you might not be so worried about Apple.

Fast forward just five years to 2012. Smartphones, which once comprised 11 percent of all mobile phone sales, account for almost half of all mobile phones sold in 2012. What's more, Apple's smartphone market share by revenue went from about six percent to 40 percent, and its smartphone profit share went from under five percent to over 60 percent. Yes, its profit share was 50 percent higher than its market share. Apple revenues soared from $24.6 billion in 2007 to $156.6 billion in 2012, while Nokia's revenue fell almost 50 percent—from a peak of nearly $75 billion in 2007 to $39 billion. In 2012, Apple earned more *profits* ($41.7 billion) than Nokia generated in total *revenue*. Worse, Apple's profits in 2012 alone were greater than Nokia's total profits over the previous ten years—yes, one year of profits beats ten.

While Nokia was surprised and devastated by Apple, in the background Motorola continued to decline. In 2011 it split itself into two separate companies with Motorola Mobility focusing on mobile phones and other related products. In May of 2012, Google completed its acquisition of Motorola Mobility that it had announced in late 2011 for $12.5 billion. Subsequently, Google sold the cable modem and set top box units that was part of Motorola Mobility to Arris Group for $2.5 billion. In 2014, Google then sold the remaining part of Motorola Mobility, which was primarily the handset business to Lenovo for $2.9 billion, but kept 15,000 patents that were part of Motorola Mobility.

Nokia's fate was equally grim. Nokia's market cap fell from a peak of $283 billion to a low of $6.3 billion in July of 2012. After that, Nokia's fortunes continued to fade, and in September of 2013, it sold its mobile devices and services business to Microsoft for just €5.44 billion ($7.2 billion). In less than a decade, Nokia's focus on the phone as a wireless means of making calls had gone from a world-beating sail to a ship-sinking sea-anchor. When Nokia's leadership failed to recognize the broader use of the phone and the importance of the phone's software, especial via "apps," and failed to respond to this and other changes imposed by Apple, its fate was sealed.

While the case study of the rise and fall of Motorola and Nokia is interesting, you may be wondering how it in particular, and the shift in competitive scope in general, relates to a change in the balance of power between employers and employees? The answer is that as the scope of competition has gone global, new competitors can emerge from virtually any country in the world and can rise up from within, as well as outside your industry. This greater turbulence means that past strategies and the associated tangible assets can quickly turn from a sail catching the wind and propelling the ship forward to a sea-anchor filling with water and holding the ship back (see Exhibit 4.2).

In the case of Motorola, its assets, capital, and competitive advantage tied up in analog technology, which previously had functioned as fantastic sails,

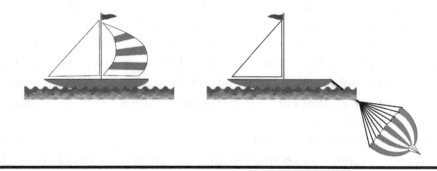

Exhibit 4.2 Shift from sail to sea-anchor.

became fatal sea-anchors. What Motorola needed was not past strategies but current *strategists*, talented executives who could recognize and respond to key changes in the weather, waves, and winds.

In the case of Nokia, its assets, capital, and competitive advantage tied up in digital but "dumb" phones (vs. smartphones), which previously had functioned as fantastic sails, became fatal sea-anchors. Like Motorola, what Nokia needed were not past strategies but current *strategists*, talented executives who could recognize and respond to key changes in the weather, waves, and winds.

With globalization, and the uncertainty that has come with it, you can no longer bank on past competitive advantages, especially those rooted in tangible assets. Increasingly, you have to bank not on past successful strategies but on observant, nimble, *strategists*. If these people are not farsighted folks who can spot potential threats and opportunities across markets, technologies, and competitors before they become obvious to everyone, you have no hope of sustaining high performance.

The uncertainty that globalization has wrought is reflected in the market. Before globalization was a real force in most businesses, past earnings and past firm performance and the stable tangible assets that the firm owned were a good predictor of future earnings and firm performance. For example, Motorola's past earnings in the 1970s were a good predictor for its earnings in the 1980s and even in the early 1990s. However, as the pace of globalization accelerated, Motorola's great past earnings lost much of their predictive power. Similarly, Nokia's past poor earnings in the 1990s were not a good predictor of its fantastic earnings in the early 2000s. And again, Nokia's great earnings in the early 2000s were a poor predictor of its huge losses a few years later. Likewise, Apple's *un*impressive earnings in the early 2000s were not a good predictor of its blowout profits just a few years after that.

This phenomenon is not confined to Motorola, Nokia, and Apple. It's reflected broadly in the market. In a world that wasn't so open, one in which competitors couldn't come at you from virtually any direction, past earnings accounted for much of the movement in a firm's stock price. As globalization has taken hold, the market's reliance on past earnings is only half as much as it once was. As Exhibit 4.3 shows, movements in earnings used to account for 75 percent of the change in stock price. That figure has since fallen to about 30 percent.

It's important to note that this chart does *not* look at the market's up-and-down movements, but examines the movement of individual stocks. It analyzes the extent to which as a company's earnings go up or down its

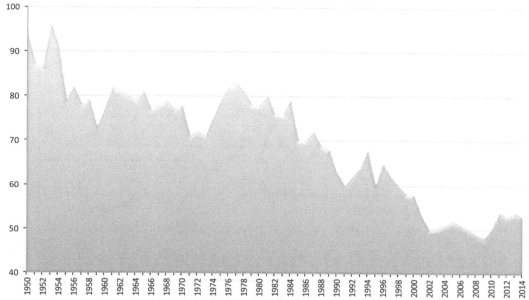

Adjust R2 of Market Value Accounted for by Earnings

Exhibit 4.3   Adjust R2 of market value accounted for by earnings.

Source: Compustat; Lev, Baruch, and Feng Gu. The End of Accounting and the Path Forward for Investors and Managers. *Hoboken (New Jersey): Wiley, 2016.*

stock price goes up or down, and the degree to which they move in sync or separately. The relationship between earnings and stock movement could range from 100 percent (meaning they are perfectly correlated) to zero (meaning past earnings and stock price are completely unrelated), or anything in between. If you like statistics, think of the relationship as a simple correlation.

When I display this chart, people are often amazed at the decoupling of past earnings and stock movement. In trying to explain this phenomenon, occasionally someone will speculate that the "Internet Bubble" is to blame. On the surface the thought makes sense because during the bubble there were many cases where as earnings went down, stock prices went up. However, you can see that this downward trend and the loosening of the relationship between earnings movement and stock price movement started long before the Internet Bubble. Others on seeing this chart speculate that it is due to hedge funds or high frequency trading. Again however, this decoupling started long before these forces hit the market. However, if you overlay the rise of globalization (as measured by FDI stock as a percentage of world GDP) on the declining power of earnings' changes driving stock price

Declining Power of Earnings and Rise of Globalization

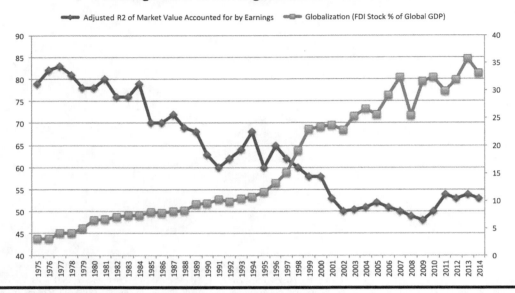

Exhibit 4.4   Declining power of earnings and rise of globalization.

Sources: Compustat; UNCTAD; Lev, Baruch, and Feng Gu. **The End of Accounting and the Path Forward for Investors and Managers.** *Hoboken (New Jersey): Wiley, 2016.*

changes, you get a very strong negative correlation of –.91, meaning that as globalization increased, the role of past earnings predicting stock price movements decreased (see Exhibit 4.4).

As I stressed earlier, for the vast majority of companies, globalization as a meaningful phenomenon is not that old—just 15–20 years. To be clear, I am not saying that there was not uncertainty before then; rather, I am saying that the magnitude was much, much less. As I mentioned, it is a bit easier to watch your domestic competitors, customers, regulators, NGOs, and the like and anticipate what they might do and how those actions might affect your future earnings than to watch, understand, and predict the behavior of these stakeholder groups across 20 or 200 nations. Put differently, it is challenging but possible to put your arms around a single country— even a big one like the U.S. in which you have a variety of competitors, customers, regulators, NGOs, and the like. As a consequence, your past good earnings would be reasonably good at predicting your good future earnings. However, getting your arms around 100 different countries and all the different competitors, customers, regulators, NGOs, and the like is a different story. Who can accurately predict all the moves regulators might make across 100 different countries? Who can reliably foresee changes in customer needs across 100 different countries? Who can anticipate all these things AND effectively react or even preempt them? How difficult is this? When I ask executives about this, they point out that it is not just 100 times more difficult to compete in 100 countries versus one country but 1,000 or 10,000 times more difficult because of the potential interaction affects across and between countries.

As a consequence, the unpredictability that globalization has introduced changed the market calculus. Though somewhat simplified, the data in Exhibit 4.3 suggests that, once upon a time, when people bought a stock, 70 percent to 80 percent of their decision was driven by past earnings. They relied on past earnings because in a more stable, constrained, and therefore knowable, domestic environment, past earnings were a good predictor of future earnings. After all, as I pointed out, within the constraints of one country you could know your domestic competitors, understand your resident regulators, and glean insight into your local customers. In addition, in a constrained, limited, and known domestic environment, deciding to turn right or left in a confined space didn't make as much difference as compared to turning left or right while operating on a wide-open world stage. In a global environment, staying committed to a proven analog technology (as Motorola did for too long) while Nokia turned left toward an unproven digital technology, made all the difference. Subsequently, for Nokia, viewing the phone as primarily a device for making calls, while Apple turned right toward the complementary world of apps, made all the difference. In a global and uncertain world, past earnings (positive or negative) are not as good predictors of future earnings as they once were. As a consequence, they now account for only about 30 percent of the movement in a stock compared to the 70 percent that used to be the case.

The bottom line implication is that now more than ever firms are dependent on people who can spot future trends among customers, technologies, regulators, competitors, and so on. Without these insights all the tangible assets in the world only serve to act as sea-anchors not sails. Even intangible assets that have been built up, such as styling for Nokia, lose their value if key human capital fail to notice that mobile phones are moving from stylish communication devices to stylish devices for music, video, texting, social interaction—oh, and also for making calls from time to time. As firms become more dependent on people to spot and respond to the quick shifting winds and waves of change, those people gain leverage and power.

Information Asymmetry

The second shift that has accelerated the move of the balance of power from employers to employees is what economists call a shift in "information symmetry," which is a fancy term for talking about how balanced or unbalanced information is between key parties. If you go back prior to 2000, the balance of information power was with employers. Today and going forward, that is not the case. The main force in this shift is the Internet.

The easiest way to illustrate this shift is to examine the role of information in the employee–employer relationship relative to labor supply and demand and prices (i.e., employee wages). In the past, employ*ers* were usually the ones who knew whether demand for a certain type of employee was going up or down, whether the supply was tight or loose, and what was happening to wages relative to those employees.

Let me illustrate. Suppose in your organization you wanted information about the supply and demand and compensation situation and trends regarding Java language programmers. In the 1990s, you would likely have hired Mercer or whomever to conduct a market study. Mercer would do the study, give you the information, and collect its $200,000 fee. While this might seem expensive, you could amortize the $200,000 market study fee across the 1,000 Java programmers you employed. Thus, the per-employee cost to you would be $200. Armed with information about Java programmer supply, demand, and prices (wages), you were in a superior bargaining position relative to employees who didn't have this information.

Theoretically a single Java programmer could hire Mercer to find out if demand for her skills was rising or falling, whether the supply was tight or loose, and what was happening to wages, but she would have to pay $200,000 for the study and would only be able to amortize the cost across one person! Even if the single employee were losing money in the negotiations with her employer because of the lack of information, it was unlikely that she was losing $200,000 in present value. As a consequence, hiring Mercer by that lone programmer was not worthwhile. Therefore, is it any wonder that employers once held a near-monopoly on information about labor demand, supply, and prices—or that this asymmetric information flow tilted the power balance in employers' favor?

Because individual employees were often unaware of trends regarding demand, supply, and compensation, they were handicapped when it came to extracting their full value from employers. With more information in their corner, employers had more power. In pointing this out, I am not accusing employers of exploiting employees; I am only saying that in general when there is information asymmetry, the party with more information typically extracts more value than the party with less information.

This may sound a bit theoretical and academic, so let me put it in a very concrete and common situation—buying a car. Prior to 2000, if you wanted to buy a new car, you had very little information about the level of demand, supply, or the true cost of a particular automobile. In contrast, the dealer knew quite a bit about these key points. Given the lack of information at your disposal, you were at a disadvantage when you walked into a show-room. However, the Internet dramatically shifted this balance of power for car consumers.

Thanks to the Internet, today you can acquire nearly as much knowledge as dealers about the supply of a particular model in your area—down to the number of fire-engine red cars of a specific make and model and its availability within a 25-, 50-, or even 100-mile radius of your home. You can learn what the average selling price is, what the sticker price is, what the destination charge is, and how much the average dealer earns on the car you want. You can also know that if you can't get the price you want from one dealer, you can go down the street to a different dealer with the same car in stock. If you want to know the financial impact of this shift in power from car dealers having the advantage to consumers being nearly on par in terms of access to information, just talk to any new car dealer. They will confirm that this shift in information has given customers more power, and with that shift in power, dealers' profit margins have declined sharply. Specifically, according to the North American Dealer Association, the average profit margin on a new car sale in the U.S. has declined by more than 50% from 8 percent in 1990 to 3.3 percent 2015.[2]

Just as the Internet changed the balance of power between car dealers and customers, it's also shifting the power balance between employees and employers.

To more fully understand this shift, we need to appreciate that information has two central qualities: richness and reach (see Exhibit 4.5). Information richness concerns the *depth* of information. In the case of employees, information about a job is richer if you know the nature of the job, the colleagues you'll work with, your boss, the culture of the company, your compensation, etc. Information reach has to do with the *breadth* of information. For an employee, information has greater reach if it covers jobs across a variety of companies, industries, and geographies.

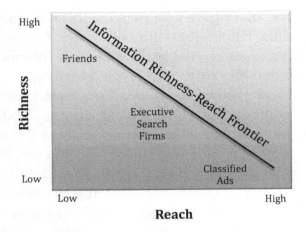

Exhibit 4.5   Traditional information reach-richness tradeoff.

For example, classified ads tend to have good reach but poor richness. Classified ads offer a good handle on the number of jobs listed in your area of expertise, but (normally) each ad contains relatively little information richness.

By contrast, a friend might provide great information richness on a particular job, but have low information reach. She might know all about the nature of the job, the colleagues you would work with, your boss, the culture of the company, your compensation, etc., but this information would apply only to the open jobs she knows.

Thanks to the high cost of obtaining both reach and richness in the pre-Internet era, there was almost always a trade-off between the two. This created an "information reach-richness frontier" that few employees could cost-effectively cross, but that most employers could.

Although the Internet didn't change everything, it *did* blow this information asymmetry apart. "Aggregator" companies, such as Monster.com, achieved global reach by aggregating jobs across thousands of companies anywhere in the world. The early version of Monster.com offered primarily text information on the jobs, so while reach was global, richness was moderate. With the subsequent (and dramatic) decline in information storage costs, Monster.com and others were able to add almost unlimited richness to every job opening, including still images, video, audio, etc. (See Exhibit 4.6).

Today, by visiting sites such as Monster.com or LinkedIn, employees can learn a tremendous amount about supply, demand, and wages in their skills markets in just 10 minutes—free of charge. This means that employees today

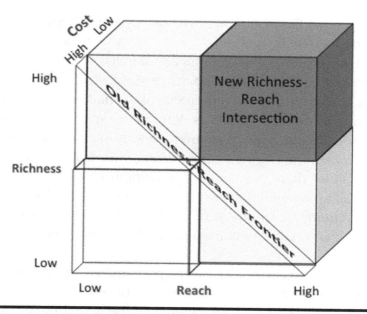

Exhibit 4.6 Simultaneous reach and richness.

know almost as much as employers, and based on my informal surveys, many employees know more. I say "know more" because whenever I ask HR or line executives, "How many of you have visited Monster.com or other sites in the last 30 days to get a sense of the market for the skills and capabilities of your employees?" only about a quarter of the hands go up. When I ask employees the same question, about three-quarters of hands go up.

This shift in information symmetry has inadvertently shifted the power in the employer–employee relationship. What used to be a balance of power on this dimension heavily in favor of employers is now at best balanced and at worst (from a company's perspective) leans in favor of employees. As I mentioned before, if you want to understand the financial implications of this for employers, just talk to someone who owns a new car dealership and has seen their margins drop by half.

Shift in Company-Specific Benefits

The third shift that has moved the balance of power away from companies and toward employees concerns company-specific benefits. The basic definition of a company-specific benefit is a benefit you lose once you leave a particular company. Given this definition, many benefits qualify as company-specific. Clearly, it isn't possible to cover them all, but of the important benefits—those that employees care about the most—few have been altered over the last several years as dramatically as retirement benefits.

In 1975, according to the U.S. Department of Labor, 75 percent of active workers participating in private retirement plans had only "defined benefit" plans—a plan in which the benefit is defined or determined in advance of retirement. For example, your retirement benefit might be defined as "65 percent of your average compensation during your last five years on the job if you worked more than 15 years for the company." If this was the definition, then it was up to the company to make sure it set aside enough money to fund your retirement, and most often these plans were "back-end loaded." By that I mean that greater benefits accrued the longer you stayed with the company.

In 1975 only 25 percent of employees participated in defined contribution retirement plans—a program in which your employer's *contribution* to your retirement is defined or determined, but the actual benefit you receive at retirement is not. For example, your employer's defined contribution might be "seven percent of your salary." By this definition, the company guarantees that it will contribute this amount to your retirement account, but it makes no promise regarding what you will receive in retirement payments. Most often, these plans are constant; in other words, the percentage contributed doesn't rise or fall, regardless of how long you've worked for the company.

In just one generation, the high proportion of defined benefit plans relative to defined contribution plans turned upside down as illustrated in Exhibit 4.7. By 2005, 73 percent of active workers participating in retirement plans had defined contribution plans and only 27 percent participated in defined benefit plans.

So why this reversal and what does it have to do with the balance of power between employers and employees? Arguably, CFOs were the key force behind this reversal in retirement plans. With defined benefit plans, employers had to invest retirement funds and earn returns sufficient to cover their defined retirement obligations. Because the investment market moves up and down, ensuring that these obligations were "funded" was not easy to predict or manage. If a defined benefit plan was underfunded, then the firm had to cover the shortfall with current earnings. This often required CFOs to announce negative earnings surprises—surprises to which the stock market often reacted with stock price declines. CFOs didn't like this. In addition, as the number of employees eligible for retirement grew and as people tended

Assets by Retirement Type

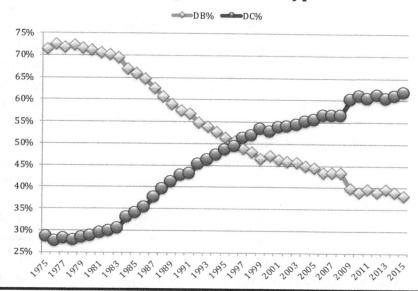

Exhibit 4.7 **Retirement plan changes 1975–2014.**

Source: U.S. Department of Labor.

to live longer, the financial obligation for the firm also increased. CFOs didn't like this either.

On the other hand, guaranteeing the company's defined contributions during any given year was pretty easy to predict, with few unpleasant surprises. At the beginning of the year, the CFO knew how many employees were employed, could reasonably estimate how many would retire and could assess how many the firm would hire. The CFO also could estimate with some accuracy how much salary the firm would pay each person over the course of the year. In combination, this meant the CFO could accurately estimate how much the firm would need to pay into the defined contribution pension. No more nasty surprises! CFOs loved this. In addition, the switch to defined contribution plans moved the "funding" obligation from the firm to the employee. CFOs loved this even more. While this is a somewhat simplified description, it makes it easy to understand why most firms switched from defined benefit plans to defined contribution plans.

This move from defined benefit plans to defined contribution plans was not just confined to the U.S. In 2005, countries such as Australia, Denmark, Iceland, Italy, Korea, New Zealand, Portugal, Spain, and Sweden had a majority of non-government employees participating in defined contributions plans.[3]

Although the financial impact of this switch for the firm was anticipated, the impact on the employer–employee balance of power was not. Because defined benefit plans were usually back-end loaded, this created an incentive for employees to stay with the firm. In some cases, the rise in benefits increased so much with tenure that they were called "golden handcuffs." Put differently, most defined benefit plans created high *switching costs* for employees because they would lose significant retirement benefits if they changed employers.

By contrast, defined contribution plans were portable and had low switching costs. The contributions paid by employers (as well as employees own contributions) could leave with the employees. As a consequence, defined contribution plans lowered employees' switching cost.

To fully appreciate what happens when switching costs are lowered, just think about customers. All other things being equal, if customers' switching costs are lowered, their switching behavior goes up. This more frequent switching behavior typically intensifies the competition for winning and retaining customers. After all, if you lose customers to your rivals because customers' switching costs go down, you don't just sit there; you go after replacement customers. Unless the market is growing rapidly, you likely have to steal customers away from other competitors. When companies' products are undifferentiated and customer switching costs are low, price wars often erupt. Throughout this process, power swings away from firms and toward customers.

The same dynamics are true for employees and employers. All other things being equal, lower employee switching costs increases employees' switching behavior (lowering average tenure). The competition to retain employees serves to increase employees' power and leverage in the employment relationship. This relationship between the rise of defined contribution plans, lowering of employee switching costs, and increase in employee switching behavior is clearly illustrated in Exhibit 4.8.

It shows that, as the percentage of total retirement funds in defined contribution accounts rose, the average tenure of men aged 45–54 fell almost in lock step with a correlation of −.96. This age group is particularly relevant because they are "within striking distance" of retirement, but not so old that their proximity dampens their inclination to change companies.

The other unintended consequence of changing from defined benefit to defined contribution retirement plans is that this change altered the psychological contract and reduced employees felt obligation to employers. Simplified, if you as an employer have to figure out how to save and earn

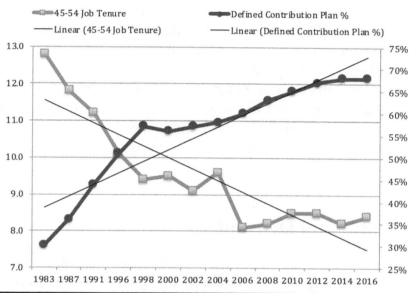

Exhibit 4.8   Company tenure and defined contribution plans.

Source: U.S. Department of Labor.

a return sufficient to cover my retirement payments, that naturally induces some level of felt reciprocal obligation or loyalty from me—the employee. However, that felt obligation and loyalty all but disappears if now the responsibility for saving and investing enough to cover my retirement payments shifts from you the employer to me. The combination of lower switching costs and lower feelings of loyalty leads to higher switching behavior whether we are talking about customers or employees.

Of course, there are more company-specific benefits than just retirement plans. For example, the *culture* of a company is a company-specific benefit. When you leave one company, you leave that company's culture behind and no longer enjoy its benefits. The new company may have a culture that is similar, worse, or even better, but it won't be the same.

Nonetheless, if you view retirement as a company-specific benefit that used to carry high employee switching costs and a psychological contract that engendered enhanced loyalty and now carries lower switching costs and lower felt loyalty, you have to ask the following question: "Has your firm's other company-specific benefits increased enough to compensate for the lowered switching costs and loyalty created by switching to defined contribution plans to yield the same retention or holding grip on employees as before this shift?" If the answer is "yes," for your firm, then perhaps you can relax. However, when I have put this question to executives, more than 80 percent indicate that their other firm-specific benefits have not increased at a rate high enough to offset the lower switching costs and loyalty that defined contribution plans have brought.

Bottom line, the switch from defined benefit to defined contribution plans has lowered employee switching costs sufficiently to tilt the balance of power on this dimension away from employers and toward employees. In particular, as it lowered employees' switching costs it raised the difficulty for firms to retain talent.

Shift in Supply and Demand

An article by McKinsey, the strategy consulting firm, published ten years ago—"The War for Talent"—was arguably the first to raise widespread awareness about the demographic shifts in the supply of and demand for talent, as well as its implications for talent competition.[4] The chart that captured most executives' attention showed that the number of 34- to 44-year-olds, as a percentage of total workforce, would drop by 15 percent from 2000 to 2015. Although that age group is important, we know that one generation can be smaller or larger than a previous one. Therefore, the fact that the number of 34- to 44-year-olds is rising or falling doesn't necessarily offer a complete picture of the labor supply. You gain a more complete picture of labor supply by looking at the trends of a country's total workforce (traditionally defined as age 15–65).

While you might think that projecting workforce levels out 20–30 years is the stuff of fortune tellers, it's not. One factor accounts for 85–95 percent of the size of a country's future workforce—births. The reason is simple; if you aren't born today, you can't enter the workforce in 15 years. It turns out that birth rates in countries are relatively stable; they don't move up or down dramatically year-to-year. This is not to say that they don't change; they do. But the change is slow and almost always from higher to lower birth rates. Between 1960 and 1980 in key developed economies, the fertility rate dropped dramatically and then stabilized at a level below the replacement rate of 2.1 births per female (see Exhibit 4.9).

After accounting for births, four factors can move a country's workforce numbers marginally up or down: net immigration, participation rate, retirement age, and child mortality rate. However, these statistics are also

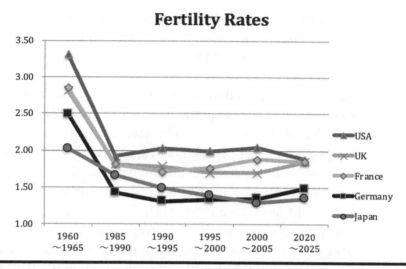

Exhibit 4.9   Declining fertility rates in developed countries.

Source: World Bank.

relatively stable within a country and do not change significantly year-to-year. Therefore, projecting their influence on the size of a country's workforce out 20–30 years is relatively reliable.

With all this in mind, Exhibit 4.10 lists key developed countries that will see their workforce population peak before 2020 and the percentage their workforce will decline from its peak by 2050.

Country	Workforce Decline
Austria	11.1%
Belgium	5.4%
Canada	5.6%
France	1%
Germany	30.5%
Greece	26.3%
Hong Kong	23.5%
Italy	21.7%
Japan	33.6%
Korea (South)	26.4%
Netherlands	13.8%
Portugal	28.3%
Singapore	12.6%
Spain	27.4%

Exhibit 4.10   Workforce declines in selected developed countries.

Source: World Bank.

Notable exceptions to this list of developed countries are the U.S. and the UK. Their workforce populations are forecast to increase from 2015 through 2050 by 10 percent and 2 percent respectively largely due to a significant net immigration.

Of course, a "working-age population decline" does not automatically lead to a "labor shortage" or a subsequent "war for talent." Much of the gap between supply and demand depends on *demand* not just supply.

However, unlike projecting supply, projecting demand out 20–30 years is a very tricky business. Nonetheless, given the magnitude of the drop in labor supply in many developed countries such as Germany, Spain, Italy, and Japan, demand would also have to drop dramatically and stay down for a long period of time to avoid a talent shortage and a subsequent war for talent. If demand does not drop in these countries, then productivity gains would have to be large enough to fill the gap between shrinking labor supply and growing demand in order to avoid a war for talent. So far there are no data to support either a significant and protracted drop in demand or such a dramatic increase in productivity. Taken together, this is why the alarm sounded by folks at McKinsey a decade ago about a war for talent in developed countries is still relevant today.

Even though McKinsey was correct to sound the alarm back then and the threat still exists today, the concern faded and is only beginning to come back into focus relative to developed countries. The main reason many people pushed aside McKinsey's warning in 2005 was because demand did drop dramatically with the Financial Crisis in 2008 and the Great Recession in 2009. The concern was slow to come back to top executives in large part because the recovery from the Great Recession was slow and weak. However, because the supply problems never went away and demand recovered sufficiently, by 2015 a Conference Board survey showed that human capital issues were the top strategic concern for CEOs.[5]

Emerging Market Supply

Compared to developed markets, the supply–demand gap in emerging markets is quite severe and will remain so over the next 20–30 years. This gap is driven by both insufficient supply and rising demand. The talent shortage and war for talent in developing markets is likely to be even more intense in the coming years than it has in the past or than it has been or will be in developed markets. This intensifying talent shortage and war is driven by both supply problems and demand or growth projections.

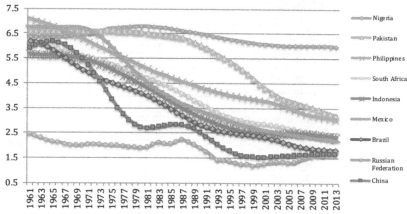

Exhibit 4.11 **Declining fertility rates in developing countries.**

Source: World Bank.

On the supply side, many developing countries have challenges related to both the quantity of talent they are projected to have (i.e., workforce size) and the quality of that talent (i.e., the extent and depth of education and training). In terms of quantity, the sad fact is that most developing countries, excepting Nigeria, have followed developed countries' trend toward lower birth rates as illustrated in Exhibit 4.11.

As a consequence, in many cases the size of the workforce population is projected to decline going forward. Exhibit 4.12 lists key developing countries that will see their workforce population peak before 2020 and the percentage their workforce will decline from its peak by 2050.

Emerging Market Demand

In emerging economies, demand for talent is surging and in most cases outstripping supply. The growth in demand is a function of both internal and external forces. Internally, local firms are growing and as they grow need more and more workers and managers. Externally, as foreign firms invest in emerging markets, they increase their need for workers and managers. In 1980, the World Bank estimated that developed countries accounted for about 80 percent of the world's GDP, while emerging economies accounted for just 20 percent. In 2014, the World Bank estimated that developed and developing countries each accounted for 50 percent.

Country	Workforce Decline
Belarus	34.5%
Bulgaria	37.1%
China	21.5%
Croatia	27.1%
Cuba	28.4%
Czech Republic	14.7%
Georgia	28.6%
Hungary	21.7%
Puerto Rico	10.5%
Romania	36.9%
Russia	28.2%
Serbia	34.5%
Thailand	26.3%
Ukraine	34.1%
Vietnam	3.1%

Exhibit 4.12   Workforce declines in selected developing countries.

Source: World Bank.

In Chapter 3, I pointed out that FDI as a percentage of world GDP has more than doubled in the last 25 years. During this period, the absolute change in FDI stock has increased nearly nine-fold from $2.3 trillion to over $25.9 trillion. In terms of the destination of those investments, Exhibit 4.13 shows that emerging economies' share of that rapidly increasing FDI has doubled. Thus, whereas in 1990, $35 billion flowed into emerging economies, in 2014 a total of $729 billion flowed in.

Is it any wonder that in developing countries that received heavy FDI flows over the last ten years, such as China, the talent shortages are intense and growing worse. For example, in China, along with growing demand from foreign multinational corporations (MNCs), former and current Chinese state-owned enterprises (SOE), and Chinese private-owned enterprises (POE) have increased their investments in China. Combined, this has fueled a rising demand for talent, especially at the senior level and across various high-skilled functions (legal, finance, HR, marketing, supply chain management, operations, etc.). For example, McKinsey estimated that the supply of effective MNC managers in China was only 5,000, but demand was 75,000.[6] It also found that while China created 1.6 million young engineers, only 160,000 were suited for MNCs because so much of their training was purely theoretical.[7] The lack of practically trained engineers is one of the factors that contributed to China ranking 40th out of 103 countries in terms of their ability to grow vocational talent according to the a new Global Talent

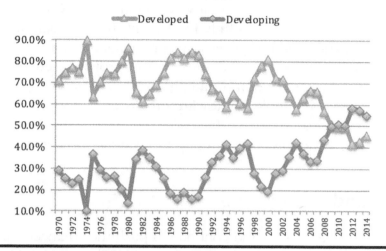

Exhibit 4.13 Percentage of FDI inflow to developed and developing countries.
Source: World Investment Report 2014; UNCTAD.

Competitiveness Index created by INSEAD. China ranked 86th in terms of its ability to grow talent with higher skills and competencies.[8]

With total supply shrinking—not just in developed countries but in emerging economies as well—and with demand, especially for educated workers growing, the net result seems to be a general talent shortage in many countries. If these trends are merely *directionally* correct, we would expect to see wages rising to offset the supply-and-demand imbalance—and this is *exactly* what we're seeing. For example, in China, managers' wages have risen 10 percent to 20 percent *per year* over the last decade.[9]

This same imbalance can be seen in other Asian countries such as Vietnam. Again, the supply–demand gap exists not because Vietnam doesn't have enough people, but because it lacks people with the experience that companies need. As in China, most of Vietnam's lack of qualified labor is due to a dearth of educational and past work opportunities—the kind of opportunities that would train the workers needed most. As a consequence, in the recently released Global Talent Competitiveness Index, Vietnam ranked 82nd out of 103 countries examined.[10] Of the 13 countries ranked in Southeast Asia, it ranked 11th with only Indonesia and Cambodia ranking lower. It ranked 91st on its ability to grow talent, especially via its education system. It ranked 88th in terms of its ability to produce talent with managerial and technical skills such as engineering.

Although improvements in the quantity and quality of education will likely increase, these are changes that vast countries like China, India, and Vietnam will require decades to fully implement. In the meantime, for virtually all industries and companies, Asia remains the one bright spot of potential growth, and, therefore, an area of ever-growing demand for talent. This shift in growing demand and trailing supply has unwittingly tilted the balance of power from employers toward employees, especially those in the service and knowledge areas. This, like the other shifts, has raised the stakes (positive and negative) of winning the war for the best people.

Summary and Implications

In summary, five forces have and continue to push the balance of power away from employers and toward employees. First, the shift in competitive advantage from tangible to intangible assets pushes the balance of power toward employees because they either are the sum and substance of intangible assets or are their principle driver. Second, the globalization of competitive scope places a premium on talent that can spot and respond to a greater array and volatility of competitors, customers, regulators, NGOs, etc. Third, the shift in information asymmetry that now allows employees to know supply, demand, and pricing (i.e., wages) conditions pushes more power toward employees and away from employers. Fourth, the lowering of employee switching costs via the dramatic change from defined benefit to defined contribution plans shifts power in the direction of employees. Fifth and finally, the shrinking labor supply in many developed and developing countries and the resurgent current and likely rising future demand also shifts power to employees.

As far as I can determine, none of the shifts described appear to be temporary. None of these genies will be stuffed back in their bottles. As a consequence, the war for talent, especially in high-knowledge industries such as education, consultancy, financial services, information technology, pharmaceuticals, aerospace, etc., is likely to get more intense before it abates.

Notes

1. Vernon Smith, 2008. *Rationality in Economics,* Cambridge University Press, Cambridge, England.
2. "NADA Data." *NADA: National Automobile Dealers Association.* N.p., n.d. Web. 26 Apr. 2017.

3. John Broadbent, Michael Palumbo, and Elizabeth Woodman, 2006. "The Shift from Defined Benefit to Defined Contribution Pension Plans - Implications for Asset Allocation and Risk Management." http://bis.hasbeenforeclosed.com/publ/wgpapers/cgfs27broadbent3.pdf
4. Elizabeth G. Chambers, Mark Foulon, Helen Handfield-Jones, Steven M. Hankin, and Edward G. Michaels III, 1998. "The War for Talent," *McKinsey Quarterly*, no. 3, pp. 44–57.
5. CEO Challenge: 2015. https://www.conference-board.org/ceo-challenge2015/index.cfm?id=28618
6. Diana Ferrell and Andrew J. Gran, 2005. "China's Looming Talent Shortage," *McKinsey Quarterly*, 4, pp. 71–79.
7. Diana Ferrell and Andrew J. Gran, 2005. "China's Looming Talent Shortage," *McKinsey Quarterly*, 4, pp. 71–79.
8. Global Talent Competitiveness Index, 2013. http://global-indices.insead.edu/gtci/
9. Jimmy Hexter and Jonathan Woetzel, 2007. *Operation China: From Strategy to Execution*, Harvard Business School Press, Boston.
10. Bruno Lanvin and Paul Evans, (eds) 2013. *The Global Talent Competitiveness Index 2013*. http://global-indices.insead.edu/gtci/documents/gcti-report.pdf

SUMMARY

1

If you take nothing else away from Part 1, I think two "takeaways" are worthwhile. First, as I documented extensively, there has been a significant shift in the primary source of competitive advantage and its chief enabler from tangible assets and financial capital to intangible assets and human capital. This shift looks to be a permanent one. To complement this, there has been a shift in the balance of power away from employers and toward employees. This shift also shows only signs of being here to stay.

To the extent that these shifts have happened and will continue, the ability to win *with* human capital and the intangible assets and the competitive advantages they supply will only grow more important. Because to win the battle *with* human capital you have to win the contest *for* human capital and because that contest is only going to get more intense, employers will have to work harder than they ever have in order to attract, retain, and motivate the talent they need. The extent and permanency of these shifts is why I argue that human capital will be the final frontier of competition (at least during my lifetime). To compete effectively, you will have to win the twin battles of competing *for* and *with* human capital. As a consequence, I predict that human capital will move out of the primary purview of human resource managers and onto the top agenda of business executives everywhere. The results of The Conference Board in its 2015 global survey CEOs I mentioned in Chapter 4 seem to support this. The following diagram illustrates the interaction between competing for and with human capital and winning the ultimate battle in the marketplace.

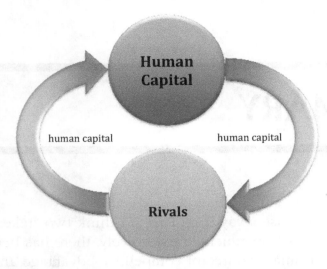

If any of the shifts in competitive advantage and in the role of human capital that I have documented in Part 1 ring true to you, then you should find Part 2 of this book tremendously valuable. Based on my research, the good news is that companies with superior employee value propositions (EVP) can achieve levels of talent attraction, retention, and engagement that are twice as good as firms with non-systematic, non-strategic and, therefore, poorer EVPs. The research also points to multiple configurations for a superior EVP. In other words, there is more than one way to win the war for talent. However, creating a winning EVP is not easy and requires deliberate and strategic discussion, decisions, and actions. Superior EVPs don't build themselves or happen by accident.

How we think about effective EVPs, how we can assess where we are, and how we should determine what actions will build a superior EVP in order to attract, retain, and motivate differentiated human capital and achieve superior business results is the subject of Part 2 of this book. In the end, Part 2 provides solutions regarding *how* to compete effectively *for* human capital—in other words it addresses the issue of how to get the people you want to want you.

COMPETING *FOR* HUMAN CAPITAL

As I mentioned at the beginning of Part 1, often we don't exercise when we know we should because we don't have a deep enough understanding of why exercise is good for us. Hopefully at this point you have additional and sufficient insights into why "people are our most important asset" is more than a nice platitude, and now you are motivated to dig into how to win the battle *for* human capital. As I mentioned, that is the main objective of Part 2.

In Part 2, Chapter 5 lays the foundation by examining how employees look at and evaluate employers. Before you can get the people you want to want you, you have to understand how they look at you—how they evaluate the value proposition you put to them.

With the foundation laid, Chapter 6 lays out the superstructure of superior and inferior employee value propositions (EVPs), much like the frame of a house. Just as you can visually see the frame of a house, Chapter 6 illustrates how you can literally graph where your EVP is today and where you need to be tomorrow. Chapter 6 concludes by highlighting the 12 years of research that underlie this framework and by documenting the empirical relationship between superior EVPs and important outcomes such as retention, turnover, absenteeism, and employee commitment.

With the foundation and frame of the house set in Chapters 5 and 6, Chapter 7 gets into the detail of finishing and furnishing the house. However, just as there are no absolute right finishings and furnishings (what's right depends on what you want), so too getting the people you want to want you is predicated on knowing who you really want and need. This turns out to be a bit more complicated than simply saying, "I want the best."

Nonetheless, Chapter 7 provides a very structured and logical way to determine who you want, which then allows you to create an EVP in nature and strength that gets the people you want to want you.

With that, let's dive into Chapter 5 and examine how employees evaluate working for you and the value proposition you put to them.

Chapter 5

How Do Employees Assess Employers?

As I pointed out at the very beginning of this book, even though virtually all business leaders *say* that people are their most important asset, few have created sound human capital strategies to attract, retain, and motivate the talent they need. Even among those with a battle plan to win the competition for talent, most don't have concrete metrics to track the progress of the campaign. Among the very few that have a strategy and metrics to measure progress, only a handful actually hold managers accountable for their performance on the human capital front.

If the trends described in Part 1 are as robust and as long-lived as I've argued, then failing to develop a good human capital strategy, not enacting concrete measures to track progress, and not holding people accountable for results is akin to the CEO telling shareholders at the annual meeting, "We are targeting a 20 percent return on capital employed, but we don't really know what this means, we have no real idea how we are going to achieve it, and we don't have any plans to hold executives accountable if we miss the target." In today's environment, no CEO would dare make such a statement for fear of being booed out of the room—or worse. Yet, this is essentially the message coming from many leaders with regard to their human capital strategies.

The good news is that it needn't be so. It *is* possible to create a superior employee value proposition—one that enables you to become the employer of choice. It *is* possible to establish concrete measures so you can know how well you're doing. It *is* possible to hold leaders accountable for human capital targets, and to build a culture in which the focus on differentiated human capital is baked into the firm's DNA. My research finds that companies with superior employee value propositions (EVP) have levels of talent retention that are twice that of companies with unsystematic, non-strategic, and ad hoc EVPs. But achieving these results requires a deep understanding of how workers assess companies' attractiveness and the value propositions they offer.

Employer of Choice: A Judged Competition

When I ask executives about differentiated human capital, they can quickly articulate what they need employees to contribute—e.g., they need employees to think outside the box, challenge the status quo, continuously improve, gain customer insights, pursue operational excellence, move from good to great, innovate, and so on. They talk about people and their contributions in the same way they talk technology, plant, equipment, and other tangible assets. This mindset leads many executives to overlook the recent changes in the employer–employee balance of power that was the focus of Chapter 4. They forget or underappreciate that the balance of power has changed—that they no longer have any choice but to understand deeply how employees decide who to join, whether to stay, and how far above and beyond the call of duty to go.

I've met many executives who, while they philosophically embrace the value of differentiated human capital, complain to me about the "wooly" or "fuzzy" nature of the topic as it is usually presented. As I've said, "Employer of Choice" is an oft-quoted phrase, but many executives would like to see strategies and plans as concrete as those they have to prepare for "CapEx" investments to ensure returns above their cost of capital. If you're one of those executives who would like to see a more concrete approach to the wooly notion of employer of choice, I think you will be very interested in the next few sections of this chapter. My objective is to remove the fuzziness surrounding how employees decide whether to join, stay with, leave, hold back from, or go the extra mile for an organization. In fact, I hope to make it as clear as understanding why customers buy or don't buy from you. Once it is clear how employees make these decisions, it becomes much easier to lay out concrete plans for creating a superior employee value proposition and becoming the employer of choice, just as once you understand how customers decide what product or service to buy (what they care most and least about), it becomes much easier to design products and services that meet their needs and fashion customer value propositions that win business. In fact, because of the dynamics described in Chapter 4, the balance of power has shifted enough away from employers and toward employees that that how they evaluate employers is very much akin to how customers make purchase and repurchase decisions. So much so, that company executives might be better off thinking of their talent as customers of employment choices rather than as traditional employees.

"What Do I Get?"

When deciding which company to join, whether to stay or leave a current employer, and whether to hold back, just do their job, or go the extra mile for the firm, employees carefully evaluate what they get from the firm. This will likely come as no surprise to any reader. This hasn't changed in the last 50 or 100 years. What has changed, however, is that because employees increasingly have more information, choice, and lower switching costs when it comes to employment, they view this part of the deal with an increasingly critical eye. In addition to appreciating this change, it is important to have a deeper insight into what both prospective and current employees look for and look at with their critical eye.

All the books and articles on GenXers, Millennials, and the like would have you believe that they are oh so different from the Baby Boomers. You get the impression that Millennials are jumping from job to job much more frequently than Baby Boomers. If you compare Millennials at 25–34 years old to Baby boomers at 55–64, then there is a big difference in "time in job" or what is typically referred to as tenure (i.e., length of time with their current employer). However, according to the U.S. Department of Labor, Bureau of Labor Statistics[1] if you compare Millennials at 25–34 years old to Baby Boomers when they were 25–34 years old, there is virtually no difference in average tenure. In 1983 Baby Boomers, age 25–34, had an average job tenure of 3.0 years and in 2016 Millennials, age 25–34, had an average job tenure of 2.9 years. In the 33 intervening years, the average only fluctuated between 2.7 and 3.2 years.

This does not mean that Baby Boomers or GenXers or Millennials change jobs or stay in jobs at the same frequency for the same exact reasons. However, fifty years of research, including my own, suggest that the basket of benefits they evaluate is fairly constant. It includes four broad baskets of

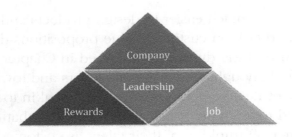

Exhibit 5.1   Dimensions of the employee value proposition.

benefits that employees care about: company, leadership, job, and rewards. What has shifted and what does shift not only across generations but even across industries and countries is the weighted value employees put on some of the specifics within these general categories.

I arrange these four baskets of benefits in a triangle with some symbolic reference. "Company" is placed at the top, not because it is always the most important, but because it is the most general. "Rewards" and "Job" are placed at the bottom because they are the most specific in nature. "Leaders" are placed in the center because they can and do influence the nature and quality of the other three (see Exhibit 5.1).

Company

This basket consists of what the company does (the challenges it tackles), how it approaches them (its values and culture), and how well or poorly it fares in its attempts (its performance and reputation). Employees working for a large pharmaceutical company may take satisfaction in knowing that they're creating drugs that save lives. They may take satisfaction in a culture of inclusiveness where employee input and opinions are valued. They may be proud of the strong financial performance of the firm and its ranking in the industry. Or they may hang their heads in shame when it's disclosed that certain side effects of a drug were hidden in order to help the drug move forward from clinical trials to commercial sale. Or they may be frustrated by an organization culture that stifles diversity of opinion or they may be embarrassed to mention who they work for when the company's large losses are dominating the headlines. Whether employees have to hang their heads in shame or can lift them with pride when they tell people where they work is something that all employees care about. Granted, not all employees care about this factor to the same degree, but they all care about it to an important degree.

Leadership

All employees care about the quality of a company's leadership, and because the leaders who are closest to them have the biggest impact on them, decades of research have consistently found that employees care most about *those* leaders. This is why the aphorism, "People join companies but leave bosses" is so widely quoted. This is also why your ability to identify and develop future leaders not just at the top of the organization but down in its bowels is a critical component of your organization's EVP. Because almost everyone has to work for someone, your company's ability to groom good leaders directly affects the quality of work life for employees. Do your leaders care about the employees? Do they spend time coaching and developing them? To the extent that employees answer "yes" to these and other related questions, the quality of this EVP component goes up.

Job

No surprise, employees also care about their jobs. They care about the extent to which it is interesting or exciting, as well as the freedom, challenges, and growth opportunities it provides. Do their jobs make them feel good about what they do today and optimistic about their prospects for tomorrow? Do their jobs allow them to develop their capabilities and work with interesting and new technology? Do their jobs enable them to use their knowledge, judgment, and skills? The extent to which companies give employees the tools they need to do their jobs well and to the extent that they structure jobs with freedom, challenge, and growth is an important part of a firm's EVP to prospective and current employees.

Rewards

The final basket of benefits is the one on which executives usually focus. It's a no-brainer that direct financial rewards are important to employees—in other words: money matters. In most cases, however, money doesn't matter in the way that we think it does. People care about how much money they make, not because they care about the money itself, but because they care about what money can do for them. People focus on money because it is so flexible. For example, if someone cares a lot about personal and family needs, money can help them buy housing, food, clothing, and the like. If they have high status or ego gratification needs, they can use money to buy a big house or a fancy car. If they care about relaxation, adventure, or entertainment, they can use money to buy a vacation in Hawaii, a safari in Africa, or a night out on Broadway to fulfill their needs. It is the very versatility of money as a means of satisfying other desired ends that makes it so powerful. Even when people have so much money that they have already bought most of what they could want, money sometimes serves to simply satisfy a status, ego, or self-worth by comparing how much money they make relative to others. The bottom line is that direct financial rewards have always been and will continue to be an important component of a company's EVP. However, in saying this we need to appreciate that in most cases it is not the money per se that is valued but rather what money can buy that people value.

In addition to direct financial rewards, people also value and assess a firm's nonfinancial rewards. Research has consistently demonstrated that people also care about career prospects, development opportunities, praise, recognition, and the opportunity to interact with "work friends."[2]

So What?

I can imagine that at this point you are saying to yourself, "These four baskets make sense but they are *not* new. In fact, our employee survey measures employee satisfaction with various items within each of these four baskets." If you are saying this to yourself, well done. However, I will add two new dimensions in this chapter (i.e., price and relative comparison) that when combined with the four "common sense" baskets of benefits described previously end up making all the difference in predicting key outcomes such as attraction, retention, and extra effort.

What Do I Pay?

The first new dimension that this more powerful approach to employee value proposition takes is the inclusion of price. As I stressed up to this point, employees (prospective and current) examine and judge what they think they will get or are currently getting across these four baskets of benefits. However, they don't stop there. They only begin there. Their calculation continues because they know that there is no free lunch; they know that they will have to pay some price for what they get. Therefore, in addition to assessing what they get from the company, they also assess what they will have to give (i.e., the price they will pay) to the company. Typically when I'm leading a discussion on this point, I don't even get the chance to explain or examine the price employees pay before someone (usually it's an HR manager) pipes up and says, "No, you've got it backwards. We pay employees; they don't pay us." Fair enough, but as I will describe in more detail later, my research clearly shows that, from employees' perspectives, there are three key points:

1. Employees pay a price to work for a given company;
2. That perceived price varies from one company to another; and
3. The perceived price has a direct impact of the attractiveness (or unattractiveness) of the firm's value proposition.

So what price do employees pay? Think about your own situation at work. What price do you feel you pay? Do you pay a price in time or hours? Stress? Fretting about work even when you're not at work? Having interviewed and surveyed literally thousands of people from clerks to CEOs, within a few seconds of asking people about the price they pay to work where they work specific examples come pouring out. At the top of this list is time. This includes the hours each day people spend on the job, as well as the time they spend commuting and the time they spend away from home traveling for their job. Next on the list of prices is that of stress and worry. This includes the stress people feel when they are at work, as well as the worrying and fretting they do about work when they are not at work. The third big category of price is that related to the energy, effort, and concentration people put into their work. In sum, the price people pay is the blood, sweat, and tears they expend on the company's behalf.

As mentioned, while it may take a moment to get this conversation about "price" going, once it gets going, it is hard to stop it. As a consequence, a few minutes into it and most people perk up and say, "You know, you're right. As employees we do pay a price for what they get. There is no free lunch." Executives, in particular HR executives, then also typically admit that they almost never measure the price employees feel they pay in any measures of employee satisfaction or engagement.

But so what if you don't measure it? Why does it matter? It matters for the very simple reason that as humans we instinctively compare what we pay to what we get and make judgments about how good or bad of a deal it is. We instinctively ask ourselves without making the question a formal or even conscious one, "Is the quality of the company, my boss and the general leaders, my job, and the rewards I receive worth the price I pay?" The stronger the answer is "yes," the more sense it makes to stay with the good deal we have. The key outcome of this evaluation is higher retention. Likewise, for prospective employees the stronger the "yes" is to the questions about whether the antici-pated quality of the company, boss and the general leaders, job, and rewards be worth the anticipated price, the more likely they are to join the company.

In contrast, the stronger current employees answer "No," to the question is what they get worth the price they pay, the less sense it makes to stay with the bad deal. This negative assessment is what causes people to look for other options and potentially leave. Obviously, the more employees who come down on the "No" side of the question, the higher the firm's overall turnover. In essence, people do some simple math in their head: Benefits/ Price = Value (as illustrated in Exhibit 5.2).

Prospective employees go through the exact same calculus but it is an anticipatory calculus not a current or retrospective one. Nonetheless, the impact of their answers is the same. The more they believe that what they get will not be worth what they have to pay, the less likely they are to join the firm.

In fact, how people as employees make this first, rough calculation of value is no different than how we as customers make initial calculations of value. To illustrate this, think back to the last time you bought a car. No doubt you evaluated what you got in terms of the car's styling, fuel econ-omy, power, reliability, fit and finish, and so on. But if someone asks you if you would go back to the dealer again or if they should go to that dealer to buy a car, I'm confident in predicting that you would not give an answer based *only* on what you got; you would also factor in what you paid for what you got. As I say, how we as humans intuitively calculate value doesn't really change much whether it is an assessment of the value proposition to us as customers or as employees. In fact, given how much more informa-tion people now have as employees, given how much lower their switching

Exhibit 5.2   Employee value calculation.

costs are, and given how the balance of power has swung more away from employers and toward employees, as I pointed out at the beginning of this chapter, we are better off thinking of employees as choosy customers of employment opportunities rather than as lucky recipients of an employment gift that firms graciously bestow.

What Are My Alternatives?

Although prospective or current employees make these intuitive calculations to determine value, they do not stop there. Before they make a final judgment about how good or bad a prospective or existing employment deal is (its value), they take a look around. Humans are by their basic nature social comparative creatures. They can't help but judge the value a present opportunity in the context of alternatives.

This need to compare is so deeply rooted in humans that we can see it even in our primate cousins. Consider the following famous experiment.[3] Two monkeys are trained to retrieve a rock placed in their respective cages and hand it to the experimenter. In exchange, each monkey receives a slice of cucumber as reward. The monkeys like cucumbers and therefore will repeat this task for the reward more than two dozen times in a row. In the context of our previous discussion, it is a positive value proposition because the *benefits* they receive (i.e., the slice of cucumber) is worth as much or more than the *price* they pay (i.e., retrieving the rock).

Once imprinted with this task–reward pattern, two monkeys are placed side by side in separate cages with plexiglass walls—allowing them to see each other. The *first* monkey has a small stone placed it its cage. It retrieves the stone and through a small opening in the cage hands the stone to the experimenter. The experimenter gives the monkey a cucumber slice as a reward. The monkey gladly eats it.

The *second* monkey has a small stone placed it its cage. It retrieves the stone and through a small opening in the cage hands the stone to the experimenter. The experimenter gives the monkey a *grape* as a reward. The monkey very gladly eats it. The first monkey sees all this. It is important to note that for both of these monkeys, grapes are more desirable food than cucumbers. In other words, they like cucumbers but they love grapes.

Again the experimenter places a small stone in the *first* monkey's cage. The monkey retrieves the stone and hands it to the experimenter. As before, the experimenter gives this first monkey a cucumber slice as a reward. The monkey takes it, looks at it, and then throws it back at the experimenter and shakes the cage, communicating his displeasure. Keep in mind that just moments before, the reward of a cucumber was perfectly satisfactory to the first monkey.

Without reacting to this first monkey, the experimenter again places a small stone in the *second* monkey's cage. The monkey retrieves the stone and hands it to the experimenter. The experimenter again gives the monkey a grape as a reward. The monkey very gladly eats it.

The first monkey sees all this a second time. Again a small rock is placed in the first monkey's cage and again he retrieves it and gives it to the experimenter. As before, the experimenter gives the first monkey a slice of cucumber as a reward. Again, even though previously he was totally satisfied with receiving a cucumber slice for the task, the first monkey rejects it; throws it back at the experimenter; and shakes his cage, displaying his displeasure at the unfairness. If you continue this back and forth, at some point the first monkey typically will simply refuse to retrieve the rock—essentially the first monkey will go on strike and refuse to "work."

It turns out that people are no different. We have this deeply embedded need to compare our deal with that of others. As a consequence, what in isolation might be a totally satisfactory "deal" can become unsatisfactory if, when compared to alternatives, the alternative looks like a better deal. In social and behavioral science this phenomenon is explained in what is called the "Equity Theory of Motivation." This theory is one of the most researched and well substantiated models of human motivation that we have today.[4]

It is important to note that while the monkeys in the experiment were able to see directly the alternative value proposition, in the area of employment much of the basis of comparison is perception not direct or full observation or experience. We think, we believe, we've heard, that someone at Company X doing the same job that we are doing is getting paid more, has a better boss, works in a nicer environment, etc. We believe but in many cases we don't know for sure. However, the fact that we make comparisons on incomplete information, even potentially inaccurate information, and therefore really have only perceptions of the available alternatives, in no way keeps us from (a) making the comparisons or (b) acting on them. Essentially, when it comes to how employees evaluate options and alternatives, *perception is reality*.

No doubt in your own experience you have seen people act on perceptions even when they were empirically wrong. For example, perhaps you have known an employee who left your firm believing that he or she was going to get a better deal (higher pay, more interesting job, better boss, more friendly company culture, less stress, etc.) at a different company. Once the person made the switch to the other company, the individual discovered that what he or she perceived and anticipated as better was in fact not; yet the person still acted on the mistaken perception and left your company to join the other. In some cases, the mistaken perception may have been so big that the individual came to you begging for their old job back. Even in this more dramatic case, it is important to keep in mind that their mistaken perception did not stop them from leaving in the first place. To repeat: when it comes to employee value propositions, perception is reality.

Obviously these dynamics can work in the opposite direction as well. People may have a vastly inferior employment value proposition when compared to what they realistically could have at another company but if they have *no* perception of this, turnover will *not* be higher, absenteeism will *not* be greater, extra effort will *not* be lower, etc.; just as the first monkey would have been happy to keep getting cucumbers in exchange for his work of retrieving the rock if he had not seen the other monkey getting a grape for doing the same work.

With this as background, a look under the hood of Equity Theory is worth a couple more pages in order to highlight more clearly exactly how prospective or current employees evaluate a company's value propositions. However, don't worry; we're only going to take a brief look under the hood. We don't need to take the engine out and completely disassemble it in order to understand how Equity Theory works in practice.

With this in mind, the first thing worth noting in the context of Equity Theory is that people are pretty good at differentiating between *equity* versus *equality*. To illustrate this, let me present to you an example that over the years I have put to literally thousands of executives from over 100 countries during various seminars, workshops, and speeches.

> *Two people get paid for their work. Person A gets $200 per hour. Person B gets $100 per hour. Is this equal?*

Essentially 100 percent of participants say, "No." Clearly, Person A is getting paid twice as much as Person B.

> *Is this equitable? Is it fair?*

Virtually 100 percent of participants remark, "It depends." "On what?" I ask. Quite quickly the ensuing discussion brings out that in order to judge the equity of the situation we need to know what each person puts "in" (i.e., the price) relative to what he or she is getting "out" (i.e., the benefits). Participants quickly ask if the two people are doing the same work. To this question, I give the following reply.

> *Assume Person A (who gets $200 per hour) does work that is twice as complicated as Person B (who gets $100 per hour). In this case, do the different "outcomes" now seem fair? Also assume that Person A put in four years of university education in order to do the complicated work she does and Person B put in no university education to do the work he does. Does the different pay per hour now seem fair or equitable?*

With rare exception, participants at this point feel that the difference in pay between Person A and B is probably equitable or fair.

This simple example illustrates the fundamental dynamic of how people and even monkey's judge equity or fairness. We look not at just what we get or put in but we compare it to others. When making the comparison, we don't just look at what others get (the benefits), we also look at what they put in (the price they pay).

As a very short side-note, I should point out that what I refer to as benefits in the formal Equity Theory are called "outcomes" (or Os for short) and what I refer to "prices" in Equity Theory are called "inputs" (or Is for short). Because these labels are essentially referring the same things, I will continue to talk about *benefits* and *price* but just be aware that if you read anything formal on Equity Theory, it will talk about *outcomes* and *inputs* and O/I (outcome/input) ratios not benefits and prices.

Returning to our monkey experiment, the reason that the first monkey in the experiment was so upset was because the other monkey was getting a better benefit for the same price. The monkey getting the grape was retrieving a rock the same size and carrying it over the same small distance to hand it to the experimenter as the monkey getting the cucumber slice. The price was the same but the benefit was different. The first monkey showed how unfair he thought this was by throwing his benefit (i.e., the cucumber slice) back at the experimenter. And by doing so actually worsened his deal—he paid the price by retrieving the rock but by throwing the cucumber at the experimenter got nothing in return.

On this fundamental principle, people and monkeys are the same. In determining if we are getting a fair deal, we compare our deal to others around us—inside and outside the company. In the process, we don't just look at what others are getting but look at what they are putting in and compare their benefit/price ratio to ours. If we feel the deal is unfair, we voice our displeasure. I will cover exactly how we typically express our displeasure a little later in this chapter.

For the moment we just need to keep in mind that in computing value we first look at what we get for what we pay and based on this we make an initial judgment as to whether it is a good or bad deal. However, we do not stop there, we only start there. We then compare our deal to that of others. This comparison can make what was in isolation a good or a bad deal flip the opposite direction. A previously good deal in comparison can seem bad and a previously bad deal in comparison can seem good.

However, to more fully understand the comparison process, we need to dig just a little deeper. This is because we make two kinds of comparisons and both can have a significant impact on the final judgment of value and our reactions to that judgment. The first is what scholars refer to as "across person, within time" comparisons. The second is what they refer to as "Across Time, Within Person" comparisons. However, don't let these phrases scare you; they are just fancy, scientific labels for two simple but powerful assessments.

Comparison 1: Across Person, Within Time

The first comparison that people make is of themselves to others at a given point in time. This is what the first monkey did. He looked at his benefit/price ratio and compared it to his neighbor and felt that he was now getting "ripped off" whereas before the comparison he was happy with his deal. He was so unhappy with the deal after the comparison and felt that his deal was now so relatively unfair that he worsened it by throwing back his reward to put an exclamation point behind his dissatisfaction.

To better understand the process, let's look at a different situation. Suppose you were paid $100 an hour for loading rocks into a crusher and someone else was paid $500 per hour for loading rocks into a crusher. Would that be fair or unfair? Before deciding, research shows that people intuitively compare not just what they get but also what they give. Returning to our example, suppose you got $100 for loading 1,000 pounds of rocks per hour and producing 500 pounds of crushed rock. Suppose the person who got paid $500 an hour loaded 5,000 pounds of rocks per hour and produced 2,500 pounds of crushed rock. Based on this added information, does the

$$\text{Benefits} \Big/ \text{Price} \quad \blacksquare \quad \text{Benefits} \Big/ \text{Price}$$

Person A; Time 1　　　　　Person B; Time 1

Exhibit 5.3　Across person, within time comparisons.

difference in pay seem fair or not? When I've used this simple example, the majority of people feel that the difference in pay is fair.

What if the person who got $500 per hour didn't load rocks? What if the other person was the company's chief financial officer (CFO)? Is the difference in pay fair? Does the fact that the company's CFO went through four years of college and then two additional years of business school come into play in assessing fairness? For the two ratios to seem fair, the six years of college would have to cause you to feel that the price in CFO's ratio is at least 5X higher than your own in order for the CFO's $500 per hour to seem fair compared to your $100 per hour.

There is no need to get carried away with numerical or mathematical precision here because in real life people don't. They don't pull out calculators and crunch equity comparisons to the third decimal place. However, the research is completely definitive in demonstrating that we make "across person, within time" comparisons (see Exhibit 5.3) and that those comparisons directly affect whether we think we have a good deal or not.

Comparison 2: Across Time, Within Person

The second comparison we make is across (or over) time but within ourselves. For example, assume that you were getting paid $100 per hour for lifting 1,000 pounds of rocks per hour into a crusher, which then produced 500 pounds of crushed rock. Assume that in Year 1 of this job you were happy with your pay and felt it was fair compensation for the backbreaking work you did.

Now assume that five years later you are getting paid $120 per hour. Is this a fair increase? You know by now that it depends on how your input has changed. Assume, now you can load 3,000 pounds of rocks per hour with nothing having changed except the strength in your back. But that is not all. With your experience, you have learned which rocks work best in the crusher and which ones don't. Now you can avoid the rocks that don't break easily or ones that break up so small that they grind to dust and gum up the gears on the crusher. So now instead of 1,000 pounds of rocks per hour you put in 3,000 (three times as much) and instead of 500 pounds of crushed rock coming out, 2,000 pounds (four times as much) come out per hour. Do you feel the $120 per hour is fair and equitable? If you are like most people I've shown this simple scenario to, you will feel that the increase of $100 to $120 for a 3X increase in rocks loaded and a 4X increase in crushed rocks produced is *un*fair. Intuitively you look at your benefits/ price ratio in Year 1 ($100 per hour/500 pounds of crushed rock per hour) and compare it to your ratio in Year 5 (120/2,000) and you feel that this "across time, within person" situation is unfair. What if the Year 5 ratio was $400/2,000 (compared to the Year 1 ratio of $100/500), would this be fair? When I've polled literally hundreds of participants on this, the vast majority see the second scenario of $400 per hour vs. $120 per hour for loading 3,000 pounds per hour instead of 500 pounds of rock and producing 2,000 pounds of crushed rock per hour instead of 500 pounds per hour as much more equitable.

Again, in providing these simple examples with numbers, I am not suggesting that people pull out calculators or punch in numbers on a spreadsheet and run "across time, within person" calculations. However, the research on this is unequivocal—we do make intuitive assessments of whether the "deal" we are getting today compared to the past is getting worse, staying about the same, or getting better (see Exhibit 5.4) and that conclusion directly affects our subsequent actions.

Implications of Bad and Good Deals

Hopefully, this all makes logical sense to you, but you may be asking, "Why do we care about these EVP assessments or these 'across person, within time' or 'within time, within person' comparisons in the context of winning the war for talent? What consequences do all these dynamics have?" The answer is simple. These assessments directly affect the judgments of prospective and current employees as to how attractive or unattractive

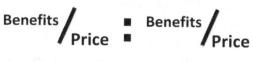

Exhibit 5.4   Across time, within person comparisons.

your value proposition is to them and subsequently affect likely actions. Specifically, the evaluations affect whether prospective employees will join your firm or not, whether employees will stay with or leave you, will diligently show up for work or look for any excuse and use every opportunity to miss work, and whether employees will go the extra mile for you or do only the minimum they feel they have to. Obviously, all of these consequences have direct impact on your firm's financial and market performance.

However, it is worth a paragraph or two to examine in just a bit more detail how prospective and current employees work through these assessments and how these assessments impact these key outcomes.

Prospective Employees

For prospective employees, they first look at the anticipated or proposed employment value proposition (EVP) in isolation. They determine whether the basket of benefits they expect to receive divided by the price they expect to pay yields an outcome that is greater than or equal to one or not. Typically, if the proposed EVP is less than one, it is "game over."

In making the "isolated" EVP assessment, some aspects of the basket of benefits or price in the EVP, such as pay or required work hours, are easier to quantify, verify, and evaluate than others. However, do not assume just because some aspects of the benefits or price are harder to quantify that employees don't pay attention to them. They do. Also, keep in mind that some elements of the EVP that might have been harder to get information on in the past are easier today. For example, let's suppose that you believe one of the key benefits of your company is its inclusive culture. In the past, it was not easy to get information on a company's culture. You could talk to current employees but often those employees are selected for you and you have to wonder if the selection was random. Conversely, you might have touted to a prospective employee that yours was a fairly stress free environment. Again, in the past it was hard for a prospective employee to verify this. To a large extent in the past, prospective employees do take your word for it. Today, sites such as Glassdoor.com and others provide insights from current employees of yours about what it is really like to work at your firm. How wonderful is the culture really? How stressful and how much travel are actually involved? Today, prospective employees can and do access information on various aspects of your EVP beyond what you supply. This means that you have to know what is out there in order to know if it is helping or hurting you. I stress this, because as I said, if prospective employees don't feel the EVP is attractive on its own, game over.

Assuming the EVP is attractive in isolation, rarely do prospective employees stop there. They almost always go on to make "across person, within time" comparisons. In other words, they look at what you are offering and compare it to what other offers they personally have or have "seen" others get. If the prospective employees are fresh graduates, they compare your value proposition to others they have received, as well as those received by their classmates.

When I stress both of these points of comparison to corporate recruiters, they invariably agree with the first but often reject the second. One recruiter put it this way, "Of course prospective employees compare what I offer them to what other companies have offered them. But why would they compare what one of their classmates was offered by a totally different company. It's irrelevant when my candidate doesn't have that offer herself." While an offer to a classmate—that a given prospective employee personally does not have—may seem irrelevant, research has shown that it is not.[5] To appreciate this, just keep the monkey experiment in mind. The offer of a grape was never made to the first monkey and yet his behavior of throwing away the cucumber slice was driven by a grape his neighbor was being offered.

Finally, before deciding that yours is *the* deal for them and you are *their* employer of choice, prospective employees sometimes then make "within person, across time" comparisons. They look at what they were getting and what they were paying in the past and compare that to what they believe they will get from your firm and what price they will pay to your firm. This is especially true of prospective employees who already have a current job versus college recruits.

As a consequence of all this, there are at least three implications for you in trying to get those prospective employees you want to want you. First, your EVP must be attractive in isolation, which means you have to have insights into how prospective employees will get information about and make assessments of both the basket of benefits they anticipate getting but also the price they expect to pay. We will dive more deeply into gaining these insights in Chapters 6 and 7. Second, you have to be very aware of how your EVP stacks up to other offers—both offers that your target candidates personally receive from other companies and ones that they don't personally receive but that they see others get. Third, for a prospective employee who is currently employed, your value proposition typically starts from a value deficit. This is simply because of asymmetric uncertainty. A prospective employee knows for certain what she currently gets and what she pays. She knows what you promise to give and she can anticipate what she will likely pay if she joins you. However, the greater the uncertainty relative to the benefits you promise and the anticipated prices, the lower the expected value. We know from decades of research, the higher the uncertainty, the more the present value of the proposed offer is discounted, and therefore the lower the practical value. Therefore, to be successful in attracting prospective employees, you have to have insights into not only what their current EVP is and how they assess it but what uncertainties they feel toward your offer. To be clear, the key is not being clear about what your EVP is, rather it is being clear about how clear and certain or how uncertain the prospective employee sees your offer.

Current Employees

While the outcome of an EVP assessment for prospective employees is binary—join or not—the outcome of an EVP assessment for current employees is more complex.

The stimulus for a current employee to examine your operational EVP is varied. It can come from an EVP that is simply unattractive in isolation. The price an employee feels she is paying is simply not worth the basket of benefits. This alone can cause an employee to start thinking about ways to somehow alter the EVP. The stimulus could come from a current employee "seeing" someone else (friend, work colleague, cousin, brother, sister, whomever) have an EVP (pre-existing or new) that seems better than what the employee currently has. The stimulus could come from making a "across time, within person" comparison in which, like the rock crushing example, the EVP has deteriorated in the mind of the employee just because the improvement in the basket of benefits has not kept pace with the price paid.

Take these various source of stimulus and multiply them by the five forces that I previously described in terms of giving employees more power and you can see that the potential for what you thought was a fine or even good EVP to not be so attractive in the eye of current employees is enormous. A key implication here is that as hard as it is to construct attractive and compelling EVPs, you must remain ever vigilant to spot perceived weakening of the EVP *before* the negative consequences I am about to describe get a chance to get going.

But suppose despite your vigilance, employees perceive a decline in the EVP, what do they do? The truth is that they do several things and the severity of the decline in the EVP largely dictates the likely behavior.

So let's start with a minor to moderate perceived decline in the EVP. Again this perception could come from any of the sources I already described. For example, it could come from no change in perceived price and only from a perceived decline in the basket of benefits. Maybe the company has had some bad publicity; their new boss doesn't recognize and reward them as much as the old one did; their job has less autonomy with the implementation of new compliance procedures; or any number of other changes. The decline in the EVP could come from no change in the basket of benefits and only come from an increase in the perceived price employees pay. They may feel that they are enduring more stress, working longer hours, traveling more, etc. Or the decline could come from changes on both sides of the equation. Independent of the source of the weakening EVP, when the decline is modest, what do employees do?

In this case, the most common reaction is for employees to try to improve the deal by enhancing some aspect of the basket of benefits. Specifically, they may seek a raise, ask for more freedom in their job, request a higher status title (even if it comes with no more money), look for more time and attention from the boss, ask for a higher bonus, and so on. This outcome is more common in countries and cultures that have direct and explicit communication styles like the U.S., Netherlands, Australia, and the UK, but is not as common of a reaction in countries and cultures that have indirect and implicit communication styles such as Thailand, Saudi Arabia, Korea, and Japan.

When you see signs of this response, even on an individual level, it is important to spend some time diagnosing the nature of the EVP change before simply responding to the effort to elevate aspects of the basket of benefits. I stress this because, if the source of the decline in the EVP is solely or even partly because of an actual or perceived increase in price, the best and least costly action may be to reduce the price employees are paying rather than increasing the benefits they are receiving.

The second common reaction to a modest to moderate decline in the EVP is for employees to try to reduce the denominator—i.e., the price paid. They might do this by being less engaged, putting in less effort, or avoiding stress and conflict. We underestimate the frequency of this reaction because it is less visible and early on can even be invisible. Unfortunately, employee efforts to reduce the price paid is a commonly trod path and can be a much more costly path than people asking for raises. Clearly if employees put in less concentration, effort, time, sacrifice, etc., results and performance typically also fall.

This is why on-going representative samples of employee engagement are needed and why it is a bad idea to rely only on comprehensive employee engagement surveys every other year. I'm not saying don't do comprehensive surveys; I'm only saying in addition, it is vital to do smaller, representative sample surveys in order to catch this stealthy but dangerous reaction to modest to moderate declines in the EVP before big problems arise.

If these are the two most common reactions to modest to moderate declines, what happens when the real or perceived EVP declines get larger? If the initial efforts I just described are not successful and the EVP declines further, or if the EVP declines in a major way quickly, then people begin to not just mentally withdraw (lowering the denominator and enhancing the over ratio), they start to physically withdraw. This is when you see absenteeism rise, and not just at the shop floor level. The costs of absenteeism at any and all levels of an organization have been well documented over the years. This is the first reason it should be closely monitored—not just because it is costly in and of itself but also because it is a sign that you have a more serious EVP problem, just as a very high fever is a sign that you have a serious infection.

Finally, if the perceived decline is severe enough, then people physically and permanently withdraw—they leave. The cost of voluntary and undesired turnover has also been well documented in both research and practice, so I won't belabor it. However, keep in mind that a severe decline in EVP can come purely from external comparisons while the internal EVP really hasn't changed at all. In other words, you cannot take comfort in the fact that your EVP has remained stable or even improved because it is its relative not absolute strength that matters at the end of the day.

Though I have stressed it before, let me hammer it home again that employees' ability to compare EVPs today is greater than ever before and is only going to increase. Even if you focus on the most visible part of an EVP—pay—the situation today is completely different than just ten years ago. In the past, it was very hard and expensive for employees to know if people in other companies were getting paid cucumbers or grapes for the same work they were doing. Now and going forward, they can know this quickly and nearly for free. Sites such as payscale.com, wageindicator.org, indeed.com, glassdoor.com, salarscout.com, salary.com, careerinfonet.org, salaryexpert.com, worldsalaries.org, totaljobs.com, monstersalary.com, jobstar.org, and careerlink.com, are just a few of the more used and useful sites for gaining information and making comparisons.

Once again, why do we care, especially in the context of winning the war for talent? The answer is straightforward. We care because if the employment deal people are getting is perceived as unfair compared to the deal someone else is getting (inside or outside the company), people again either look for a better deal or look to make their current deal better. If they look for a better deal (passively or actively), you can only hope that you would have wanted them to leave anyway, otherwise you get dysfunctional turnover—i.e., voluntary and undesired. If they look to make their current deal better, you can only hope that they chose the path of actually asking for a raise or some other increase in their basket of benefits rather than lowering their price paid.

Summary

Before moving on to Chapter 6 and examining how all of this translates into a concrete way of measuring, mapping, and assessing the strength or weakness of your firm's value proposition to employees, it is helpful to briefly summarize how employees view and assess your firm's value proposition.

First, employees do care about and evaluate what they get—the basket of benefits. Most of what they care about falls into four baskets of benefits: the company, its leaders, their job, and the rewards.

Second, employees don't stop there, they only begin their assessment of how good or bad the value proposition is by looking at these four baskets of benefits. They then make assessments about the price they pay to get the benefits. The blood, sweat, and tears they give. Combined, the relationship between what they get and what they pay forms the initial assessment of "the employment deal" and whether it is a good one or not.

Third, before employees land on a more definitive assessment of the employment "value," they make mental comparisons. They compare what they received and the price they paid in the past relative to what they are getting and the price they are paying in the present. Based on that comparison, they assess whether the employment deal is getting better or worse or staying the same. They also compare their deal to feasible alternatives regarding both the benefits they could receive and the price they would pay in other organizations or what they "see" others getting and paying.

Fourth, these judgments are typically based on incomplete and often inaccurate information and therefore lead to less than perfect perceptions. However, the Internet has made and will continue to make gaining information on what others are getting for the work they do easier and easier. Whether the normal anecdotal sources of information or Internet sources lead to more accurate perceptions or not will *not* change the fact that in this context perceptions are reality and employees will act— right or wrong—on what they perceive as unchanging, improving, or deteriorating EVPs.

Fifth and finally, if the current deal starts to become unattractive in isolation or is too much worse than the past or too inferior to what they believe they could get or see elsewhere, employees will start the process of (a) trying to improve the numerator (getting more and better stuff in their basket of benefits), (b) trying to reduce the denominator (putting in less and lowering their price), or (c) will replace the EVP altogether and leave you and join someone else. Any and all of these outcomes hurt the performance of the company, especially if the sentiment is widespread among employees.

Notes

1. http://www.bls.gov/home.htm
2. D. Pink, 2009. *Drive: the Surprising Truth about What Motivates Us*, Riverhead Books, New York.
3. S. F. Brosan, and F. B. M. de Waal, 2003. "Monkeys Reject Unequal Pay," *Nature*, 425, pp. 297–299.
4. M. Hitt, J. S. Black, and L. W. Porter, 2012. *Management*, (3rd edition) Pearson.
5. A. E. Barber, 1998. *Recruiting employees: Individual and organizational perspectives.* Thousand Oaks, CA: Sage.

Chapter 6

How Can You Make Your EVP Concrete?

Given the shifts that have happened and tilted the balance of power away from employers and toward employees, I argued earlier that firms are better off thinking of employees more as choosy customers of employment offerings than as lucky recipients of employment gifts. To recap, I make this case because today, like customers, employees have more information, more choices, lower switching costs, and more power than ever before. As a consequence, your firm's EVP must be sufficiently alluring compared to realistic alternatives that desired prospective employees will choose you over the competitors and once they join you will remain with and be devoted to you. No doubt this makes sense and you are hopefully more convinced than ever that your firm needs a superior EVP. But what does a "superior EVP" look like? How can we translate these general ideas into something more concrete?

Graphing Your EVP

The good news is that all of the ideas about benefits, price, and relative comparisons can be captured in such concrete ways that you can literally graph your EVP. From that graph you can visually see how strong or weak your EVP is. As a consequence, you can more easily discuss and determine how to best improve your EVP. As a reminder, the reason for assessing and improving your EVP is not just for the fun of it, but because its strength or weakness dramatically affects your ability to attract the new employees you want, to hold on to the current employees you need, and to ensure that the employees you have are highly engaged and motivated.

To graph a firm's EVP, we start by examining the two core dimensions—price and benefits.

The first dimension is price. As I pointed out earlier, just as all customers pay a price for your products or services, so too do your employees pay a price to work for you. Unfortunately, whereas it is relatively easy to compare the price you charge for a given product to the price your competitors charge, it is not so easy to compare the prices employees pay across organizations. However, don't despair; reasonable approximations can be made, and I will explain how I do this from a technical perspective later. For the moment, simply think of the price your employees pay as either being at a discount, on par, or at a premium compared to the average.

The second dimension of the tool looks at the benefits. As discussed before, the benefits consist of four big baskets—the company, the leadership, the job, and the rewards. Again, it is not just the absolute value of these benefits but their perceived relative value. Just as with the monkeys, it not just if you get a cucumber slice in exchange for producing a rock, it is whether others get a cucumber or a grape for doing similar work that matters.

Using the tool, the value of the proposition is the intersection of the price paid and the benefits offered (see Exhibit 6.1). Literally you plot the intersection of these two dimensions. As I mentioned, I will explain later how you can measure both of these, but for now it is important to understand that, just as for a customer, the intersection between price and offering is dynamic. This simply means that as you change one dimension, it affects the overall value of the proposition. Intersections in which the price paid is commensurate with the benefits offered fall along the "fair value" diagonal line.

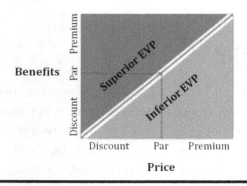

Exhibit 6.1   Two-dimensional EVP.

Intersections above the line are superior and intersections below the line are inferior. The right-angle distance between the intersection and the fair-value line gives you the magnitude of the superior or inferior value.

To illustrate this in a common context, imagine that you walk into a store and they are offering a plain white dress shirt. The quality of the shirt (i.e., its fabric, cut, seams, etc.) all seem about average to you. Let's assume, therefore, that a price of $40 seems fair to you. Let's further assume that if you went into the market, that you in fact could find this quality of white dress shirt for an average price of $40. Let's assume, however, that when you look at the actual price tag, the shirt costs $80. At that price, you likely judge the value proposition as unattractive or inferior. However, what if when you looked at the price tag it was $20? You would likely think that this was a very attractive or superior value proposition. By the way, this is precisely why "sales" or discounts work. What we might feel is not a good deal at one price is attractive at another, even though nothing has changed in the product itself.

The dynamic works the other way around as well. Suppose that for $80 you are offered not just a plain white dress shirt but one that is custom tailored to fit you and has a fabric that lasts twice as long. Now what was unappealing at $80 (i.e., a plain white dress shirt) might be very appealing—the price is the same but what you get is more than before. This is why at the same price one shirt is unappealing and another shirt with different features is a great deal.

In this simple case, I changed only the price or the offering, but in real life, you can simultaneously change both price and offering. With all this in mind, let's walk through the plotting of a couple of case study EVPs. The case studies are real but the companies requested their names be disguised.

The first case study is a technology firm based in California. I will call it TechnoServ. TechnoServ has lower than average turnover and its recruiting yield is better than average. However, TechnoServ sits in a very competitive landscape for talent and cannot afford to find out too late that its EVP has deteriorated. To start with, I gathered data on their EVP (benefits and price) via a standardized survey I created and validated. However, one could get a sense of the key dimensions by using structured interviews or focus groups.

Based on the survey data, TechnoServ's employees on average assessed the price they paid at about 30 percent higher than the average technology firm. This number simply reflected the fact that most TechnoServ employees felt that they had to work longer hours, fret and worry more about work even when not at work, and endure above average stress while at work

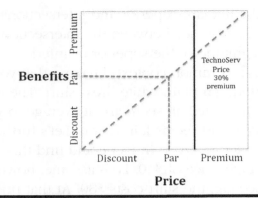

Exhibit 6.2   TechnoServ's price plot.

compared in their minds to employees in similar firms. In order to graph this, I simply drew a vertical line that approximated the 30 percent price premium (see Exhibit 6.2).

The next task was to plot TechnoServ's benefits. In aggregate, TechnoServ's offering was about 40 percent higher than the average. In particular, compared to other firms in its competitive space, employees felt that TechnoServ had a very strong reputation and culture. In addition, employees felt that the leadership had a strong focus on employee development. While the results concerning the job were about the same as the competitors, the rewards, especially financial rewards, were significantly higher. In order to graph the composite of these four baskets of benefits, I simply drew a horizontal line that approximated the 40 percent offering premium (see Exhibit 6.3) until it intersected with the price line.

Given the favorable intersection of price and offering for TechnoServ, I was not surprised that it had turnover that was significantly lower than

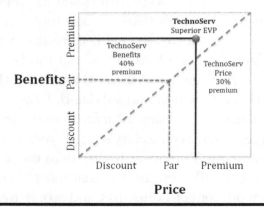

Exhibit 6.3   TechnoServ's price and benefit EVP plot.

its peers. In addition, as expected, its new hire yield rate (i.e., job offers accepted/job offers made) was much better than its rivals. Finally, as expected, its level of motivation and engagement was also much higher than its peers.

What alarmed TechnoServ executives was the high price premium its employees felt they paid. This mattered because TechnoServ did not believe that it could just keep increasing the value of the basket of benefits if the perceived price increased. As we dug into the numbers and comments more deeply, it became clear that there were certain sources of price that could and should be reduced. For example, employees were experiencing significant job stress in part because they did not have certain software tools for key activities. These tools would not only make their jobs easier but would increase the probability that they could hit project deadlines. This mattered because employees were experiencing significant stress relative to the ever-present possibility of missing deadlines. This stress came both from the pressure they experienced from their bosses but also the stress they put on themselves for fear of falling behind competitors in the marketplace.

A statistical analysis of the current EVP using multivariate techniques showed that a 10% increase in price (in particular, stress due to worry about missing deadlines) would likely result in a 17% increase in turnover. The cost of that turnover compared to the cost of acquiring the needed software tools made it an easy decision to buy the tools. Not surprisingly, afterward, the EVP actually improved and undesired turnover went down, recruiting yield improved, as did employee motivation and project deadline achievement.

Obviously, EVPs can go in the opposite direction as well. To illustrate this, we will take the example of a financial service firm; I'll call it FinServ. This company found itself in an inferior value proposition position. Similar to TechnoServ, FinServ employees assessed the price they paid at about 30 percent higher than the average financial firm. This number simply reflected the fact that most FinServ employees felt that they had to work much longer hours, endure significantly more stress, and travel much more for work than what they perceived to be the case at other financial service firms. In order to graph this, I simply drew a vertical line that approximated the 30 percent price premium.

The next task was to plot FinServ's benefits. In aggregate, FinServ's offering was about average. Employees perceived the four benefits of leaders, jobs, and rewards as about par with comparable firms; they perceived the company (i.e., its reputation, culture, performance, etc.) as above average. However, the significant price premium combined with benefits led to an inferior EVP (see Exhibit 6.4).

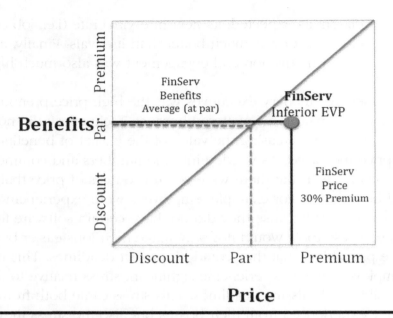

Exhibit 6.4   Plot of FinServ's EVP.

Because its offering was seen by the firm and by its employees as competitive, and because prior to this consulting, FinServ executives had never really factored in price, they were puzzled as to why the firm's turnover rate was higher, its new hire yield rate was lower, and its employee motivation and engagement were worse than its peers. Once the plot of the EVP, which included price, was presented, it was much easier for FinServ executives to understand what was going on and what they had as options in order to improve the firm's EVP and the associated outcomes.

In FinServ's case, executives determined that lowering the price was simply not possible. There were no obvious time savings that could reduce hours. There were no obvious sources of stress that could be relieved. The higher level of travel was tied directly to the firm's strategy of stronger customer relationships. In short, the top executives determined that enhancing the basket of benefits was the only way to improve their EVP. However, you don't just want to increase benefits randomly but want to increase those where there is the best "bang for the buck." In other words, you want to increase benefits that will yield the greatest improvement in the EVP.

To determine this, we used multivariate statistical analysis. Without getting into the technical details, we determined that for their employees the biggest improvement in EVP would come from improving financial rewards and leadership. In terms of leadership, the key issue was feedback—which employees felt they rarely got and only when something went wrong. A well-structured development program for leaders helped improve this element in the benefits. In terms of financial rewards, it turned out that it was not so much salary or even bonuses that needed to be increased but rather per diem allowances when traveling to visit clients. FinServ was almost as fanatical about keeping travel costs low for each trip as they were about ensuring that there were enough total trips that their clients felt more loved by them than any competitor. Some small changes in travel allowances in combination with the change in leader behavior made a significant improvement in the EVP and lowered turnover and increased employee engagement.

While the two examples both had "price premiums," you can create superior or inferior EVPs with price at a premium, at par, or at a discount. Whether the EVP intersection will be superior, on par, or inferior depends on the strength or weakness of the firm's benefits in concert with price.

Readers with marketing backgrounds may, at this point, recognize this EVP tool as similar to what has been used to graph product and service value propositions in marketing for years. With no shame at all, I freely admit that the entire notion of this approach to EVP came to me when talking with a marketing colleague. We were discussing how marketers graph the strength of a product's value proposition and use that to predict the likelihood of customer repeat purchases. During this conversation, it occurred to me that employee retention was analogous to customer repeat purchase. Employees "repeat purchase" their employment when they decide to come back to work each day. Just as this two-dimensional model in marketing was good at predicting customer repeat purchase because it captured not just what customers got but what they paid for what they got, it seemed to me it would make sense that looking at the intersection of benefits and price relative to a firm's value proposition to employees would also do a better job of predicting employee outcomes than the traditional employee satisfaction approach. As noted earlier, this in fact turned out empirically to be the case.

The other innovation this approach provided compared to traditional measures of employee satisfaction was the notion of relative comparison. As I mentioned, most employee satisfaction surveys take no measure of "price," but they also take no comparative measures relative to what they do ask employees about. For example, in a traditional employee satisfaction survey, it might ask, "How satisfied are you with the level of autonomy you have in your job?" The survey would then have response options ranging from

1 = Not Satisfied to 5 = Very Satisfied. If it were the case that employees had no information or zero perceptions of job autonomy at other companies or had very high switching costs, this "absolute, internal" rather than "relative, external" approach would be fine. But as I have stressed, employees do have information and do form perceptions about price and benefits at other companies, including such factors as job autonomy. In addition, as I demonstrated in Chapter 4, today employees have lower switching costs than ever before. As a consequence, the normal "absolute, internal" survey approach underestimates the likelihood of turnover, absenteeism, and declines in engagement.

It turns out that you can get a good measure of relative perceptions just by changing the wording of the questions a little. For example, you simply rephrase the question on job autonomy from "How satisfied are you with the level of autonomy you have in your job?" to "Compared to other organizations you know, what is the level of autonomy you have in your job?" The survey response options then range from 1 = Significantly Less to 5 = Significantly More.

In quick summary, traditional employee satisfaction surveys (or even the ones that are now called "employee engagement" surveys) have only a weak to moderate relationship to key outcomes such as turnover, absenteeism, and productivity because they miss key information. First, virtually *none* of the traditional employee satisfaction or engagement surveys measure price. The few assessments that do measure price almost never examine the intersection between price and satisfaction and therefore can't truly position the EVP. Second, virtually none of the traditional employee satisfaction or engagement surveys get at any relative comparisons that employees in fact take into account. It is simply logical that if you measure only part of the picture and in that process leave out critical components, what you measure will have only a modest ability to predict key outcomes.

This new approach not only measures just one but all three key factors that affect employees' assessments of a firm's EVP—benefits, price, and relative strength of each. By placing these measures in a graphic model, it makes the model not only easier to visually understand but empirically more powerful in predicting key outcomes.

Up to this point, I've shared the model at a conceptual level and provided some high-level case examples to illustrate the principles. However, some readers may want a more in-depth understanding of the research that is behind this new approach. I present that in the following section but do away with all the scientific jargon and simply explain it is normal terms.

The Data and Results

Over the last several years, I've collected data from nearly 10,000 employees across 20 countries to test the power of this approach for measuring EVPs and the impact of superior and inferior EVPs on key outcomes. The results of my empirical analyses support three important conclusions. First, there can be and are significant variations in the strength or weakness of EVPs across firms. Second, even within large firms, there are usually vast difference by countries, division, and departments even when these firms think they have a common employee value proposition. Third, these variations matter in that stronger EVPs have a significant impact on lowering turnover, lowering absenteeism, increasing retention, increasing engagement, and increasing efforts by employees to go the extra mile.

It is important to stress at this point that being able to predict critical outcomes such as employee commitment, extra effort, and intent to leave or stay with the company by the strength of a firm's EVP is important not only because these outcomes matter but also because these outcomes affect even larger company results and performance. For example, 25 years of research conducted by a host of scholars demonstrates that employee commitment and extra effort are important drivers of employee performance, and that employees' intent to stay or leave a company is the most proximate predictor of actual employee turnover.[1] In addition, employee turnover and absenteeism can have significant impacts on a variety of key outcomes including employee productivity, costs, customer satisfaction, revenue growth, and profits.[2]

However, the fact that the new approach has twice the predictive strength of transitional approaches simply on its own may not matter that much in the world of practice. The reason that what scientists call "predictive validity" matters to a practicing manager is that that stronger relationship means that a manager can more intelligently and effectively change factors and thereby more directly avoid undesired results and achieve desired outcomes.

With that in mind, the empirical relationships between and among EVP and key outcomes are captured in Exhibit 6.5.

As Exhibit 6.5 illustrates, an attractive EVP will increase employee commitment, and will also increase extra effort, such as helping other employees perform activities even when offering such help is not part of their normal job descriptions. Both higher employee commitment and extra effort have a positive impact on performance.

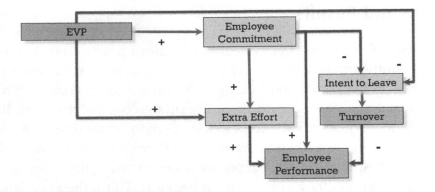

Exhibit 6.5 Impact of EVP.

Moreover, an attractive EVP will decrease an employee's intent to leave the company. Obviously, the stronger an employee's desire to leave, the more likely he or she is to leave. In addition, a higher the intent to leave typically brings down performance in the near-term as the employee emotionally and psychologically separates him or herself from the organization in anticipation of physically leaving. In addition, turnover can hurt the overall performance of the organization as knowledge and capabilities are lost and time and money have to be spent to replace them.

Theoretical relationships are all well and good, but what are the empirical results of my research? Exhibit 6.6 illustrates the empirical relationships, but interpreting the results without a Ph.D. in statistics requires a bit of explanation.

First, it's important to note that all the relationships were in the predicted direction and all were statistically significant. The "+" or "−" sign in front of the numbers in Exhibit 6.6 tells you whether the relationship was positive or

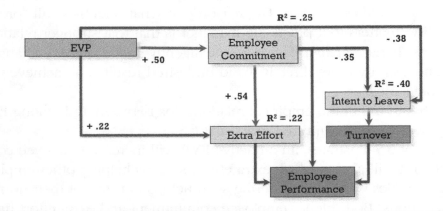

Exhibit 6.6 Effects of EVP.

negative. The number after the "+" or "−" sign indicates the strength of the relationship based on a multivariate regression analysis. All you really need to know about the regression analysis is that a number between .25 and .50 indicates a strong empirical relationship when it comes to humans and human behavior and outcomes.

Second, the number following the "R2" tells you how much of the variation in that variable is explained by the indicated drivers. For example, EVP explained 25 percent of all the variance in employee commitment, and in combination, the firm's EVP and resulting employee commitment explained 40 percent of the variation in employee intent to leave. EVP and employee commitment in combination explained 22 percent of all the variation in extra effort. Not only are these results statistically significant, but in the context of social science research, they are quite strong.

While not as sophisticated, there are other ways to illustrate the quantitative power of having a strong versus weak employee value proposition. Exhibit 6.7 shows the composite EVP for a set of companies in a recent study of mine. Each company had at least 200 employees participating in the research. As you can see, there was a fair bit of variation in the composite EVP. The "winning" company (Company K) had an EVP of 4.29, while the weakest had an EVP of −1.66 (Company A). Although the exact algorithm for computing the composite EVP is not critical for our purposes at the moment, it's important to appreciate what the numbers mean. The more positive the EVP number, the more employees felt they were getting great value from the company in terms of the four dimensions (i.e., company, leadership, job, and rewards) relative to the price they were paying. EVP numbers close to zero

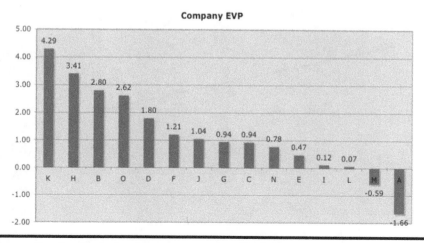

Exhibit 6.7   Distribution of company composite EVP scores.

indicate that employees felt they were getting about what they paid for. A negative EVP number indicates that employees felt they were paying more than they were getting.

It is important to keep one other thing in mind when it comes to positive or negative EVP numbers. Positive numbers do not mean that these companies had the highest absolute values in terms of company, leadership, job, and reward scores. Positive numbers mean that these companies had the highest relative values—i.e., their employees believed that, relative to what they were paying, they were getting a lot. Conversely, negative numbers don't mean that these companies had the lowest absolute values in terms of company, leadership, job, and reward scores. Negative numbers mean that the companies had the lowest relative values—i.e., employees believed that relative to what they were paying they weren't getting much.

Exhibit 6.8 allows us to visually appreciate the relationship between a company's composite EVP score and the likelihood that employees will leave the company.

Again, you don't need a Ph.D. in statistics to appreciate the relationship. As you can see, the higher the EVP score the lower the intent to leave (or conversely the higher the intent to stay). The diagonal line shows the perfect trend line, which makes it easy to see how close the actual data points are to a perfect relationship. The actual data points are very close to falling exactly on the trend line.

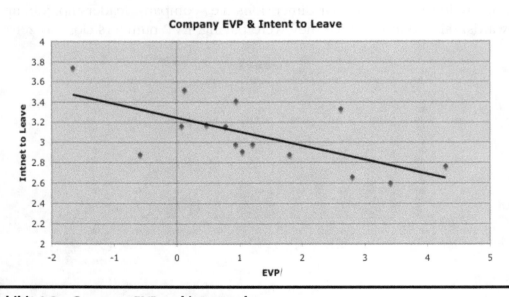

Exhibit 6.8   Company EVP and intent to leave.

EVP Variation

Although the composite EVP had a significant impact on employee commitment, extra effort, and intent to leave or stay with the firm, not every company with a superior EVP got high marks for all four dimensions (company, leadership, job, and rewards), and not every company with an inferior EVP received low scores for every dimension. In many cases, companies with strong composite EVPs scored average or above average on most dimensions but had outstanding scores on one or two dimensions.

In some cases, this "unbalanced" configuration was deliberate. For example, one of the companies had only an average score on rewards—by design. Because its business was relatively labor-intensive, the company didn't want to increase labor costs relative to the market by paying premium wages. In contrast to its average reward scores, its scores on leadership and job were somewhat above average. However, its scores on company (especially its culture) were among the highest in the study.

Obviously, the impact of this profile relative to the benefits can only be fully understood when the price employees felt they were paying gets factored in. In this case, the employees felt that they were paying an average price in terms of hours, stress, sacrifice, etc. Therefore, relative to the price the employees felt they were paying, they were getting a fantastic value on company and a good value on the other three dimensions, and a par value on rewards, resulting in a strong overall EVP.

At one of the high-tech companies, scores on company, leadership, and rewards were just slightly above average, but scores on job were among the highest of any firm. On further analysis, it was clear that these employees valued the job dimension more than the other three. To be clear, employees at this company valued all four dimensions, but they cared most about the job dimension. The fact that the company scored highest on the dimension that employees cared most about, and the fact that this high score was among the highest scores in the entire study, meant these employees were getting more of what they valued most. Because this premium value was not eroded by an equally premium price, the overall EVP was among the strongest.

However, once again, the total value of the employment proposition to the employees can only be fully known by factoring the price they felt they were paying. As stated earlier, value is NOT just in what you get. It's what you get relative to what you feel you paid. In this case, employees felt that they were paying only a slightly above average price; thus, yielding a superior EVP.

In contrast, another high-tech company in the study also had a very high score on job, as well as average or above average scores on the other three dimensions. However, the company's composite EVP was not high, and its employees didn't score well on commitment or extra effort, and they were more likely to leave. What was the problem? Employees felt they were paying a very high price for what they were getting. They felt they were working significantly longer hours, enduring more stress, sacrificing more personal and family time, etc. In effect, the premium offering was more than offset by a premium price. For these reasons, many of the employees were actively seeking alternative employment.

Conclusion

What can we make of all this? I think there are five key takeaways:

1. What you offer matters. It matters what employees feel they get: the company, its leadership, their jobs, and the rewards. These four categories capture about 80 percent of what matters most to employees.
2. Price matters. Like customers, employees don't just care about what they get, they care about what they have to pay for what they get. Employees pay attention to the price they pay to work for a company in terms of hours, stress, sacrifice, blood, sweat, and tears, and that calculus affects their overall sense of value of the employment proposition.
3. Configuration matters. A winning EVP does not need to offer equally superior value across all four EVP dimensions. A superior EVP can be comprised of average or slightly above average offerings on some dimensions, provided there's an outstanding offering on the remaining dimensions and that outstanding benefit is not offset by an equally outstanding high price.
4. Matching matters. The most powerful EVP configurations occur when the highest offering is provided on the dimension(s) that employees value most. Knowing what the employees you want to attract and retain value most, and then matching your EVP to those criteria yields the greatest ROI.
5. EVP drives key outcomes. A superior EVP is not just a nice thing to do for people. It has direct and indirect effects on outcomes such as employee turnover and performance, and these outcomes directly affect

overall business outcomes. Therefore, line executives (and not just HR managers) must measure, monitor, and enhance their employee value proposition.

People are a company's most important asset, but the truth is (even if it's an inconvenient one) the balance of power has shifted from employers toward employees. Today and going forward employees (a) make greater and more direct contributions to competitive advantage, (b) have an significantly enhanced ability to know the value they add, (c) have lower switching costs to change employers when they don't feel they are getting the value they deserve, and (d) are in higher demand than ever before. Companies that recognize this, and executives who proactively seek to measure, monitor, and enhance their employee value proposition, will be the ones that win the war *for* human capital and that is necessary in order to win the competition *with* human capital.

Notes

1. R. T. Mowday, L. W. Porter, and R. M. Steers, 1982. *Employee-Organization Linkages: The Psychology of Commitment, Absenteeism and Turnover*, Academic Press; R. M. Steers, L. W. Porter, and G. A. Bigley, 1996. *Motivation and Leadership at Work* (6th edition), McGraw-Hill.
2. W. Cascio and J. Boudreau, 2011. *Investing in People: Financial Impact of Human Resource Initiatives*, Pearson Education, Upper Saddle River, NJ.

Chapter 7

How Can You Get the Employees You Want to Want You?

Up to this point I have stressed that employees judge the value of working for you based on an assessment of what they get from you (benefits) relative to what they give to you (price) and then compare that to the past and to external alternatives. The strength of your employee value proposition (EVP) is essentially the intersection of benefits and price in a comparative context. Obviously, if your EVP is strongly positive, you are in great shape—*today*. I say *today* because even if your EVP looks great today, given all that I have presented on the war for talent and the shift in power between employer and employee, it is wise to keep a close eye on your EVP to ensure it remains strong tomorrow. Obviously, if your EVP is simply average or inferior, then you need to make some changes.

In this chapter, we want to look at how you assess and make needed changes consisting of a simple but powerful four-step process (see Exhibit 7.1). The first step involves gathering baseline data so that you know how strong or weak your EVP is. The second step focuses on determining what matters most within all the factors of the EVP to your people. What matters to your people can easily be different from what matters to employees in other companies. The third step involves gaining deeper insights into the factors that matter most and can have the biggest impact on improving the EVP and subsequently impacting key outcomes. The fourth and final step brings the first three steps to fruition in determining what specific

Exhibit 7.1 Getting who you want to want you.

actions you are going to take to improve your EVP and thereby get the people you want to want you and be motivated to work hard for you.

To help illustrate these four steps, I introduce and walk through a fairly detailed case example for which I served as a consultant. The company is a large logistics firm with operations around the world. We will call it Global Delivery. Recently, Global Delivery had made big investments in China. Soon after, it was struggling with high employee turnover, especially among delivery personnel. Its turnover rate was 34%. This rate was slightly higher than its competitors in China. Despite having only slightly higher turnover than rivals, turnover was having a big and negative impact on recruiting and training costs. In addition, turnover was hurting delivery quality, customer satisfaction, and ultimately revenue and profit growth. While Global Delivery's operations in China were growing at a rapid pace, both country and regional executives wanted to ensure that it was profitable growth and were determined that a 34% turnover rate was not just a cost of doing business in China but something that could be changed. Most importantly, their experience in general told them that reducing turnover and raising employee engagement, especially among delivery drivers, could make a major contribution to the general business objective of profitable growth.

Step 1: Gather Baseline Data

For all companies and executives, knowing where your EVP currently stands is *the* starting point. As with any journey, you cannot effectively navigate to your desired destination without knowing your starting point. The easiest method to do this is using the validated survey I've created and tested.

In the case of Global Delivery, senior executives at the country and regional level were already convinced that getting the people they wanted to want them was not just a nice thing to do but a business-critical objective to achieve. Therefore, they were more than willing to survey their employees. Yet, at the outset they were somewhat nervous or perhaps even skeptical that this new approach would give them insights that their normal employee engagement surveys had not.

I almost can't stress enough the challenge of helping executives, not the least of which are HR executives, appreciate that (a) value is in the eye of the beholder—employees in this case, (b) value is judged by the intersection of what the person gets and what they feel they pay for what they get, (c) increasingly employees can compare the value you offer with that of alternatives, and (d) because of lower switching costs, employees are more willing to switch than ever before when they don't feel they have a competitive deal. Executives completely accept these four points in the context of customers, but for many it does not quite compute in the case of employees. As I have already highlighted that the reason executives are reluctant to view value this way for employees when they readily accept this concept for customers is because many simply do not yet fully appreciate the shift in balance of power that has occurred between employers and employees. In particular, most senior executives in their 40s or 50s today started working and went through the formative years of their careers when the balance of power was strongly in favor of employers not employees. So it is understandable that their recognition of this shift has been much slower than the actual shift itself. That being said, because the shift is undeniable and irreversible, the recognition will come. Nonetheless, part of the key in helping executives recognize and appreciate this new perspective is to literally help them see it. That is why how the baseline data are first presented is as important as gathering it. To illustrate all of this, let's return to Global Delivery.

Global Delivery decided that it wanted to survey all of its employees in China. The EVP survey is relatively short and required only about 10 minutes to complete. The CEO of the country sent a note to all employees encouraging them to complete the survey and promising them that (a) their responses would be completely anonymous and (b) the results would be shared with them within six weeks. The actual administration of the survey was carried out by my consulting firm. The response rate was higher than for their previous employee engagement survey in part because the EVP survey was much shorter.

The general results were fairly consistent across site locations and other organizational segments within the company. As a consequence, the overall results were shared with all employees without any breakdowns by typical demographics such as location, job, gender, and the like.

Price

For the executives, one of the most surprising results related to price. Overall employees felt that compared to other rivals and companies they knew they paid a price premium. In particular, employees felt that they were under greater stress even though the hours worked were not perceived to be higher than the competition.

Leaders

The other surprising result was related to leaders, especially at the local level. Employees' assessments were significantly lower than the company executives expected and lower than their peers. Employees did not feel that leaders were good at providing feedback or performance guidance. They also rated leaders low on the level of care and concern they showed to employees.

Rewards

The assessment relative to rewards was slightly below average. This somewhat surprised executives, especially HR executives, because the company had gone to great lengths and spent considerable money on compensation studies and consultants to ensure that their pay and benefits were competitive. What the executives didn't factor in and what showed up in the survey was that while employees viewed direct financial rewards as competitive, they saw nonfinancial rewards, such as praise and recognition, as significantly worse.

Job

The results concerning the basket of benefits related to job were average, but this was somewhat disappointing to executives. They thought that they had done an outstanding job making jobs clear and well defined, which the results showed that they had. However, employees viewed the amount of freedom and discretion as much less than rivals. The results also showed that employees did not feel they had all the resources required to do their jobs well.

Company

Global Delivery executives were surprised in the opposite direction relative to the company results. On this dimension, employees judged the company as significantly better. In particular employees felt that the reputation, values, and performance of the company were much higher than other firms.

These general results were presented in a simple graphic form to executives with each of four specific baskets of benefits intersecting with the price line (see Exhibit 7.2).

This enabled the executives to immediately see whether a particular aspect of the "offering" to employees was superior or inferior or on par relative to price—just as it would be with customers. The executives knew and accepted that customers judge "overnight delivery" at one price a great value and at another price as an unappealing value. The same principle was true for their employees. This simple graphing of the separate components helped executives literally see this point.

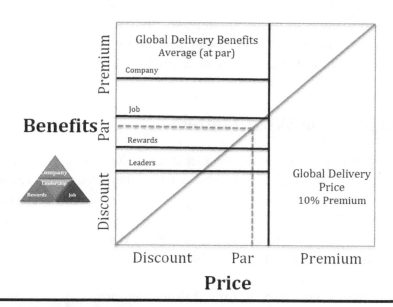

Exhibit 7.2   Global Delivery's EVP.

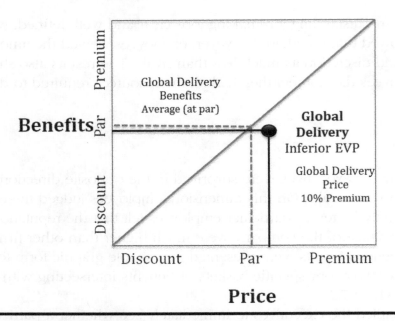

Exhibit 7.3   Global Delivery's inferior EVP.

When taken together, Global Delivery's overall EVP was slightly inferior (see Exhibit 7.3).

This was completely consistent with their slightly higher than average turnover rate. It also matched well with an employee engagement survey of some months prior that showed lower than peer group results, especially for delivery drivers. While this consistency was good, the practical purpose of the entire exercise was to more intelligently change and improve things in order to bring down turnover, its associated direct costs, and improve customer satisfaction and enhance profitable growth.

Step 2: Determine What Matters

Just based on this general description of the results, you can see that at Global Delivery there were any number of possible areas to address or to dive into deeper. However, at Global Delivery time and money were limited. They could not afford to address everything. In my experience, this is the case for virtually every firm. As a consequence, you can't afford to address everything that might seem to be problematic but does not have a high impact on targeted outcomes.

However, even if you had unlimited time and money, you should not address everything. This is simply because not everything matters—or at least doesn't matter equally. Some factors are critical while others are merely important. Vilfredo Pareto, an economist at the University of Lausanne in Switzerland in 1896, published a paper that put forward this overall notion. It began with the simple observation that a small portion of pea pods in his garden actually accounted for a very large portion of the peas the garden produced. With further investigation, he found this true across many phenomenon. His notion that generally 20% of inputs account for 80% of a given outcome became known as the "Pareto Principle."

This is really the guiding principle behind Step 2. We want to understand what 20% of the factors if changed could achieve 80% of the desired improvement. The good news is that statistical analysis has advanced since 1896 to the point that with survey data we can fairly easily determine which elements are in fact the most important. Sometimes these are the ones that you might think are powerful, but quite often they are not. As a consequence, having gathered baseline data, it is important to use data analysis to zero in on what is critical and separate those items from ones that are merely very important.

In the case of Global Delivery, it was a good thing that we conducted the sophisticated statistical analysis because what turned out to be the most powerful and important factors were not exactly what the executives expected. Specifically, the executives saw price at 10% higher than *par* as "not what we want or would have expected but not that bad." However, the statistical analysis showed that all other things being equal, a small improvement in price (i.e., lowering it) would have an outsized impact on the overall EVP and on the other measured outcomes such as intent to leave, engagement, and going the extra mile for the company. In addition, without the analysis, because "company" was rated high, the executives would have left it alone. However, the statistical analysis revealed that even though people saw the company's reputation, values, and performance as significantly better than the average, improvements in that dimension would significantly improve the EVP and subsequently impact the key outcomes. Finally, without this analysis, the executives' instinct was to "fix" the lowest scoring item, which was "leaders." Actually the analysis showed that improving this dimension would help improve key outcomes but not nearly to the extent as the other variables already discussed.

The bottom line is that in this case if the executives of Global Delivery had gone only with their instinct to fix the lowest scoring item, they would not have been completely wrong, but they would have missed out on making changes that would have had given them a much bigger bang for their buck. In summary, the analysis showed that improving a close to average item (i.e., price) could have an outsized impact, and that strengthening a strength (i.e., company) could as well. It also showed that the fixing a weakness could have an important impact but not as big an impact as addressing the other two.

One of the key "takeaways" here is that data and analysis are usually better than gut instincts. It is hard to know in advance what the relative relationships are between and among variables without multivariate statistical analysis. That being said, while the data and analysis get you started on the right path, they don't complete the journey for you. In other words, the statistical analysis can tell you where you ought to spend your time and energy; it can tell the "target-rich environments;" but, it cannot tell you exactly what to change. For that you need to move to Step 3.

Step 3: Gather Insights

With the "target-rich environments" identified through the statistical analysis, it was time to gather some deeper and richer insights. This required some interviews and focus groups. These were conducted with a random but representative set of employees.

In interview employees to get deeper insights into "price," I would not recommend using that exact term—certainly not in Chinese. However, using the term "price" in English, or its equivalent in any language, can be confusing to regular employees. However, if you ask them what it costs them to work at the company in terms of things like time, worry, stress, etc., they easily get the concept and can provide quite illuminating insights.

However, I don't recommend nor do I ever just rush into open-ended interview questions. I always set the questions up with a very brief summary of the survey results. I then ask two types of question in sequence. The first type of question tries to get them to articulate some specific issues, challenge, or problems related to a particular dimension of the EVP model, such as the company, the job, the rewards, etc. The second type of question asks them to describe the cause-effect relationships among these issues. Let me illustrate all of this by describing what transpired at Global Delivery.

In Global Delivery's case I started by reminding people that the survey found that employees felt that it cost them a bit more to work at Global Delivery than people thought was the case at other companies. In particular employees felt that the stress they experienced was higher. In interviews and focus groups, people tended to nod their head in agreement with this statement.

At this point, I asked a very simple open-ended question, "So what types of stress do you experience?"

In the case of Global Delivery, the most common response was that employees experienced stress relative to the pressure their supervisor put on them in meeting shipping deadlines every day.

I then probed further, and asked about why delays happened or what caused deadlines to be missed. In response, employees most commonly talked about the inefficient warehouse sorting processes. I followed up asking, "How could the sorting process be improved and beyond that how could supervisors put less negative pressure and stress on employees?"

I followed the same approach in order to gain insights relative to the company. Recall that this was a significant strength but that the statistical analysis demonstrated that if this strength could be strengthened that such a change could improve the EVP and the related outcomes. Again to begin, I reminded the interviewees or focus group participants that the survey showed that employees felt that the reputation, values, performance of the company were significantly better than rivals and that employees valued that. I followed up with several simple open-ended questions. For example, "So what specifically about the values of the company do you like?" or "What about the reputation of the company do you think is so much better than other firms?" In response to these questions, employees disclosed that they valued the long-standing positive reputation of the company and its values, especially its focus on safety, which was they felt in great contrast to many domestic Chinese delivery companies.

I then asked employees how they could feel even better about the positive values of the company and its reputation. What came out of the interviews was fascinating. Although the employees valued the general reputation of the firm and appreciated its corporate values, especially its value for safety, employees did not feel that non-employees really knew the reputation of the company. Of all the non-employees' opinions that mattered to employees, it was those of their own family members that mattered most. Thus, if the company could get employees' family members to know the company's reputation and appreciate its corporate values, especially regarding safety, the employees could feel even better about being a part of Global Delivery. With this insight, the key question was: How could the company's reputation in general and its value regarding safety in particular be reinforced effectively to employee family members?

The final area to address was the issue of local leaders, and in particular supervisors. Keeping to the standard structure, I first reminded interviewees and focus group participants that the survey results showed that employees overall felt that local leaders and supervisors were not quite as good as those in comparative companies. In particular, the results found that employees did not perceive that local leaders cared about them as much.

I followed this with a more probing open-ended question: "What types of things do local leaders and supervisors do that indicates to you that they don't care?" The most common response by far was that employees felt that leaders criticize them too harshly and too often in public. This is something that likely no employee likes anywhere but which was particularly painful in China given its cultural value of saving face. What was perhaps most interesting is that when I probed about the causes of public criticism of employees, the most common sited trigger of harsh criticism in public was delays or missed deadlines.

Taken together, the 20% of issues that needed to be focused on in order to achieve the desired results was coming into clear view. First was the issue of "price." Somehow the sorting process in the warehouses had to be improved in order to reduce the principal source of extra stress, and thereby lower the EVP price. Second was the issue of "company." We had to think of ways to help others, especially family members of current employees, know about and appreciate the company's reputation and values, especially its value on safety. Third, we had to determine what actions to take relative to supervisors to help them stop criticizing employees publicly and start exhibiting behaviors that showed that they cared about employees. With these issues in front of us, it was obvious that improving the sorting process would both lower price and improve the value employees got from leaders. However, the data analysis, the interviews, and the focus groups suggested that simply eliminating this negative aspect of supervisors would not deliver the full potential improvement in the EVP. Capturing the full potential required not just eliminating a negative but adding a positive.

Step 4: Take Action

Based on both the statistical analysis and the qualitative data gathered in interviews and focus groups, Global Delivery decided to improve both key aspects of the numerator (i.e., company and leadership) and lower the denominator (i.e., price) in order to more substantially enhance the EVP and thereby dramatically reduce turnover. The statistical analysis in particular showed that a 20% improvement in the overall EVP could cut turnover by more than 50%. This would not only save Global Delivery literally millions of dollars in recruiting and training costs but would also increase customer satisfaction and revenue growth because new delivery employees in particular made more mistakes that hurt customer satisfaction.

The reason for the significant relationship between reduced turnover and revenue in Global Delivery's business was fairly straightforward but important. Most businesses had contracts with multiple delivery companies. However, the staff at these client companies who actually put express items together had some level of discretion as to which carrier to use each day. Delivery personnel who consistently picked up from and delivered to these clients got to know the staff and the client's needs. That in combination with pleasant interpersonal interactions could easily cause client staff to swing more business Global Delivery's way. The more items picked up and delivery to a given client substantially increased margins because the marginal personnel, fuel, or delivery truck costs for the increased volume were near zero.

With these potential business outcomes in mind, we set about working on the specific actions Global Delivery might take to reduce EVP price and increase the benefits. Because my experience over the years is that often those who could benefit most from an enhanced EVP (i.e., the employees) often have the best insights into what specific actions might be the most effective, we involved a small set of employees in a brainstorming session regarding potential actions.

The discussion regarding price was purposely focused on understanding exactly what the problems were with the sorting process in the warehouses and which issues were having the biggest impact relative to any delays or missed deadlines. In other circumstances, this focus might be viewed as just another operational improvement exercise, but not framing it in the normal operational improvement way made all the difference. Rather than talk about what changes would be needed so that the company could meet deadlines and commitment to clients, we framed it in terms of what changes would have the biggest impact in eliminating the stress to employees that came from delays and missed deadlines. Without being this blunt, we framed the challenge as: "What changes would most reduce the chance of a delay or missed deadline causing your boss to 'get on your case?'" Framed this way, employees in very short order identified several improvements. These were easily and quickly approved by management.

As discussed earlier, these delays and missed deadlines were the principal driver of bosses criticizing employees in public, which was both a source of stress that increased price and also a roadblock to employees feeling that their bosses cared about them. However, based on the interviews and focus groups, it was clear that bosses were publicly criticizing employees not just because of delays and missed deadlines but also because the model of a good boss that they held in their head was one who was tough and pushed employees. Therefore, we weren't convinced that just eliminating delays and missed deadlines would lead eliminate this negative behavior in bosses. As long as bosses thought they needed to be tough and criticize employees in order to be good bosses, they would find something to fault. If it weren't missed deadlines, they would find something else. Consequently, we were not convinced that just eliminating delays and missed deadlines would magically lead bosses to positive expressions of care and concern for employees, which was what employees wanted in order to feel they were getting positive benefit from their bosses. To add maximum impact from this variable in the EVP, we needed to both eliminate a negative and add a positive.

For the leadership component of the EVP, we did not engage workers in brainstorming or problem solving sessions. Rather, we worked with HR (local and regional) to create a high impact development program that would help supervisors see the downside of open criticism and the benefits of coaching and positive reinforcement. For this session, we created a video of the undesired behavior and consequence, as well as, the desired behavior and consequence. We also provided simple but effective frameworks and tools to help bosses understand the new model of leadership and then used role plays to ensure that supervisors not only intellectually understood what to change and why but also could put them into behavioral practice. For the three months after this training, the managers of the supervisors made it a point to visit operations more frequently and during those visits would reinforce with supervisors the desired behavior.

In amplifying the "company" dimension of the EVP, we once again engaged employees in a brainstorming and problem solving session. We structured the session by clarifying that the objective was to figure out a way to help employees' family members have a greater appreciation for the reputation and values of Global Delivery. Employees came up with a variety of suggestions, but the one that got the greatest collective reaction was a proposed "ride-along." One young driver said, "If my parents could see how we are taught to drive and how other delivery drivers behave, they would know that I'm with the very best company."

An actual ride-along was infeasible but it quickly gave rise to the idea of creating a short virtual ride-along video and then sending it directly to employee family members. In short, the video showed unsafe and discourteous drivers of competitors (with the company names and logos blotted out) zipping through the streets of Shanghai, honking their horns, coming dangerously close to pedestrians, running red lights, etc. It then contrasted this with images of the company's own safe and courteous drivers with Global Delivery's logo prominently displayed.

The response from the employees' family members was strong and positive. Here it may be worth noting that while people in any country seem to care what family members think of them and their work, culturally in China, family opinions matter to a great extent. While nothing in the company actually changed, workers felt significantly greater pride in working for Global Delivery because of how people they valued now felt about the company.

In fact, the impact was so great, that Global Delivery began to use the video with great effect in recruiting new delivery personnel. New recruits would take the video home and show it to their family. Often the family would react positively enough that they would nearly command, not just recommend, that the person join Global Delivery. No surprise then that new hire yields increased dramatically, and with this, recruiting costs dropped significantly.

Even without changing the denominator, this improvement in the numerator significantly enhanced the overall EVP.

Outcomes

In combination, the changes to the numerator and denominator improved the overall EVP by 40% when the target was 20% (see Exhibit 7.4). This resulted in a drop in turnover from 34% to 9%—a drop of 74% when the target was 50%. Importantly, the turnover rate for rivals remained above 30%. As anticipated, there were spillover effects on customer satisfaction. It improved by more than 25%. Also as modeled, more satisfied customers gave Global Delivery more business and revenue and profits grew by an additional 12% above the previous trend lines. Again what is perhaps most important is that revenues and profits grew significantly more than the competitors. The entire engagement produced an ROI of nearly 900%.

Effectively Global Delivery became the employer of choice by taking this very practical approach. There were no long sessions discussing what it meant to work for Global Delivery or debating its employer brand

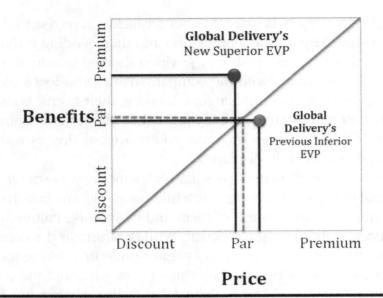

Exhibit 7.4 Global Delivery's superior EVP.

positioning. There were no fuzzy conversations about brand communication strategies. There was just very down-to-earth data gathering, analysis, and action. Don't get me wrong, all the brand work that marketers do with products or even companies can be valuable, but when it comes to being an employer of choice and constructing an effective EVP, such general discussions and debates are not necessary and are not effective.

This matters because as I mentioned at the outset of this book, virtually all managers and executives believe and accept that "people are our most valuable asset" and they almost always think that being the "employer of choice" is a good idea. However, perhaps because this domain does not have the history, track record, or direct outcomes that product brand discussions do, in my experience many (maybe even most) executives do not have the patience for long and esoteric discussions of what it means to be employer of choice. This approach takes into account how employees actual choose their employer, is data driven, and is relatively straightforward to put into practice.

Summary

In summary, getting the people you want to want you is the essence of winning the war *for* human capital. You need them to want you and therefore choose to join you; you need them to want you and choose to stay with you; you need them to want you and choose to be engaged and go the extra mile for you. While achieving this is not easy, it can be a structured and fairly straightforward process.

The first step in getting those you want to want you is simply to find out where you are. How strong or weak is your current EVP and on what dimensions. A survey is the best way to get this baseline information. Plotting the four baskets of benefits individually relative to the price can give you a very quick visual sense of your current position. The aggregate plot can bring it to a finer focus.

The second step is to determine which factors have the greatest impact. The most efficient and reliable way to do this is through multivariate statistical analysis. This is most easily done with the survey results. Sometimes, the poorest scoring items are the ones that if improved could have the greatest impact. However, this is not always the case, as illustrated with Global Delivery. Sometime strengthening a strength is the way to gain the biggest bang for your buck. Once you know which factors your employees value the most and which elements if improved could have the biggest impact, you are ready for the third step.

The third step involves diving a bit deeper into those dimensions that the statistical analysis has shown to be the highest impact. As illustrated in the Global Delivery example, this almost always requires data gathering beyond the survey—including interviews and focus groups. When price is problematic, you have to find out what is driving up stress, strain, hours, frustration, etc. No survey can tell you this but employees, if asked, can. If reputation is a strength but improving it can yield significant impact, what is it about reputation that employees value? No survey can tell you this, but again, employees can. If there are both negative leader behaviors that if eliminated and positive behaviors that if added could enhance this benefit, no survey can get effectively at this, but conversations with employees can. Quite simply the survey results and statistical analysis tell you where your target-rich environments are. Interviews and focus groups help you gain insight into what specific things in your situation with your people need to be changed.

The fourth step is where you take action. While there is no formula for what action to take, Global Delivery helps illustrate that on some issues it is very beneficial to involve employees in brainstorming and problem solving activities. In other cases, the problem has to be addressed from more of a "top-down" approach.

Taking these four steps is a simple but powerful way to ensure that the people you want, want you.

COMPETING *WITH* HUMAN CAPITAL

Up to this point we have covered an impressive amount of ground. In Chapter 1, we examined the fundamental shift in the source of competitive advantage from tangible assets to intangible assets. Importantly, we explored the chief enabling role of human capital relative to intangible assets as either the sum and substance of intangible assets or their principal driver. In Chapter 2, we reviewed how and why this shift from tangible to intangible assets has happened. In the process we shined a bright light on the role of increased competition in general and globalization in particular in driving competitive advantage from tangible to intangible assets. In Chapter 3 we dug deeper into why intangible assets have taken over the starring role in competitive advantage. We put the spotlight on the attractiveness of intangible assets' exponential curve compared to tangible assets' traditional "S-curve." We accentuated not only the fact that intangible assets' fundamental return curve is more attractive but also that the "S-curves" of traditional tangible assets are largely tapped and have reached the point of diminishing returns in many, many companies. This is partly why intangible assets have exploded from 25% to 65% of the average firm's value over the last 20 years. With the shift in source of competitive advantage clearly established and the mission-critical role of human capital firmly set in the equation, in Chapter 4, we examined why winning the battle *for* human capital has gotten tougher and looks to get only more intense going forward not just because more firms are competing for human capital but because that capital is in a stronger position. Specifically, we looked at four forces that have tilted the balance of power away from employers and toward employees.

These first four chapters constituted Part 1 and essentially answered the question of *why* the battle *for* human capital is so critical and *why* winning it has been recently, and will be going forward, so difficult.

With these questions of *why* answered, in Part 2, we examined key *how* questions. Specifically, *"How* can you get the people you want to want you?" In the process, I introduced a new framework for thinking about, measuring, and modifying a firm's value proposition to its employees. We explored why the new components of this framework (i.e., price and relative comparison) matter and how they more than double an executive's ability to understand and influence key EVP outcomes, such as attraction, retention, and engagement.

In summary, Parts 1 and 2 solved the challenge of competing *for* human capital. Parts 1 and 2 answered the questions of *why* competing *for* human capital is important and *how* to succeed. Once you have won the competition *for* human capital, you then have to win the competitive battles *with* human capital. That is the focus of Part 3.

The reasons why firms increasingly have to win with human capital have already been addressed but are worth restating. In many, if not most industries, the competitive power of economies of scale and the associated tangible assets have reached the point of diminishing returns. This is why firms are increasingly focused on intangible assets and why a majority of most firm's value today is tied to their intangible assets. As I have reinforced many times, human capital is either the sum and substance of intangible assets or the principle driver. Therefore, firms must compete *with* human capital. They must ensure that they have the right people, with the right capabilities, focused on the right issues, and following through consistently enough to deliver the right results.

However, this is easier said than done. Winning the final frontier of competition *with* human capital requires answers to several key questions:

- How do I link up my business strategy with the type of human capital and capabilities I need?
- If I don't have the right human capital to support the intangible assets that I target as my competitive advantages, should I buy, borrow, or build that capital?
- How do I align key processes and systems within my company, division, unit, team to ensure that my human capital indeed delivers and supports the intangible assets I have targeted as my competitive advantages?

- How can I lead effectively the necessary changes once I know what the alignment should look like?
- How can I make sure the changes stick?

Part 3 is designed to address and answer all these critical questions, so let's dive in.

Chapter 8

Business Strategy: The Fundamental Building Block

Getting the right people in place, with the right capabilities, doing the right things in the right way, depends on how you are trying to win. How you are trying to win is the essence of your competitive strategy and your competitive advantages. Today there are almost as many frameworks for business strategy as there are authors of the frameworks. Despite all the variations and differences, they all share a commonality. Strategy is about choices.

Perhaps this commonality stems from the origin of the notion of strategy. The word strategy comes from the Greek word *strategos* (στρατηγός), meaning military general. From a military standpoint, a strategy is a plan for how to defeat the enemy. That plan is fundamentally a set of choices, such as where to engage the enemy, when to engage, what armaments to use in the engagement, and the like. Today competitive strategy is not just about how to defeat an enemy—a competitor—but how to win customers. Nevertheless, just as a general had to decide where to fight or not fight, what armaments to use or not use, when to move forward or slip to the side, and so on, so too do executives formulating business strategies have to make choices about where to compete, which customers they want to win, what competitive advantages they are going to compete with, and so on. Any business strategist has to make choices.

But given all the different business strategy frameworks out there, how do you decide which one to use to guide the strategic choices you have to make? I think the decision begins with establishing some grounded selection criteria. Looking across all the academic work, as well as 30 years of practice, I think there are three simple criteria for selecting the right framework:

1. The framework should be one that organizes key choices.
2. The array of those choices should be reasonably comprehensive.
3. However, the array should also be simple enough to use in the real world.

If the framework does these three things, then it is a winner. Shortly, I will propose such a framework. However, in advance of that, it is important to keep in mind that because business strategy is a defined set of key choices, as those choices change, so too does the needed human capital. In this sense, the nature of your human capital follows the nature of your business strategy. For example, strategy that has a focus on innovation doesn't need the same sort of human capital as one focused on operational excellence. The types of people needed are different; the required knowledge is different; the required capabilities are different. Therefore, if you ultimately are going to compete effectively with human capital, you first must have clarity of strategy. This is why business strategy for our purposes is the foundation upon which the human capital structure has to be built.

With this in mind, let's return to what framework you should use to create or clarify your business strategy. Despite the number of business strategy frameworks out there, when it comes to selecting one that organizes a reasonably comprehensive set of choices into a simple enough structure that executives can use it effectively in practice, I think there is a clear winner—the Strategy Diamond.[1]

Formulating a Business Strategy

The Strategy Diamond focuses on five areas of choices that arguably every business executive must make in formulating a strategy. I simplify those choices from their original labels into five everyday words: Where, Which, What, When, and How (see Exhibit 8.1). While the original academic authors of the framework might not appreciate this simplification, nearly a decade-and-a-half of work with companies suggests that real world executives do.

With this simple, but reasonably comprehensive, set of questions in mind, let me walk through each of them and examine how you can use them to either assess an existing business strategy or formulate a new one.

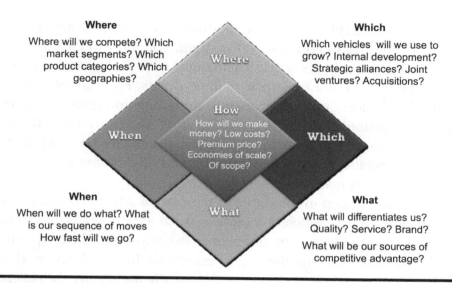

Where

Where will we compete? Which market segments? Which product categories? Which geographies?

Which

Which vehicles will we use to grow? Internal development? Strategic alliances? Joint ventures? Acquisitions?

How

How will we make money? Low costs? Premium price? Economies of scale? Of scope?

When

When will we do what? What is our sequence of moves How fast will we go?

What

What will differentiates us? Quality? Service? Brand?

What will be our sources of competitive advantage?

Exhibit 8.1   Strategy Diamond.

Where to Compete

The first strategy choice concerns where you will and won't compete—i.e., the competitive terrain. However, the competitive terrain is not composed of just one dimension. Among the various dimensions are what I will call the Big Three: customers, geography, and value chain.

Customers. Because it is impossible for one company to be all things to all possible customers, you must choose which customers you are going to focus on and which ones you are not going to worry about. You have to choose because not all customers want the same thing or put the same value on particular aspects of a product or service. In fact, the entire discipline of customer segmentation is based on the premise that customers have different needs and therefore can be grouped (i.e., segmented) based on those differences. As a consequence, one of the first questions you must answer in formulating a strategy is whom do you see as your customers.

Geography. Just as companies cannot be all things to all customers, they cannot be everywhere with equal presence—the world is just too big. You have to decide in which geographic markets you are going to put more or less emphasis. Even companies like Nestlé that operate in nearly 200 countries and territories across our planet cannot and does not put equal emphasis in every country. It decides that some countries are more important than others. As a consequence, part of your strategy is choosing where geographically you will place more or less emphasis.

Value Chain. Finally, because it is difficult for a single company to compete along every link in an entire value chain, you have to choose where along the chain you will compete. That could mean that you chose to compete only at a given point or across multiple points. For example, Nike puts significant time, effort, and resources into designing and marketing great products to consumers but not in manufacturing and distributing them; Nike essentially contracts for others to do those activities for it. In contrast, BASF focuses specifically on manufacturing and distributing its products and places little focus on marketing.

It is important to keep in mind that in the case of a large company with different businesses in very different industries (such as light bulbs and jet engines within GE), there are likely to be different answers to the "Where" question for each of the businesses within the overall enterprise. In fact, the more diverse the businesses' units within the enterprise, typically the greater the differences in their answers to the "Where" question. This point aside, it should be clear that where you decide to compete in terms of customers, geography, and value chain has a direct impact on the human capital you need.

Which Vehicles to Use

After you have decided where your business will and won't compete, you have to decide *which* vehicles you will or won't use to grow the business. Will you use primarily organic growth, mergers and acquisitions, joint ventures, licensing and franchising? Obviously, the answers to the "Which" questions are not necessarily determined by the answers to the "Where" questions. For example, you might determine that you are going to compete more in emerging international markets than developed ones. However, this answer alone does not determine the vehicles you will use to expand into those targeted emerging markets. You could decide to expand primarily through M&As, greenfield start-ups, licensing deals, or JVs. While any one of these vehicles might be feasible, and of course they are not mutually exclusive, they do require different capabilities. Therefore, the relative weight that is put on one vehicle over another is a critical strategy question to answer and has direct implications for the human capital you need.

What Competitive Advantages to Target

The third set of choices concerns the competitive advantages on which you will focus. We addressed competitive advantages at great depth earlier in the book. We established that something is a competitive advantage when it meets three key criteria: superiority, inimitability, and expropriability. We also discussed in some detail how and why the sources of competitive advantage and the chief enablers have changed over time, even though the three criteria have remained the same for three million years. Most importantly, we established that if any of the competitive advantages you select to be part of your business strategy are based in intangible assets, then human capital moves from a resource you may need to the key enabler you must have; human capital moves from being in the cast of characters to being in the starring role. The exact intangibles you target as your competitive advantages have a direct bearing on the human capital you need.

When to Do What

These first three areas of choices are critical but rarely does it make strategic sense to do everything at once. Often you must stage and sequence actions as well as determine the speed of that sequencing. For example, your strategy may call for expanding internationally into 20 emerging market countries (*Where*) primarily through acquisitions (*Which*) while leveraging your competitive advantages of brand and innovation (*What*). However, you may not be able to expand into all the targeted countries and leverage or build your brand power simultaneously. As a consequence, you have to make a strategic choice about the sequencing and speed. As an illustration, you have at least three major choices:

  A. Move into all the countries quickly, and then build your brand power over time
  B. Build up your brand power today in a few countries and then move into the other countries tomorrow
  C. Build up your brand power and expand into countries gradually over time

These three different paths are illustrated in Exhibit 8.2.
   The sequencing of strategic actions also has direct bearing on the human capital you need and when you need them.

How

The fifth and final set of choices concerns how the business will in fact make money as it follows these initial four strategy choices. While the term "make money" seems straightforward enough, I have a very particular

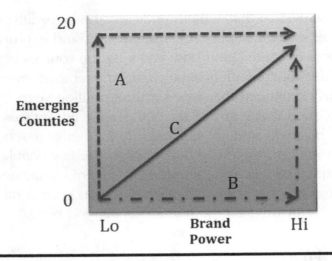

Exhibit 8.2 When: Sequencing of moves.

definition in mind. Making money means at a minimum earning profits that exceed your cost of capital *and* ideally are significantly higher than any of your rivals. Fundamentally, this final choice involves decisions about how the different elements of the business will be configured in order to create and capture economic value. Some refer to this final component of strategy as the business model. Whatever you want to call it, it is the economic road-map of how you will make money. Here I should note that while the choices made in the other four categories influence this final choice, they do not dictate it. Even if you decide that you are going to focus on price-sensitive customers in emerging markets through organic growth leveraging the competitive advantages of quality and design and move into these markets gradually over time, there is more than one way to organize your business model to ensure you make money and deliver superior returns. This is why this final category is indeed a category of choice and not one of determinism.

Strategy in Action: Southwest

As I mentioned, the Strategy Diamond is a widely accepted framework and I personally use it quite frequently in my consulting work. When I use it, I find that it makes intuitive sense to almost all executives. Nonetheless, it comes to life a bit more when illustrated with a real company example. Since I utilized Southwest Airlines earlier, let me now come back to it and use it to illustrate the Strategy Diamond framework and in the process bring the Strategy Diamond a bit more to life.

Where

As mentioned, the first question concerns where you will compete and not compete. As highlighted, there are often multifaceted answers to this question. When you talk with Southwest executives, they determined early on that "*Where*" in terms of customers would be those who, without a low airline ticket price, would travel by car or bus or not travel at all. Also, they decided that they would focus on domestic air travel. In terms of that domestic air travel, they determined they would fly primarily point-to-point routes that were over-priced and under-served. In serving these point-to-point destinations, Southwest determined that it would fly in and out of "secondary airports" such as Midway in Chicago or Love Field in Dallas rather than the major airports. In terms of the value chain it focused almost exclusively on the flight portion of the value chain—not before or after.

As I mentioned, deciding where you will compete also requires deciding where you will not compete. Even though Southwest decided to compete only domestically, within the domain of domestic travel, it decided to *not* compete for first-class business customers. As a consequence, it put in place only an economy-class cabin of service with no first-class seating. Clearly, a decision to focus on domestic service does not automatically preclude focusing on first-class customers and Southwest could have installed a limited number of first-class seats, but it chose not to.

Southwest remained very true to this business strategy for more than 40 years, until in 2010 when they acquired Air Tran. In addition to domestic routes, Air Tran also had flights to "near international" destinations in Mexico and the Caribbean. Southwest kept most of those destinations and in doing so changed part of their "Where" strategy from purely domestic flights to near-international flights as well.

In summary, Southwest chose to focus on price-sensitive customers primarily in the United States flying point-to-point on underserved and over-priced routes in and out of secondary airports primarily in the U.S. but to a limited number of near-international destinations.

Which

In the Strategy Diamond framework, the second set of choices concern the vehicles the business will use to grow in the areas in which it will compete. Southwest chose to grow primarily organically. In its over 40 years of existence, Southwest made two rather small acquisitions and only one notable acquisition—the purchase of Air Tran in 2010, which I mentioned earlier. In addition, as part of Southwest's strategy, it chose not to join any of the alliances such as Star, Sky, or OneWorld. Southwest chose to grow primarily on its own.

You can make the case that to some extent Southwest's "Where" choices influenced some of its "Which" choices. For example, given that Southwest chose to focus on point-to-point routes between secondary airports, to some degree this made it difficult to form alliances with any of the major U.S. airlines, all of which had "hub-and-spoke" structures, especially since the hubs in those structures were at major airports such as O'Hare in Chicago or DFW (Dallas/Fort Worth International Airport) in Dallas and not at secondary airports such as Midway in Chicago or Love Field near Dallas. In addition, not being in many of these major airports or not having a strong presence in these airports made it difficult for Southwest to join any of the global alliances, such as OneWorld or Star. This is because the major international partners in these alliances flew into major airports in the U.S., such as Chicago's O'Hare or Dallas' DFW, where Southwest had little presence. As a consequence, if Southwest were part of these alliances, the passengers of those international carriers would have to transfer from one airport to another, such as from O'Hare to Midway in order to take an onward flight on Southwest.

What

The third set of choices concerns the competitive advantages that the business determines it will focus on. For the first ten years of operations, Southwest was determined that its plane utilization (i.e., hours in the air per day) would be a competitive advantage. As mentioned earlier in the book, Southwest's plane utilization was at the beginning and remains today distinctively superior to its competition and despite their best efforts, even after more than 40 years, the competition has not been able to copy Southwest. While potential customers don't care about Southwest's high plane utilization, they do value the low fares that high utilization allows Southwest to offer. And customers have rewarded Southwest with volume premiums as evidenced by Southwest's growing market share over those years.

Because planes are such an expensive tangible asset, you could argue that Southwest had little choice but to ensure it managed this key tangible asset well. However, as evidence that it had pushed about as far up that traditional tangible asset "S-curve" as it could and had reached the point of diminishing returns, plane utilization was 11.17 hours per day in 1996 and 10.26 hours per day in 2016. During that 20 years the range only fluctuated between a high of 11.65 hours (2013) and a low of 10.2 hours (2010). Granted Southwest was still better than all the major U.S. airlines and than virtually all the other U.S. low-cost airlines, but it wasn't making any material improvements.

As a consequence, Southwest determined that it wanted an intangible asset to also be a competitive advantage—friendly service. For friendly service, Southwest was dependent not on the planes it flew, or the seats it installed, but on the people it employed, especially those that interacted with customers. The fact that Southwest's customer ratings that have been substantially higher than all the other major U.S. airlines over the last 15 years is testimony to its distinctive superiority. The fact that despite time, money, and effort the major U.S. airlines have never been able to get close to Southwest on this dimension, let alone pass them even for one year, is testimony to how inimitable this advantage has been. Southwest's high level of repeat business, positive word of mouth, and market share are all evidence that customers have rewarded Southwest with more of their business for this competitive advantage speaks to its expropriability.

When

Southwest could not do everything at once or become all that it desired to be overnight. It had to make important sequencing and speed decisions. In the 1970s, it concentrated its flights in Texas and then expanded primarily into the "southwest" area of the U.S. Over time, it gradually increased its flights in the eastern portion of the U.S. Its purchase of Air Tran in 2010, with its major hub of operations in Atlanta and flights to Mexico and the Caribbean, both accelerated Southwest's expansion into the east and southeast of the U.S. and launched its expansion into near-international destinations.

How

As discussed, the fifth and final set of choices concerns how the business will in fact make money as it follows these initial four strategy choices. Regarding this part of their strategy, Southwest had a very simple but powerful economic logic that divided into two parts—driving revenue up and driving costs down. To drive revenue up, Southwest determined it would use prices low enough to stimulate *new* demand, not just low enough to steal existing customers away from competitors. In other words, it determined it would use low prices to get people to fly Southwest who otherwise would have taken the bus, driven by car, or simply not traveled to their destination. This was a critical choice because rivals respond differently when they see their customers leaving and their revenue declining because of a new competitor as compared to when they see a new but small competitor growing but don't see any decline in their own numbers.

Obviously as more people flew Southwest for the first time, its revenues increased. However, Southwest anticipated that low prices would be necessary but insufficient to drive revenues over the long term. Its executives recognized that as the company entered markets with lower prices than its rivals, the competition would eventually respond and lower their prices. As a consequence, Southwest needed people to not just fly them once because of a low price but to fly them repeatedly because they enjoyed the experience more than on rivals' flights. In fact, Southwest wanted the customer experience to be good enough that customers would not only come back to fly them again but would recommend Southwest to friends and family (i.e., positive word of mouth). To secure this repeat purchase and positive word of mouth, Southwest determined that it would create a customer service oriented culture and provide distinctively friendlier service than its rivals. As already mentioned, it was quite successful at this and as repeat purchases increased, so too did Southwest's revenue.

However, Southwest could only offer prices low enough to stimulate demand and still make money *if* its costs were even lower. To drive costs to the lowest level, Southwest concentrated on high plane utilization. An important part of this was the quick turnarounds of its planes at the gates. This was in turn driven to a large extent by the productivity and efficiency of its staff—gate agents, cleaning crews, baggage handlers, etc.

In addition, Southwest drove costs down by utilizing only one type of plane—Boeing 737. This lowered pilot, mechanics, and other personnel training costs, made for more efficient maintenance and repair operations, and made it quick and easy to switch customers from one plane to another if a plane unexpectedly had to be taken out of service or if it had to be substituted because of a significantly delayed arrival of another flight.

Also, flying into secondary airports such as Midway in Chicago rather than O'Hare or Love Field near Dallas rather than DFW substantially lowered landing and slot fees. In addition, these secondary airports were not as crowded with flights, enabling Southwest to turn its planes around more quickly and get them back into the air. Because Southwest chose to focus on domestic passengers, it did not have to worry about connecting passengers to international flights serviced out of the major airports.

Clearly life is more complicated for Southwest than this portrayal of their business model might seem. After all Southwest Airlines has nearly 4,000 departures per day with over 700 planes serving 97 destinations and enplaning nearly 400,000 passengers per day (over 145 million passengers per year). Nonetheless, about 20% of all the business model factors explain 80% of how Southwest makes money. (See Exhibit 8.3 for an illustration of the Southwest business model.)

While applying the Pareto Principle to the "how" of a business strategy is helpful in its own right, as I will illustrate later, knowing what matters most is critical when you link the human capital needs and EVP to the business strategy. Without a clear sense of strategy and what matters most within the business strategy, it becomes nearly impossible to intelligently and economically determine who you want and why, and figure out how you can get

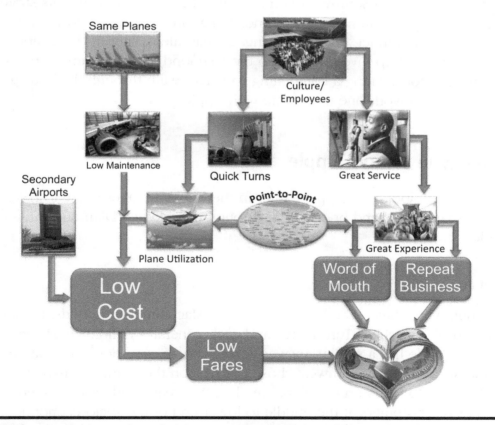

Exhibit 8.3   The how of Southwest's strategy: Its business model.

them to want you, plus then determine how to deploy your human capital in ways that win competitive battles.

As highlighted earlier, Southwest did a great job of not only formulating a winning strategy but ensuring that it had the right human capital with the requisite capabilities to implement the strategy. This is in large part why Southwest made money in years when most of its rivals lost money. To appreciate how effectively it both formulated and implemented its strategy, we need to keep in mind that not only did Southwest outperform all its major airline rivals over more than 40 years, but it also beat literally 100 different low-cost rivals that popped up over this time. Importantly, more than 90% of these low-cost start-ups not only failed to make returns close to Southwest's but they lost so much money that they went out of business. As a consequence of its effective strategy formulation and implementation, Southwest saw both its market cap and its stock price grow exponentially faster than its rivals and actually grow faster than the overall U.S. market in general.

We will return to Southwest and examine the implications that its strategy had on the type of human capital it needed and the value proposition that was required to attract, retain, and engage that talent, later in this chapter. But in order to help dive deeper into the Diamond Strategy framework as a precursor to formulating a compelling EVP, let's walk through the Strategy Diamond framework one more time with Apple.

Strategy in Action: Apple

Since we also looked at Apple earlier in the book, it makes sense to leverage that familiarity and briefly walk through the Strategy Diamond to dissect Apple's strategy.

Where

Although Apple has several businesses (e.g., Mac computers, iPods, iPhones, iPads, Apple Watches, iTunes, etc.) and each generates billions in annual revenue, Apple has a similar answer to the *"Where"* question across all its businesses. Whereas Southwest chose to focus on the domestic market, Apple chose to focus on the global market. Whereas Southwest decided to focus on customers at the middle to lower end of the socio-economic scale, Apple decided to focus on customers at the middle to higher end of the socio-economic scale. Whereas Southwest selected to focus on only the activities connected to flight link in the value chain, Apple selected to be directly involved in both upstream and downstream activities, though not all. In terms of upstream activities, Apple put great focus on the design of products. However, it chose to outsource most manufacturing. In the downstream, Apple chose to operate both its own brick and mortar and online stores, as well as cooperate with retailers who would also sell Apple products. Further downstream, Apple operates most of its service activities and outsources very little. Thus, Apple is engaged in both upstream and downstream activities but not all the various activities along the entire value chain.

Which

Like Southwest, Apple has chosen to grow primarily organically. While it has made a number of small acquisitions, it has eschewed large ones despite having enough cash on its balance sheet to buy any number of competitors such as HP, Lenovo, or Dell.

What

Identifying and trying to agree on Apple's competitive advantages is the best way I know to get an intense debate going among even best of friends. Nonetheless, there are some areas of agreement. For example, the ecosystem within which all Apple products work and the relative seamlessness of the interface among Apple's various devices is a competitive advantage on which most can agree. Apple's ecosystem is distinctively superior to its rivals in part due to its scope. Apple's ecosystem includes devises, operating platform, services, applications, and infrastructure. Apple owns many elements within each component of the ecosystem and has a combination of ownership and partnerships in other components. For example, Apple owns more than 90% of all the devices and hardware it sells but it owns less than 10% of all the applications that it approves for sale. It owns its operating platform for mobile and non-mobile devices, but directly owns only some of the infrastructure elements in its ecosystem. Virtually none of its competitors even come close to a similarly broad ecosystem and copying the breadth and depth of Apple's ecosystem would be a significant financial and technical challenge. In addition, Apple's ecosystem is hard to copy because Apple owns patents on many aspects of it and much of the ecosystem is in the software not the hardware of the devices, making it difficult to reverse engineer and replicate. In terms of the third criteria of competitive advantage, as previously discussed, Apple's high market share and significant price premium across its ecosystem is evidence that it has been able to expropriate significant value.

When

Even though Steve Jobs envisioned and talked about the "digital hub" and integration of devices many years before his passing, Apple could not rush to it all at once. In fact, even its success with the iPod required not just innovating the device but securing agreement with artists and record labels on DRM (digital right management) and allowing for greater penetration of broadband Internet access before the product could take off. To appreciate this sequencing, consider that even if Apple had come out with the iPod in 1998 when the first commercial MP3 player arrived, Apple's sales would have languished with all the other makers until a significant number of record labels and artists agreed to license their songs, which required acceptable DRM technology. Similarly, even if Apple had come out with the iTunes Store in 1998, this would not have spurred sales of the iPod as it did in 2003 because Internet speeds were just not fast enough in 1998 to prompt legions of people to order and download songs. After all, who wants to wait ten minutes to download *one* song, which is how long it took in 1998. So Apple made important sequencing decisions even within the iPod product category and the mini-ecosystem related to iPods. With high integration across Mac computers, iPods, and iTunes by 2007, bringing the iPhone into the ecosystem was much easier and made the ecosystem that much more difficult for rivals to copy and that much more valuable to customers.

How

Like Southwest, Apple has had a very simple but powerful economic logic for making money. In general Apple has pursued both price and volume premiums. Its pursuit of and success with price premiums is well known. By offering products that were simpler to use, more elegant in design, and more seamlessly integrated into the ecosystem than the competition, Apple has maintained across all the life cycles of all its products a 20% to 100% price premium. With the exception of computers, in general Apple has also pursued and enjoyed leading volumes. Although people often cite Apple's low market share of computers in terms of units sold, it is worth noting that among laptops costing $1,000 or more, Apple enjoys over a 90% market share in the largest market in the world for such laptops—the U.S.

Apple, however, has not been satisfied with securing margins primarily through price premiums; it has also sought to enhance profits by driving down costs even lower than many, if not most, of its competitors. In order to lower its costs, Apple has leveraged its volumes. For example, because it uses flash memory in so many of its products and has high volume across those products, Apple is the largest buyer of flash memory on the planet. As a consequence, it leverages its top purchaser position to extract the lowest possible prices from flash memory suppliers. In addition, it leverages its size to obtain significant decreases in manufacturing costs from its strategic partners such as Flextronics.

In combination, the core factors that help drive both price and volume premiums and the elements Apple leverages to drive down costs, enable it to make more money than virtually any other company on the planet (see Exhibit 8.4).

To illustrate the power of this combination of premium prices, superior volumes, and low costs, consider that Apple's computers have only a 10% market share in terms of units shipped and yet Apple makes more money off its Mac computers than its six largest competitors make off theirs *combined*! This is also why even though in 2017 iPhones had only 32% of the

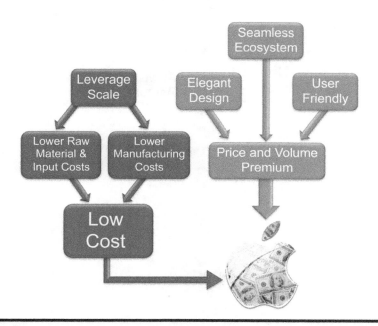

Exhibit 8.4 The how of Apple's strategy: Its business Model.

market by sales, they captured 92% of all the profits globally made on smartphones. Earlier, I highlighted what this stellar performance has meant in terms of shareholder returns. As a reminder, if you had invested $10,000 when the iPod was launched and another $10,000 when the iPhone hit the market, your stock would have been worth over $2.4 million toward the close of 2018.

Strategy Summary

Hopefully, at this point you can see the utility of the Strategy Diamond framework just in its own right. However, in the context of competing *with* human capital, the Strategy Diamond is fundamental. You can't really identify the human capital you need until your business strategy is clear. Once

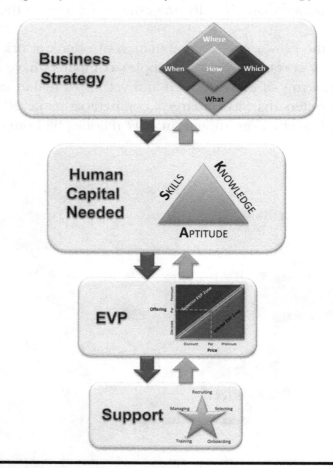

Exhibit 8.5   Linking business strategy and human capital.

you know the type of human capital you need, then you can think more intelligently about how to construct an EVP that will attract, retain, and engage them. After you know who you want and you have constructed an EVP that gets them to want you, then you can determine what aspects of the company you need to change in order to ensure the needed alignment and support are in place to sustain the human capital that drive your competitive advantages that in turn drive your business strategy (see Exhibit 8.5).

Conversely, without a well-structured business strategy, the nature, scope, and direction of your human capital strategy is all but impossible to formulate. You wouldn't be able to figure out who you wanted, and without knowing that, you couldn't determine what EVP would get them to want you.

Note

1. D. C. Hambrick and J. W. Fredrickson, 2001. "Are you sure you have a strategy?" *Academy of Management Executive*, 15, 4, pp. 48–59.

Chapter 9

Linking Human Capital Capabilities to Strategy

Once you have clarity regarding your business strategy, then you can start to link your human capital requirements to it. Fundamentally this involves determining who you want to want you. However, this requires drilling a bit deeper into the notion of human capital and human capital capabilities. Fortunately, this journey does not need to be complicated or filled with fancy jargon. A majority of what matters in terms of people's capabilities can be divided into three related but separate components: Aptitudes, Skills, and Knowledge, (see Exhibit 9.1 ASK framework). An easy way to remember this framework is to think "What am I 'ASK'-ing of my human capital?" Together these three components capture the vast majority of what I keep referring to as human capital capabilities.

Aptitudes

The best way to think of aptitudes is as endowed capabilities. For example, you likely know from your own personal experience that some people have a natural ability to carry a tune and others don't. People who can carry a tune can "hear" a song in their head and then they can have it come out of their mouth on key. Others are not endowed with this ability; they are often called "tone deaf." However, the term "tone deaf" is a bit of a misnomer because it is not that these people can't hear the tone, notes, or melody of the song in their head, it is that somehow what they hear in their head gets lost in translation by the time it comes out of their mouth.

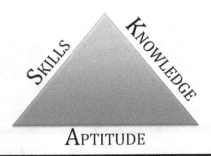

Exhibit 9.1   The "ASK" human capital capabilities framework.

Likewise, you may know people who have a "natural sense of direction." You can put them in a new city and they seem to just naturally calibrate distance and direction and find their way around. Others, if you put them in the middle of a city they know and have them close their eyes and turn around once, they're lost.

With this simple but practical definition of aptitudes, one of the first things to assess is whether your strategy requires certain aptitudes in your people. If so, you have to assess which aptitudes in which people? Clearly the more your people need aptitudes to implement your business strategy, the more successful your value proposition has to be in attracting the right people because you cannot adequately make up the deficit of not having the right people with training, development, and the like.

For example, if you are building a choir, you must attract people who can naturally carry a tune. Creating an EVP that gets the choir seats full, keeps them full, and has the choir members loving being in those seats is not very helpful if most of those seats are filled by people who love to sing but are tone deaf. Just because someone is enthusiastic and loves music and even loves to sing is no guarantee that they can sing. If they can't sing, it is hard to build a first-class choir no matter the amount of study, training, coaching, etc. that you provide. Your value proposition has to be effective at attracting people who can naturally carry a tune—otherwise all the retention and engagement in the world will be wasted.

Skill

The second category is skill. Generally, the term skill refers to the ability to do something well. However, in this context, I use the term skill to mean an ability that most people can acquire. For example, driving a car is a skill, and it is a skill that most people can acquire. Of course, some people can develop this skill to a higher level than others, but virtually anyone can develop a functional ability to drive. To ensure that people have a minimum level of driving skills, most countries have a practical driving test. You go out with an inspector who assesses your skills maneuvering the car on the road. As mentioned, but it is worth reinforcing, in my stating that skills are those abilities that most people could acquire, I am not assuming or implying that everyone can reach the same proficiency level. I am merely defining a skill as something that most people could develop to an acceptable level of proficiency. If most people can't develop a functional level of a particular skill, then there is a good chance that there is an underlying aptitude that is required as a foundation upon which high-level skill proficiency can be built.

Knowledge

The third aspect of human capital capability is knowledge. Knowledge is exactly what you would think it would be. It is the information, facts, and understanding that someone needs about a particular topic, discipline, activity, place, etc. in order to do their job. You can appreciate that some strategies by their nature are higher or lower in their overall knowledge requirements of human capital than others. For example, a strategy that focused on cutting edge technological innovation as a competitive advantage would require more knowledge than a strategy that focused on speed to market. In addition, some strategies require particular areas of knowledge than other strategies. Depending on how sophisticated, complex, and deep the knowledge requirements, there may be some requisite aptitudes, such as cognitive complexity, that will determine, or at least influence, the extent to which even with motivation and opportunity someone could master the required knowledge.

Capability

For our purposes, I use the term capability to refer to the overall proficiency to execute a complex task, which includes some combination of aptitude, skills, and/or knowledge. Clearly the mix of required aptitude, skills, and knowledge can and does vary from one capability to another. In addition, within a given capability the actual level of proficiency could vary from one employee to another.

For example, even with an equally high level of aptitude for singing, one person might obtain a higher level of proficiency by practicing more or getting better coaching and thereby raising his or her skill level. Or that person might attain a higher proficiency than another by attaining higher knowledge, such as how the vocal cords work, how breathing affects singing volume, and so on.

At the end of the day, proficiency is a function of the match between the degree of aptitude, skill, and knowledge required and that possessed by the employee multiplied by the motivation of the employee. Obviously, there are many things that an individual or an organization can do to accelerate, amplify, or augment knowledge, skill, and motivation and thus enhance ultimate proficiency. However, if an aptitude is needed but is missing, there is very little that can be done to compensate for that deficit. This is why it is critical to assess what aptitudes are required within key groups of employees. If you miss the need for aptitudes or misidentify the need, then you are relying on Lady Luck that the people you need will actually join you. If you don't recruit people with the requisite aptitudes, all the education, training, coaching, and incentives in the world will not make the needed difference. Just like if someone cannot carry a tune, all the study, knowledge, practice, and coaching in the world will not turn that person into Luciano Pavarotti.

The Five Steps to Linking Capabilities and Strategy

I recognize that conceptually creating the linkage between business strategy and human capital capabilities is not that hard to comprehend. However, hitting a golf ball is also not that hard to understand; you swing the club and hit the ball. Nevertheless, anyone who has tired golf knows that hitting the ball far and straight is easier said than done. Despite being easy to understand, hitting a golf ball takes some practice to get good at it. The same is true for linking your human capital capabilities to your strategy and then aligning your EVP to your human capital needs. It is not hard to understand but it takes some practice to get good at it. Therefore, in this chapter I will lay out the concepts and the various steps you need to take (see Exhibit 9.2), and then apply the framework to the Southwest and Apple case studies as virtual practice rounds.

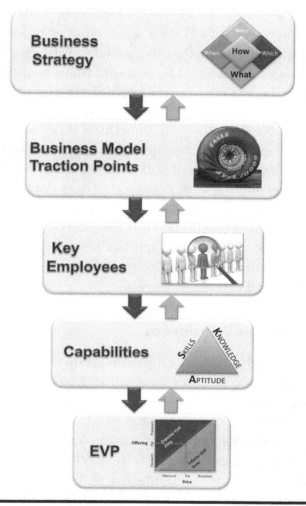

Exhibit 9.2   Linking your strategy and your human capital capabilities.

Step 1: Create or Clarify Your Business Strategy

The overall framework of linking your business strategy and your human capital needs starts with your business strategy. In Chapter 8, I reviewed the Strategy Diamond as a great framework to use in creating a clear strategy or in clarifying an existing strategy. Going through all five questions in the Strategy Diamond framework is a critical activity.

Step 2: Identify Traction Points

Once you have your business strategy, the second step in linking your strategy to your human capital needs is to determine what I call the strategy "traction points." Just as only about 5–7% of the surface of the tire accounts for traction at any moment, so too do a small number of key points have a disproportional impact on whether the strategy grips and the company moves forward or not. In practice I have found that examining the business model is often the easiest means of identifying the traction points. Ask yourself, "Where are the most critical points in the business model that must get traction?" or conversely "Where, if something slips, will this business model fail to move forward and we will fail to earn extraordinary returns?" For example, if you are a restaurant and your business model calls for premium prices for mind-altering delicious food, if you don't get traction in the kitchen, you don't move forward; in this case, it doesn't matter how wonderful your décor is or how professional your food servers are or how spotless your bathroom is. If the food coming out of the kitchen isn't mind-blowingly good, which is at the core of your strategy, then the strategy will slip and the restaurant will spin its strategic wheels.

Step 3: Determine Key Employees

The third step is to identify the key employee groups relative to the identified traction points. Typically, to help zero in on this, I work with clients to look closely at their targeted competitive advantages. This helps shine a light on who the key employees are. You can guess that there is a general correlation between the key traction points for your strategy and key employee groups. In the restaurant example I gave in which the kitchen was a critical traction point for its business model, you can imagine that the kitchen staff, especially the chefs in that case, are a critical group of employees. In contrast, a fast food restaurant has a different business model and therefore chefs are not critical.

Often when making this point, I have executives point out that there are many, many activities that may not be key traction points but nonetheless have to be done, and you need employees to carry out those activities. There is no argument about this. However, when pressed virtually every executive I've ever spoken with will subsequently admit that not all activities make equal contributions to a given strategy. As a consequence, they accept the logical conclusion that not all employees make equal contributions to that given strategy. Put directly, for a given strategy, all employees are important but some employees and their actions are critical. Looking carefully at the traction points in the business model and the targeted competitive advantages are the two most efficient and effective means of determining the critical, versus merely very important, employee groups.

Step 4: Identify Key Capabilities

Once key employee groups have been identified, then the fourth step involves using the ASK framework to identify the needed human capital capabilities for those targeted employee groups. The fundamental principle of prioritization that applies to the first three steps also applies within the fourth step. While all three components of the ASK framework matter, the "A" (aptitudes) matters the most. This is because you cannot afford to miss or misidentify needed aptitudes. If you miss or misidentify required aptitudes, it can undo all the time, money, and effort that you correctly might put into identifying the needed skills and knowledge.

Step 5: Determine EVP Priorities

The fifth and final step is determining which elements within the EVP matter most to your identified key employee groups. As I discussed earlier, having an overall "employee brand" is a nice ambition but there is little empirical evidence that such efforts really pay dividends. This is largely because you don't have generic employees who work for you doing generic jobs with generic contributions to your strategy. You have specific people doing specific things and some of those activities and people make a much bigger difference in your strategy's success than others. As a consequence, it is much more effective to an EVP that matches the needs of your key employees well and is only of average appeal to your other employee groups than to have an EVP that is of average appeal to your most critical employee groups.

Exhibit 9.2 provides a graphic illustration of these five steps for linking your human capital capabilities to your business strategy. In the exhibit, the down arrows indicate the sequence and the "macro to micro" logic and flow of the steps. The up arrows indicate that in practice the effective implementation of a human capital strategy is a bottom-up process. As a consequence, if there are weaknesses in the EVP, the needed capabilities, or the key employees, the strategy is unlikely to gain the desired traction almost regardless of how brilliant its formulation has been.

One important downside of "downstream" problems relative to implementing an EVP is that often poor strategic results get misinterpreted as evidence that the strategy was wrong or somehow inadequate. While you can certainly have a bad strategy, and if you do, you should change it, often the problem is not with the strategy itself but with the linking of human capital capabilities needed to implement the strategy. Following the five steps out-lined here, is the best way I have found to avoid prematurely and incorrectly changing a business strategy.

Applying the Framework to Southwest

As I mentioned earlier, these five steps are not that hard intellectually to understand. Hopefully, they even seem quite logical to you. However, like golf, it takes some practice both to appreciate the subtleties required to actually execute the steps and to get good at implementing them. As a consequence, let me walk through the first four steps in the context of Southwest Airlines.

Step 1: Create or Clarify Your Business Strategy

Since we effectively used the Strategy Diamond in Chapter 8 to articu-late Southwest's business strategy, there is no need to go through it again. However, it may be worth noting that despite all the ups and downs in regulations, competitors, the economy, fuel prices, and the like, Southwest has not had to modify its strategy much in over 40 years. This is not to say that strategies should never change; they should. It is only to point out that great strategies well formulated and well implemented may have longer life cycles than the go-go, disruptive, paradigm-shifting, whitewater business environment that the media and others like us to think we live in and must constantly adapt to. Indeed there may be many tactical adjustments that need to be made more frequently today than 20 years ago, but changes in fundamental strategy may not be needed as frequently as we suppose if the human capital strategy is well formulated and implemented.

Step 2: Identify Traction Points

Step 2 involves the identification of the key traction points in order for the strategy to move forward effectively. As mentioned, these are often best discovered by closely examining the business model and competitive advantages of a company's strategy. In the case of Southwest, I presented in Chapter 8 a simple diagram of its business model that divided it into two separate but related parts: those key factors that were designed to drive revenues up and those intended to drive costs down. As we quickly walk through their business model to identify the most critical traction points, we can also zero in on the related competitive advantages.

In terms of generating more revenue, Southwest had determined that it would use price to get people to fly the first time but then rely on friendly service to get them to come back. In fact, relative to this portion of the business model, the company had targeted friendly service as a competitive advantage. The key question for Step 2 is, "Where are the traction points for this portion of the business model?" Put more specifically, "What interactions with customers does friendly service make 80% of the difference in whether customers come back or not?" You don't need a $500,000 marketing study or Ph.D. in Customer Relations to figure this out. It turns out that Southwest's customers care most about their interpersonal interactions—how they are treated. In order of importance, they care about (a) how they are treated on the plane (the longest part of their experience), (b) how they are treated just before and while boarding the plane, and (c) how they are treated when they are checking in. These three interactions account for 80% of a customer's interpersonal experiences, and their interpersonal experience determines the majority of their satisfaction and whether they are satisfied enough to come back and fly Southwest again or not.

Often when I present this or when Southwest presents this, people argue that on-time departures and arrivals also matter to customers. This is true, but this matters somewhat less to leisure travelers going from point-to-point than business travelers. This is the case for three reasons. First, business travelers typically have "tighter" schedules than leisure travelers and therefore delays have bigger consequences for them. No one likes to keep a friend or family member waiting because of a delay but it is not the end of the world. It is a different story when 200 salespeople are waiting for the regional V.P. to arrive. Second, point-to-point system delays tend to have overall lower total delays than hub-and-spoke system delays. This is because in a hub-and-spoke system a delay in any spoke can get compounded via missed connections through the hub. This is not the case with point-to-point routes. Third and most importantly, it turns out that even if there is a delay, either before or after Southwest customers board the plane, what matters more than the actual delay is how they are treated relative to the delay. Specifically, what matters most is if customers feel they have been respected enough to be given honest and accurate information regarding the delay. No information, dishonest information, or inaccurate information essentially says to the customer, "We don't respect or value you or your time enough to take our time to tell you what is really going on." To be clear, no one likes delays. However, delays matter more to business travelers than leisure travelers. In addition, what matters as much or more than the delay itself is how customers feel they are treated regarding and during the delay.

The other key aspect of Southwest's business model is driving down costs. Arguably the single most important aspect of this piece of the business model is plane utilization, which I have noted a few times previously. While maintenance, optimal scheduling, and the like are important to plane utilization, it turns out that quick turns at the gate have the biggest impact. You don't have to be an operations management expert to understand this. All you have to do is think about the nearly 4,000 departures per day that Southwest undertakes with a fleet of a bit over 700 planes and it is easy to appreciate why a quick turn at the gate is the single biggest driver of plane utilization.

If Southwest cannot get its planes turned quickly at the gate, the productivity of its most expensive and largest tangible asset goes down and its cost per available seat mile goes up. If its costs go up high enough, Southwest either loses money or has to raise its prices. If it raises prices enough, it could see fewer customers and its total revenue could go down and the entire business model could begin to crumble.

With these key traction points in mind, we can then progress to Step 3 and identify key employee groups.

Step 3: Determine Key Employees

In terms of driving revenue up by ensuring positive interpersonal interactions, three key employee groups pop to the front: flight attendants, gate agents, and check-in agents. Clearly there are other points of interaction between Southwest employees and customers, but these are the key ones where positive interactions can boost customers' experience to the point that they intend to fly Southwest again and tell others to fly Southwest.

In terms of driving costs down, we simply have to ask which employees have the biggest impact on quick turns at the gate. Again, you don't need to be an expert in the industry to figure this out. The biggest issue affecting quick turns is you have to get customers who have just landed off the plane and get the boarding customers on. Again, you don't have to be an expert to understand that it is easier and quicker to get customers off a plane than to get them on it. With that in mind, you ask the question, "What employees have the biggest impact in getting customers on the plane and seated quickly?" The answer is gate agents and flight attendants. Of course, the efficiency of cleaning crews matter, the catering crew, the re-fuelers, and the baggage handlers also matter. However, the short overall length of most flights means that typically not that much trash accumulates for the cleaning crews to clean. The fact that Southwest serves only drinks and snacks, means that there is not much for the caterers to take off or put on the plane. Re-fuelers don't take long to do their job, but if they are late arriving at the plane, the plane cannot pull back until the re-fueler's job is done. Baggage handlers on the other hand can have a big impact on the turnaround time. Baggage handlers have a similar number of bags to load and unload for each plane. Also, because Southwest doesn't charge for checked bags, unlike most airlines, Southwest baggage handlers often have more checked bags to load and unload than their rivals. The positive side effect of no fees for checked bags is that Southwest customers have fewer carryon bags, which makes boarding go faster.

With this simple analysis, Southwest knows that gate agents and flight attendants are important both for supporting its friendly service competitive advantage, which drives revenue up, and also for facilitating quick turns and plane utilization, which drives costs down. In addition, check-in agents are important on the friendly service side of the equation and baggage handlers are important on the cost side of the ledger.

This does not mean that Southwest doesn't need pilots or engine mechanics or managers or marketing specialists or a dozen other categories of employees; it does. However, Southwest's strategy does not require 737 pilots or engine mechanics that are vastly different from those flying 737s or fixing their engines at other airlines. Now Southwest will argue that its pilots, engine mechanics, managers, marketing specialists, and janitors are different and special. They may be. But the strategy does not live or die on whether these employees have differentiated capabilities. However, the strategy does live or die depending on whether its flight attendants, gate agents, and check-in agents are distinctively more friendly and whether its gate agents, flight attendants, and baggage handlers are distinctively more productive.

Step 4: Identify Key Capabilities

With these employees in mind, the next critical question to ask is whether there is an aptitude or a set of aptitudes that are key for these employee groups and what they need to do. Let's take this step-by-step and first examine friendly service and then productivity.

In terms of friendly service, the first question to ask is whether it is an aptitude or not; does friendly service rely on endowed abilities or orientations or can anyone master it? To make a long and somewhat complicated scientific exploration of this subject short and sweet, let me jump to the punch line. While anyone can learn how to smile or how to ask a question or provide an answer in a friendly tone, to do that for hours on end, day after day turns out to require an aptitude. That aptitude is the extent to which a person naturally gains energy from interacting with people. For some people, interacting with others is naturally energizing and for others it is naturally draining. From a scientific point of view, when we are naturally energized by interacting with people, this is the essence of extroversion, and when such interactions are draining, this is the foundation of introversion.

The common misconception of extroversion or extroverts is that they are "friendly, outgoing people." While this is often the case, the true defining aspect of extroversion is not how outgoing someone is but the extent to which the person gains or loses energy from interacting with others. Also, it is important to highlight that even if someone has a high level of this aptitude, they may not have a high level of skill or knowledge. Specifically, someone could gain energy from interacting with others but not necessarily be skilled as doing so in a friendly or effective manner. Likewise, someone could be skilled at friendly service but naturally be drained by these social interactions. In this case, we would label this person a "socially skilled introvert."

All that being said, the research on extroversion strongly suggests that it is a very stable personality trait—meaning it doesn't really change in a person over time.[1] Furthermore, by the time people are in their late teens or early 20s, the level of extroversion is largely set. Fortunately, there are fairly simple but quite accurate assessments of this attribute. With this in mind, Southwest knows that relative to these three important categories of employees, their EVP must be compelling in attracting extroverts. They need people who are energized by interacting with others almost regardless of their skills at doing so. The skills of friendly service can be learned, taught, and developed; sustaining that behavior day in and day out requires an aptitude.

Assuming that employees with this aptitude are attracted to join and stay with Southwest, the requisite friendly service knowledge is not that difficult to impart to key employee groups. In other words, Southwest does not need its employees to be neuroscientists and understand the anatomy, biology, and chemistry of friendly customer service. It simply needs employees to understand that smiling at and greeting customers under normal circumstances and showing empathy and solving customers' problems when difficulties arise are the keys to having customers feel like they were given friendly service.

In terms of skills related to friendly customer service, virtually anyone can learn to smile and greet customers. Skills related to showing empathy, such as saying, "I can understand that you are frustrated with missing your flight. In your situation I would also be frustrated," can also be acquired by almost anyone. Solving problems like finding the next available flight for the person who missed their flight, takes a bit more training on Southwest's computer system, but most people can acquire this skill as well.

The bottom line for friendly service is that Southwest needs to attract, retain, and engage employees who have a high aptitude for friendly service (i.e., people who are extroverts) but whose ability to take on knowledge and skills relative to friendly service is average.

Now let's look at the capability of productivity. How much of productivity is based on aptitudes? As before, one way to approach this is to ask, "What do people need to be naturally good at or need to naturally like in order to be productive (if anything)?" Unlike friendly service, there does not seem to be a distinctive productivity aptitude—attitude, yes, but aptitude, no. Anyone can learn to be productive.

However, there may be an aptitude behind the drive to be productive. Scientists have labeled that drive "need for achievement." Some research has found a positive relationship between this personality trait and job productivity.[2] As a consequence, in areas in which productivity matters, such as baggage handling, Southwest may be well served by attracting and retaining employees who in general have high achievement needs. However, in areas in which productivity matters but safety matters more, such as aircraft and engine maintenance or ground operations, skill and knowledge likely trump any potential aptitude.

Assuming that an achievement aptitude job matters for baggage handlers and gate agents, the requisite skills and knowledge are not extraordinarily high. Southwest doesn't need baggage handlers that calculate the standard deviation of loading and unloading bags over a day across 50 different enplanements. Southwest simply needs employees who can understand how the speed and efficiency at which they do their job affects Southwest's overall productivity and costs.

Obviously, this productivity requirement is separate from technical knowledge and skill requirements in any number of other jobs. For example, the skill and knowledge requirements for a certified airplane engine mechanic

are substantial. Similarly, the skill and knowledge requirements for someone involved in flight scheduling and operations are non-trivial. These and
other jobs are highly technical and can have an impact on key operational
determinants of cost such as plane utilization. However, on an hour-by-hour,
day-by-day basis, jobs such as baggage handlers, plane cleaners, gate agents,
and ground operators have a more consistent and immediate impact on
turnaround times and ultimately plane utilization.

In terms of productivity in these job categories, the skills and knowledge
required to do their jobs well and efficiently are those that can be acquired
by most people. The bottom line for productivity is that Southwest needs
to attract, retain, and engage gate agents and baggage handlers who have a
higher than average need for achievement but whose ability to take on skills
and knowledge relative to productivity is nothing above average.

Linking Needed Human Capital Capabilities to EVP

Once you have a picture of the needed capabilities by key job categories or
groups of employees, then you can begin the process of creating or modifying EVPs that ensure you get the people you want to want you. Also, by
knowing the extent to which aptitudes are required or not, you can more
intelligently start the work of ensuring that the EVPs get and retain the right
people. Here it is worth being a bit repetitive and pointing out that if aptitudes are required and you can't attract and retain the right people, all the
training, coaching, rewarding, scolding, empowering, etc. in the world will
not compensate for the lack of aptitude sufficiently to ensure the desired
competitive advantage is produced. Put differently, if you can't attract people who can carry a tune and your competition can, all you compensat-
ing actions will not make up the gap and the competition will in the end
outsing you.

Top-Down vs. Bottom-Up EVPs

Assuming this makes sense, there is still a fundamental choice in the
approach of linking EVPs to the required capabilities that you have logically derived from the strategy. You could take a top-down or a bottom-up
approach.

Most consulting firms and purveyors of paths to "employer or choice"
take a top-down approach. They typically start by asking what you want

your employer of choice brand to be? What do you want to be known for? This almost always leads to a fairly generic set of responses, such as "we want to be known as a place of inclusion and empowerment" or "we want people to think of us as one who respects and develops people to their fullest extent." Who could argue with such statements and aspirations?

However, my research and experience suggest that taking a bottom-up approach is much more effective. Why? As we just demonstrated with Southwest, the odds that all your employees have the same configuration of required aptitudes, skills, and knowledge is quite low. As a consequence, trying to create an EVP that applies equally and powerfully to a diverse employee population is just not very high. It is like giving everyone the same size shirt. There is just no way it is going to fit everyone well.

Also, there is no need to treat everyone equally. The reality is that just as not every activity in the company is equally important given a specific strategy, neither are the people performing those activities. The fundamental principle of strategy is choice. You chose which customers are more important to you over others—domestic travelers or international travelers; price-sensitive travelers or luxury travelers. You chose what competitive advantages you are going to focus on—friendly service or interior colors, design, and lighting. Those choices move some activities, the people who perform them, and the capabilities they need to do it well, to the front and push others to the back. Change the strategy choices and the priorities change as well.

This does not mean that you would broadcast to employees, "Hey you folks over here really matter and make critical contributions to our competitive advantages and strategy and you employees over there—not so much." That would be crazy. However, it would also be crazy to pretend that all employees matter equally and as a consequence create a generic EVP. You want your EVP to be attractive to the employees you most need to attract, retain, and keep motivated.

Does the bottom-up approach mean that there can't be common, universal, company-wide aspects to an EVP? No, not at all. It only means that those common aspects are discovered after the bottom-up process rather than determined at the beginning of a top-down declaration.

Linking Capabilities and EVP

To the extent that aptitudes matter for certain key groups of employees, that is where the strongest and tightest link between capabilities and EVP needs to be. But how can you know what aptitudes correlate strongest with which aspects of the EVP? In the case of Southwest, does extroversion have its strongest link with company, with job, with leaders, or with reward? Within any one of these are there specific elements with which it might have a stronger link? For example, within rewards, is extroversion more strongly related to salary, variable pay, stock grants, recognition, or something else? I wish there were enough academic studies done on the relationship between various aptitudes and components and subcomponents of EVP to give you specific answers. The reality is that there is not. And actually, I don't think there ever can be.

The reason is simple. Even for a given aptitude like extroversion, there is not just one type of extrovert. The type of extroverts attracted to the airline industry could easily be somewhat different than those attracted to the hotel industry. Both need to smile, greet people, and most importantly derive energy from interacting with people hour after hour, day after day. After all, there are only so many variations of interactions when giving someone some peanuts and a drink on Southwest or checking someone in at the front desk of a Marriott Hotel. However, there is a fairly big difference between being gone 13–17 days a month as a Southwest flight attendant and being home every night if you work the day shift at the Marriott front desk.

The good news is that you only have to understand the relationship between your people and the components and subcomponents of an EVP; you don't have to understand the relationships for all extroverts in the world. That's the good news. The other good news is that the process of making the connection between your key people and what needs to be the strongest elements of your EVP is not that hard or time consuming.

To illustrate this, let's go back to the case of Southwest Airlines and make it simple by just focusing on flight attendants for the moment. Assume that Southwest didn't systematically assess for extroversion before hiring flight attendants in the past, and as a consequence, today they have a mix of flight attendants who range from highly introverted to highly extroverted. Assume further that the EVP Southwest has is good but not superior to other airlines. In other words, Southwest's ability to attract, retain, and engage employees is about as good as the rest of the airlines. (By the way, Southwest would argue that it is better, but let's put that aside for the moment.) How should Southwest begin the process of determining what aspects of its EVP should be given higher or lower priority? It is a simple five-step process:

1. Random, representative sample. First, Southwest would select a representative and random sample of flight attendants.

2. Measure the aptitude. Second, within this sample, Southwest would measure the characteristic of introversion-extroversion.
3. Measure the EVP preferences. Third, Southwest would have this same sample rate or rank the EVP categories and subcategories in terms of preference—what do they value most?
4. Examine the relationship. The fourth step involves a simple examination of the relationship. An easy way to do this it to divide the sample into strong introverts, strong extroverts, and mixed based on their assessment scores and then look at the percentage of each of these three groups of employees that prefer different EVP categories and subcategories. In particular, you would look to see which EVP categories and subcategories your strong extroverts most preferred.
5. Test the relationship. Sometimes the preferences are so clear that you can stop at Step 4, but often you have to go to Step 5 and look at the relationships with some simple statistical analysis—correlations and regressions.

Once you have walked through all five steps, you typically have what you need to determine the nature of your EVP. Let's peak under the hood of Southwest for a moment in the case of the EVP for flight attendants by looking specifically at all five elements of the EVP.

Price. The maximum hours that a flight attendant can work are largely regulated and therefore the same from airline to airline. The stress of angry passengers, weather delays, mechanical delays, etc. are largely outside of the control of any airline and to some extent common across all airlines. The point here is that Southwest can only do so much to alter the price flight attendants pay to work for Southwest. The price Southwest flight attendants pay is not radically higher or lower than that of flight attendants at other airlines. Therefore, if Southwest is going to have a superior EVP for its flight attendants, it largely needs to come from having superior offering on one or more of the four baskets of benefits.

Job. The job of a flight attendant also does not vary that much from company to company. Clearly how a flight attendant carries out that job can vary, and Southwest clearly wants its flight attendants to be distinctively more friendly than its rivals. But the freedom, autonomy, challenge, etc. of the job turns out to be something that Southwest cannot dramatically elevate. The good news is that the basic nature of the job fits extroverts—there are lots of opportunities to interact with people and gain energy from those interactions.

Rewards. The basic pay of flight attendants is fairly similar across the industry in the U.S. However, given that flight attendants can influence both the revenue and cost side of Southwest's business model, they are a particularly important category of employees. As a consequence, to the extent that they value money at all as part of the EVP and you can tie some of the money they receive to the performance of their job and the company's performance, you can use this aspect of the EVP to get the people you want to want you. As a consequence, Southwest has a profit sharing plan that includes flight attendants. In a typical year, the profit sharing bonus can constitute 10% to 20% of a flight attendant's total compensation. This is a very appealing part of the reward's portion of Southwest's EVP for flight attendants.

Leaders. There are always two levels of leaders that matter to most employees—the visible leaders at the "top of the house" and the leaders that employees live with each day (i.e., their boss). At the top of the house, Herb Kelleher was CEO from 1981 to 2001. He was beloved and admired by all employees for his down-to-earth style. He continued as Chairman of the Board until 2008. Colleen Barrett took the reins of the company in 2001 through 2004 when Gary Kelly took up the role of CEO. In 2008 he also took on the role of Chairman of the Board after Kelleher retired. Kelly has the same down-to-earth style as Kelleher and flies coach on Southwest and waits to get on and off the plane just like everyone else. Southwest employees, including flight attendants, feel that their top executives can and do relate to them and that top executives appreciate that flight attendants are the ones who really make Southwest fly. At the more immediate level of direct supervisor, the positive benefits that these leaders add to the EVP of flight attendants is directly tied to the focus in the final element of the EVP—the company and its culture.

Company. Clearly employees take pride in Southwest's unbeaten record of profits and stock performance compared to all their domestic rivals. Its solid track record also gives employees confidence in future profit sharing bonuses, which I discussed earlier. However, it is its culture of fun and friendly interactions with each other (not just customers) that distinguishes Southwest and provides a valuable benefit to flight attendants. As mentioned, flight attendants need to get energized by interpersonal interactions. They need to keep up a sincere and friendly attitude with customers, even when customers are not so friendly or nice. This is much easier to do if the other employees you interact with, including your boss, are fun and friendly. This is what Southwest seeks to do by modeling this desired behavior at the top of the house and then reinforcing it down through the house. The details of how you ensure that you have alignment throughout the organization relative to your human capital strategy and EVP is the focus of the final chapter, so I will leave the details of how to do this until then.

Step 5: Determining EVP Priorities at Southwest

So what does Southwest's EVP look like when you pull it all together? While the EVP looks similar for most groups of employees, we will continue to focus on the EVP relative to one of Southwest's most important categories of employees—flight attendants.

First, as illustrated in Exhibit 9.3, Southwest's price is effectively on par with that of its domestic rivals. Southwest flight attendants work about the same hours, endure the same types, and amount of stress and strain, etc. as their peers at other airlines. On the benefits side of the EVP, the benefits of the job are not dramatically better or worse than other airlines. It too is about on par with the competition. However, the rewards are better, primarily driven by the profits Southwest generates and the flight attendants get through the profit sharing plan. Its leaders, both at the top of the house and directly related to employees, are perceived as better—more caring, more

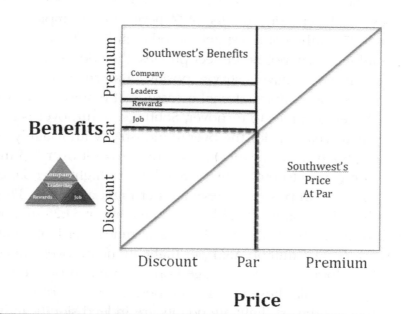

Exhibit 9.3   Southwest's raw EVP.

down to earth, more friendly and fun. The company, its reputation, and in particular its culture, are seen by employees as vastly superior to what they could experience elsewhere—certainly within the airline industry.

Given that flight attendants care most about the rewards and company, the weighted EVP is strongly superior. But given that it is strongly superior, is there evidence that it is producing the desired benefits? Understandably, this is a little difficulty to perfectly layout because Southwest, as well as other airlines, do not publish certain performance details such as turnover, absenteeism, employee satisfaction, and the like. However, this does not mean that there are no indicators or proxies we can use to at least make a general assessment of whether the EVP is producing positive results.

First, let's take a general measure of employee satisfaction. Each year for the last six years, Glassdoor.com has conducted a very extensive online survey of employee satisfaction to determine its Top 50 Glassdoor Employee Choice rankings.[3] Glassdoor is one of the largest websites that gathers and posts job descriptions, salary levels, employee reviews, etc. and has over 41 million unique users. Over the last six years, Southwest is the only airline to make the list of the most preferred employers as assessed by employees. Over the last six years, Southwest's average rank is #23 among all companies in the U.S. No other airline has an average rank that puts them in the Top 50 over the last six years. Another workforce website, Indeed.com, also recently started a "Best Places to Work" ranking and in 2017 ranked Southwest #2 overall. Forbes also has produced a list of "America's Best Employers." In 2017, Southwest was #35 on the entire list and no other airline made the top 50. While these rankings may not be perfect proxies, they do seem to indicate that Southwest employees have a strong, positive assessment of the company.

Next, let's think about more internal measures of employee satisfaction and behavior. When it comes to turnover, Southwest's turnover is about 4.5%, which is half what it is for the overall industry. With roughly 14,000 flight attendants, Southwest's lower turnover rate saves it over $13 million per year. When it comes to productivity, Southwest's flight attendants average about $1.5 million in passenger revenue per flight attendant. Flight attendants at the other major U.S. airlines average about $1.25 million or almost 17% less. In terms of ASM (available seat miles) per flight attendant, Southwest averaged 11.6 million ASM per flight attendant over the last five years, while their domestic rivals averaged on 10.3 million or about 11% percent less. Again, while these may not be perfect proxies of productivity, they indicate that Southwest flight attendants are indeed significantly more productive than flight attendants of other airlines.

I have already talked about Southwest's customer satisfaction rating that is 15% to 20% higher than its rivals (excepting JetBlue) and has been for more than a decade. Sadly, I know of no data or studies that show the relationship between airline passenger satisfaction and either repeat purchase behavior or positive word of mouth to others. As a consequence, estimating the value of Southwest's friendly flight attendants relative to revenue is impossible.

Summary

We traversed quite a bit of territory in Chapter 9 and so it may be worthwhile to summarize some key takeaways. First, in competing with human capital, you have to know what type of capital (i.e., capabilities) you need and that directly flows from your business strategy. To zero in on needed capabilities, you have to have a simple but reasonably comprehensive framework of what a capability is. I use a simple one called ASK (Aptitudes, Skills, and Knowledge).

Second, in linking strategy and required human capital capabilities, I offered a simple but effective five-step process:

1. Create or clarify your business strategy.
2. Identify key traction points for the strategy to succeed.
3. Determine key employee groups for the strategy to gain traction.
4. Identify key capabilities within those target employee groups.
5. Determine EVP priorities for the target employee groups.

The second major process in being able to compete with human capital involved the more detailed process of linking the EVP to the targeted human capital. This also involved a simple but effective five-step process:

1. Select a random but representative sample of the existing employees in the targeted employee group.
2. Measure the key aptitudes.
3. Segment the employees based on different aptitude levels and then measure their EVP preferences.
4. Examine statistically the relationship between targeted employee segments and EVP components.
5. Statistically test the strength of the relationships in order to know what aspects of the EVP to target.

Finally, in coming up with exactly how to create or strengthen the specific components of the EVP, I proposed a bottom-up rather than a top-down approach. In this approach you interview and talk with employees to get at concrete elements of the EVP so that in the end, the people you want to want you get what they most want from the EVP.

Notes

1. P. J. Howard and J. M. Howard, 2009. *The Owner's Manual for Personality at Work:: How the Big Five Personality Traits Affect Your Performance, Communication, Teamwork, and Sales.* Bard Press, Austin, TX.
2. B. Yehuda, M. F. O'Creevy, P. Hind, and E. Vigoda-Gadot, 2004. "Prosocial Behavior And Job Performance: Does The Need For Control And The Need For Achievement Make A Difference?" *Social Behavior and Personality,* 32, 4, pp. 399–411.
3. https://www.glassdoor.com/Award/Best-Places-to-Work-LST_KQ0,19.htm

Chapter 10

Aligning Key Processes to Support Your Human Capital Strategy

Once you have an EVP that causes the people you want to want you, then the task is ensuring that key parts of the organization are aligned to reinforce your human capital strategy. While this may seem like an extra step, I have seen many companies that have essentially done all the right things to attract, retain, and motivate their targeted human capital and restructured their EVP to that end, but then unwittingly undermined those costly efforts because other aspects of the organization were not aligned. This happens most often when the organization has shifted its needed human capital and when it has constructed or reconstructed its EVP. This misalignment is like putting a new, more powerful engine in your car so you can go faster but then leaving the old wore out tires, the limited transmission, the soft brakes, and the loose steering in place. At best, this misalignment keeps you from realizing the full potential of the new engine and at worst, because the tires can't corner, because the brakes can't handle the new speed, because the transmission shifts too slowly, and because the steering is not responsive enough, you crash and burn.

The key processes that need to be aligned to the human capital strategy in order to ensure that it does what it is supposed to in supporting the business strategy are not new ones I invented (see Exhibit 10.1). In fact, you can easily make the case that they are old. The issue is not their newness or their oldness but rather their power in supporting all the work done to

Exhibit 10.1   The key supporting processes.

build a human capital strategy and optimizing the impact. In general, this means ensuring that all the key actions inside each process can be tied easily and directly to getting the human capital you need and building the targeted capabilities required. At the end of the day, every activity within the "Support Star" should be clearly and directly tied to supporting the targeted human capital, building the required capabilities to drive the business strategy.

Recruiting

Although it may seem obvious, who you recruit and how you recruit them needs to be aligned with your new or refined human capital strategy. Even if the business strategy has not changed, my experience is that when companies go through the process of clarifying their strategy, assessing the traction points, identifying the key employee groups, determining the required capabilities, and aligning their EVP to all of that, who they need to focus on recruiting and how they need to go about it almost always needs to be somewhat to substantially different than it was before. If the strategy is also different from the past, then it is virtually guaranteed that the recruiting targets and process will have to change as well.

However, just as the EVP does not need to be tailored to all employees but should be focused on the key employee groups, so too should any changes in the recruiting process focus on these same key employees. It is just too big of a task, and an unnecessary one, to try and revamp the entire recruiting process. Rather it is much more effective and practical to focus any and all changes on the already identified key employee groups.

The key to success in revamping the recruiting process is to focus on (a) the needed aptitudes, (b) the type of people who have the targeted aptitudes, and (c) where you might find those people. The traditional recruiting approach starts by looking at the experience and knowledge people need to do the job. However, starting here will almost certainly limit the net cast in the recruiting process and cause you to miss out on some of the best talent you need.

Let me illustrate this by looking at recruiting flight attendants for Southwest. If Southwest started with skills and knowledge as the basis for recruiting flight attendants, it would logically go after individuals with previous flight attendant experience. This has two important and likely negative consequences relative to Southwest's business and human capital strategy. First, most of the people with previous flight attendant experience likely got that experience working for other airlines. Although this might not seem problematic of the surface, it could easily hurt rather than help support both Southwest's business strategy and its human capital strategy. This is because most other U.S. airlines have not had nearly as strong of a focus on friendly customer service as Southwest, in part because at most of the other airlines, friendly service has not been a part of their business strategies. Without this focus, it is highly likely that the other airlines did not screen for aptitudes or even attitudes that drive and sustain friendly customer service behavior. In the worst case, these individuals with experience at other airlines might have adopted not so friendly customer service behaviors and patterns that then Southwest would have to "undo." Undoing or unlearning past attitudes and behaviors is always a difficult task. In fact, in most cases, unlearning an old behavior is harder than learning a new behavior. Second, starting with a focus on skills and knowledge and related experience could easily cause Southwest to miss people who have the required aptitudes for friendly service but no airline experience, knowledge, or skill. However, because the knowledge needed and the skills required to be a flight attendant are not exceptional, Southwest cannot afford to miss out on people who have the right aptitude but don't have the experience, knowledge, and skills. Furthermore, given how core the right flight attendants are to Southwest's human capital strategy and how directly its human capital strategy supports its business strategy, missing out on the right talent for flight attendants would be a serious business impediment to Southwest.

In contrast, if Southwest starts with a focus on the required aptitudes rather than skills, it can cast a wider and more effective recruiting net. For example, it might find that candidates who currently work in retail, especially those with high customer interface opportunities, might have the underlying needed aptitudes for friendly customer service. Those high-aptitude candidates, if selected and hired, can be given the knowledge and can acquire the skills required for flight attendants. Because Southwest does, in fact, focus first on the right aptitudes and attitudes for prospective flight attendants, it has discovered that their best flight attendants in fact do come from a wide variety of work experience backgrounds, and the vast majority do not have previous flight attendant experience.

Southwest's current focus on recruiting for the right inherent aptitudes and attitudes versus skills and knowledge for flight attendants goes back to its founder and first CEO, Herb Kelleher. Kelleher once said,

> We'll train you on whatever you need to do, but one thing we can't do is change inherent attitudes in people. I've often said, if I could do that, if I could change [inherent] attitudes, I'd be on Park Avenue making $5,000 an hour as a psychologist. But you can't. Once we've got the people with the right attitude, we can do almost anything....[1]

Selecting

Once the right pool of candidates for the key employee groups have been generated, then it's time to select the best from that pool. Just as the recruiting focus should be first and foremost on the required aptitudes, so too should the selection activities. Again, this may seem intellectually obvious but in practice it is often not done. To illustrate how to do this most effectively, I first need to highlight very briefly a few scientifically validated best practices relative to selection and then illustrate them via Southwest.

There are whole books on best practices when it comes to selection of candidates to hire. There are stacks and stacks of scientific studies that now illuminate what practices work and don't work and why. Let me try to condense 40 years of research into just one paragraph. First, validated tests that measure a particular aptitude or personality trait are much more efficient and reliable than interviews despite the fact that interviews are *the* most used selection technique.[2] Second, structured interviews, meaning that the questions are standardized and not idiosyncratic to the interviewer, are about twice as reliable and predictive of later job performance as unstructured interviews despite the fact that unstructured interviews are used nearly three times as often as structured ones.[3] However, even though structured interviews are significantly better than unstructured interviews, structured interviews on average are only about 25–40% accurate in predicting who will be successful in a job.[4] Therefore, the best selection results are achieved when adding other selection mechanisms to structured interviews. Third, in structured interviews, behavior-based questions are much more effective than other forms of questions.[5] Simplified, behavior-based questions require interviewees to describe either what they have done in specific situations in the past ("retrospective behavior") or what they would do in a given circumstance in the future ("prospective behavior"). An example of a retrospective behavior question would be, "Tell me about a time when you went above and beyond the call of duty for a customer." An example of a prospective behavior question would be, "What would you do if you had a customer who was taking a long time to get settled in the plane and the customer's behavior risked a late departure as a consequence?"

There you go; 40 years of research in one paragraph. With this as a backdrop, let's examine what Southwest does and doesn't do and what changes it might make to ensure its selection practices were optimally aligned to its human capital strategy, at least relative to flight attendants. First, Southwest typically doesn't administer any tests of aptitudes or personality traits like extroversion or need for achievement to flight attendant candidates. Given the long and strong scientific foundation for assessing these aptitudes and the well-established relationship these aptitudes have for key behaviors Southwest needs from flight attendants, Southwest may be missing out on important input into their selection of flight attendants. In Southwest's case, or in any company's case, if there are aptitudes for which there are validated tests, the past 40 years of science says that they should be used. Second, Southwest does use interviews as a principal means of selecting candidates and in general uses structured interviews. Many, but not all, of the questions in the interviews are behaviorally based questions. What is equally, if not more, important than having structured interviews with behaviorally based questions is ensuring that the weight of the questions (and therefore the answers) is proportionally and appropriately allocated to the key attributes. Put differently, although all the questions may be informative, they are not all equally relevant to selecting the right talent.

Let me give you some examples for Southwest. Given that emergencies can happen on a plane, you can make the case that how a person has handled emergencies in the past is a relevant selection criteria. As a consequence, in Southwest flight attendant interviews candidates have been asked, "Tell me about how you handled an emergency in the past?" While this question and the candidate's answer may be informative and relevant, they are not as important as other questions and answers. This is in part because emergencies are relatively infrequent and what flight attendants need to do in the event of an emergency can be taught (and in fact by statue is required to be taught). In contrast, given how often flight attendants interact with less than pleasant or cooperative passengers and given how important friendly service is to Southwest's business strategy, a much more important question is, "Tell me about a situation when you were able to effectively handle an upset customer." Consequently, the answer to this question should also be given more weight than how the candidate has handled an emergency in the past.

While aptitudes can be very important in selecting the right employees, often high levels of skill and knowledge are also required of certain new employees. Clearly in these cases, candidates' current level of both aptitude and ability should be assessed in the selection process. Knowledge is much easier to assess than skill in the context of the normal selection process. You can literally test a person's knowledge level. However, a true measure of skills can only be gained through a demonstration of proficiency. As an illustration, you can easily test how well I know the rules of golf. You can also ask me to describe my skills as a golfer, and my description may tell you some things, but you can only truly and accurately assess my skill level by watching me play (often referred to as behavioral demonstration). However, actual demonstration of skills can be expensive in both time and money. If the required level of skill proficiency is high enough and if skill proficiency has a big enough impact on business outcomes, the cost of assessing that skill in action may be worth it. However, often there are ways to simulate the real world demonstration of skills at a lower cost that still give you a reasonable assessment. For example, in the case of Southwest, being friendly is not just an aptitude but is also a skill the company wants in flight attendants. While it would be costly to observe a candidate's friendly service skills with real passengers, it is not expensive to watch candidates behave with each other. As a consequence, Southwest often conducts group interviews in which they observe and assess how the candidates behave toward each other.

In summary, there are five main points in terms of ensuring that your selection processes are well aligned to and supportive of your human capital strategy. First and most importantly, whatever the selection tools and techniques used, they should be focused on and weighted toward those aptitudes that are most critical to your key employee groups. Second, to the extent possible, validated tests that provide insight into the core aptitudes should be used in the selection process. Third, structured rather than unstructured interviews should be used and the questions in the interview should be behavioral in nature and again weighted in favor of core aptitudes. Fourth, in cases in which knowledge level is critical to job performance, direct tests of that knowledge should be conducted. Fifth and finally, in cases in which current skill level is critical, to the extent of possible demonstration of the skill, even in simulated situations, is always better than having people simply describe their skills and levels of proficiency.

Onboarding

The old saying, "You never get a second chance to make a first impression," is oft quoted because it is true. This adage holds for the outsized impact of onboarding new employees. Again, there are literally tons of research on onboarding, but let me highlight just a few key statistics.[6] First, about half of all hourly workers leave their job within the first three months. Much of this is due to ineffective onboarding. The total replacement costs of these employees are roughly 25% to 50% of the hourly employee's annual compensation. Moving up the organizational hierarchy, half of all executives hired from the outside leave their jobs within 18 months. About 60% cite failure to establish effective relationships early on in the onboarding process as a principal reason. For executives, the replacement costs on a percentage basis are about twice as much as for hourly workers, averaging about 50% to 150% of annual compensation. In contrast to these costs of poorly executed onboarding, effectively implemented onboarding leads to a variety of positive outcomes, including higher satisfaction, more commitment to the organization, lower turnover, higher performance, and less stress.

This naturally raises the question: How can onboarding be done right or what are the keys to doing it effectively? Again invoking the Pareto Principle, there are four things that account for achieving 80% of the desired positive results: crystalizing the strategy and employees' role in it, clarifying job expectations, enhancing understanding of the company culture, and facilitating social integration.

Strategy. First and foremost, employees who are in "traction points" in the company strategy need to understand their position and role relative to the strategy from the outset. Only through that understanding can they use their brains and discretion to make wise decisions every day to help advance the strategy when they are doing their jobs even if no one is watching. If you want baggage handlers at Southwest to not just throw bags on the plane and kick them off, they need to understand how their productivity fits in the strategy, and in particular, how their performance impacts the company's business model. They also need to understand how their productivity comes back to benefit them in higher bonuses that come directly from higher company profits. If you want flight attendants to be friendly on their last flight after four days of being away from home and dealing with more than 3,000 customers during that time, they need to understand the strategy and their role in it. Unfortunately, too often new employees are told about the company policies, the rules and regulations, their specific jobs, and so on but are told nothing about the company strategy or their role in it. When they are told the strategy and their role in it, from my experience, this is best done by the CEO or a similar top executive and not by someone in HR. No one has more credibility when it comes to articulating the company's business strategy than the CEO and no one lends more symbolic importance to the topic in the minds of new employees and creates a more powerful first impression than the CEO. Over the years, I've seen many CEOs do this. Among all of them, one of the real masters of this is David Neeleman, the founder and former CEO of JetBlue, which incidentally is the only U.S.-based airline to ever beat Southwest in customer satisfaction. Neeleman would explain in simple language (a) the most important factors that drive revenue up, (b) the most important activities that drive costs down, and (c) how both those outcomes helped JetBlue make money and share those benefits with workers. He was then great at helping each key category of workers understand how they could do their job in a way that supported the business model and strategy.

Job Expectations. Clearly new employees need to understand their jobs, but in the context of key human capital, the job clarification should be an extension and continuation of the strategy conversation. In other words, the objective of clarifying job expectations is not just so new employees understand what their jobs are but understand how to do their jobs in a way that supports the strategy. Here the best work I have seen involves not providing dry, written job descriptions but video tapes of on-target and off-target behavior, war stories from star employees, and role plays. Why use these techniques versus the traditional long, written job description? The answer is simple and tied to human biology. Humans are remarkably symbolic creatures, and as such, if they are provided vivid examples of on-target and off-target behavior, they can fill in between the lines. This is why we tell children stories and highlight the "moral of the story" and don't dive deeply into all the rules and regulations, policies and procedures, etc. People, even children, can see examples of the right and wrong behaviors and color in the rest of the picture. In addition, the relational structure of stories, videos, examples, role plays all have the added benefit that they fit how the human brain is organized and structured and therefore are much better remembered and recalled than a long list of bullet points in a PowerPoint presentation or meticulously detailed in a written job description.

Organization Culture. The third area to properly convey during the onboarding period is the culture of the company. Although most companies have formally espoused values and it can't hurt to tell people these, that is not the essence of helping new hires understand the organization's culture. There are two reasons for this. First, sometimes what are espoused as the values of the company are just that—espoused but not really lived. Actually, making too much of espoused values that are not lived can be dangerous. Specifically, if leading new hires to believe the culture is one way when it is not is a sure way to lessen commitment to the organization and increase turnover. Why? While it may not be the intent of the organization to "lie," often when people are told one thing and reality turns out to be another, they feel they have been deliberately mislead at best or lied to at worst. Neither of these conclusions leads to higher satisfaction, commitment, and performance or to lower turnover; they lead to the opposite. As a consequence, the best way to convey the culture is again to provide vivid examples of it in action. The rationale for this approach relative to helping people understand the culture is the same as for taking a more symbolic rather than descriptive approach to helping people understand their jobs; it fits with how the human brain is structured and consequently is what works best in terms of making an impression and making a lasting mark.

Networks. Finally, because not everything can or should be conveyed to new employees on the first day or even in the first week, it is important to help them make the social connections that can help fill in the blanks as time goes on and can help reinforce all the pictures and colors that were painted during "orientation." On this point, sometimes executives will comment, "Yes, helping people make social connections and integrate makes great sense, but you can't force these things. Not everyone clicks with everyone. Don't you have to let the natural fits between people just happen?" The short answer is, "No." The point of these early social connections is not to match people up to form friendships. It is to ensure that newcomers know and have connections to the people you want them to; you want them connected to those employees who are exemplars of desired behaviors. You do not want to leave it to chance that newcomers will link up with people who understand the strategy, understand key jobs support and enable the strategy, and understand what the cultural values are that need to be reinforced. These issues are too important to leave to Lady Luck or Charlie Chance.

Training

Training is an inevitable part of onboarding and an important opportunity to reinforce key elements of your business strategy in general and your human capital strategy in particular. Even when the people you hire already have the experience and skill you need, the chances are good that you need to train them to employ that experience and those skills in somewhat unique ways that best fit your strategy. For example, Southwest generally hires pilots that know how to fly planes (good thing, right?) and they often have thousands of flight hours. What may be different, however, is that for Southwest often those pilots are going to fly many more shorter routes as part of Southwest's point-to-point flight strategy compared to other airlines. As a consequence, its pilots have more takeoffs per day than pilots at other airlines. This matters for two reasons. First, takeoffs are the most fuel-consuming part of any flight. Second, fuel consumption is the second largest expense within Southwest. As a consequence, Southwest trains its pilots in how to take off safely but economically.

Training that is aligned with the company strategy is required for other job categories within Southwest as well, such as baggage handlers. Because Southwest doesn't charge a fee for checked bags, on average it handles more checked bags per customer than other airlines. In addition, because it tries to turn planes around almost twice as fast as most other airlines (in about

35 minutes), passenger bags have to be loaded and unloaded more quickly at Southwest than at other airlines. Combined, these two factors mean that Southwest baggage handlers must load and unload more bags per minute than any other baggage handlers working for virtually any airline anywhere in the world. At the same time, no matter how friendly the service before, during, or after the flight, if customer's bags are damaged or lost, they are unlikely to feel great about their experience and subsequently may be less likely to fly Southwest again or may even complain about Southwest to friends and family, who in turn might then be less likely to fly on Southwest. As a consequence, Southwest baggage handlers (a) have to get more bags on and off planes faster than their peers at other airlines, (b) have to do this higher volume in less time, and (c) have to do this at least as well (in terms of damage or lost luggage), if not better, than their peers at other airlines. Clearly, within this strategic and human capital context, Southwest's training of baggage handlers cannot be just average. It has to be done in such a way that baggage handlers see the connection between how they do their job and the company strategy and develop the knowledge and skill to move more bags per minute at a comparable or higher quality level than those at any other airline.

Managing

The task of managing employees needs to focus primarily on three things: feedback, rewards, and development. Books have been written on each of these topics, but what really matters can be condensed into just a few paragraphs.

Feedback. There is no need to explain in any detail why feedback matters. Every manager or top executive understand that humans need feedback both to continue doing what they should the way they should and to make changes or corrections. Where the greatest discussion takes place is in how to effectively give feedback. Again let me condense decades of research into a few simple rules.

- Give feedback as soon after the positive or negative incident as possible.
- Positive feedback designed to reinforce desired behaviors and performance can be given in private or in public.

- Corrective feedback designed to change behaviors and performance should be given in private.
- Feedback (positive or negative) should be specific in terms of the situation, the behavior, and the consequences.

As an example of the last point, assume you had a conference call with your team yesterday. Brad interrupted people during the call and you want to have him stop this behavior and listen more carefully to people. You could say, "Brad, I think you need to work on your interpersonal and listening skills." No surprise, decades of research and practice find that this feedback will have little impact on changing Brad's behavior. You could be a bit more specific and say, "Brad, you sometimes interrupt people." This is better in that it has some specificity regarding the interpersonal behavior or interrupting but the situation is not specific and neither are the consequences. A much more effective wording of the feedback would be: "Yesterday when we had our conference call (situation), you interrupted Lisa and didn't let her finish her comment on the sales report (behavior) and I noticed that after that she didn't say much else (consequence)." You could then use the same three criteria for effective feedback for constructive change: "Brad, on our next call, if you let Lisa finish her point, and in fact if you ask one or two questions of her, she is likely to not only fully share her ideas but be much more willing to listen to and be interested in your ideas."

Rewards. The phrase, "What gets rewarded get repeated" is often said because it is true. To understand how powerful rewards can be, consider the following case. Several years ago I was doing some consulting with a package delivery company that had customer service as a key part of its strategy. It did a good job of recruiting and selecting new employees for the call centers with a customer service orientation, of onboarding them, and training them. However, they rewarded them for the number of calls they answered per hour. This created a financial incentive not to solve customers' problems but to get customers off the phone or passed on to another department as fast and possible, which as you can easily imagine did not lead to satisfied customers. In this case, misaligned rewards essentially undid all the time, effort, and money to get the right human capital. In this case, the reward had to be changed from being based only on efficiency (i.e., number of customer calls answered per hour) to that plus a measure of effectiveness (i.e., customer satisfaction). By combining these two measures and rewarding call center employees on the combined results (with customer satisfaction weighted about 50% more heavily than number of customers served per hour), call center employee behavior changed, customer satisfaction improved, and revenue also increased. It may seem simple but rewards, both financial and nonfinancial, need to be aligned to reinforce the behaviors among the key employee groups that support the strategy.

Development. Finally, because employees typically do not stay in the same job forever, ensuring that the human capital are aligned with the strategy requires developing people for their next responsibilities that also align with and contribute to the strategy. On this topic as well, scores of books have been published. However, again, the key principles can be condensed into just a few points. First, there is no substitute for finding out what other responsibilities employees themselves want. People typically do best what interests them most. Therefore, the first step in effective development is to find out what individual employees want to do. Second, there is also no substitute for candid descriptions of what is required to do, what employees might be interest in, and how close or far away you as the manager feel they are. For example, moving from being a customer service agent at a package delivery company to being a supervisor of other agents requires a shift from just a customer service focus to also an employee focus. As a supervisor you can just focus on delivering good customer service but you have to focus on what will inspire and motivate your agents to deliver superior customer service. This is a very different capability than simply trying to understand and solve customer problems. Third and finally, effective development requires giving employees structured opportunities to build and demonstrate the aptitudes, attitudes, skills, and knowledge required in the new responsibilities. Waiting until after the promotion to see if people can do the new job is a high-risk strategy. It is much better for the person and the organization to give that person some small opportunities to demonstrate the key capabilities required in the new responsibilities. For example, having an employee step up to the team manager role while you are on holiday could be an effective means of not only helping the individual really understand what new capabilities are required but to see if the individual can switch from only thinking about how they personally can serve customers to thinking about how to motivate and inspire others to serve customers.

The following assessment tool can be used to get a more empirical sense of how aligned or not your practices are to the human capital strategy.

Recruiting & Selection

	1	2	3	4	5	6
Recruiting & Selection						
1. We know where to find the best people for key positions at the entry level.	Strongly Disagree	Disagree	Somewhat Disagree	Somewhat Agree	Agree	Strongly Agree
2. At the entry level we get the people we want; our "yield rate" is high (80%+).	Strongly Disagree	Disagree	Somewhat Disagree	Somewhat Agree	Agree	Strongly Agree
3. Our reputation as an employer is so strong that often the best people seek us out.	Strongly Disagree	Disagree	Somewhat Disagree	Somewhat Agree	Agree	Strongly Agree
4. We are successful at recruiting and integrating great outside hires from the middle manager to executive level.	Strongly Disagree	Disagree	Somewhat Disagree	Somewhat Agree	Agree	Strongly Agree
5. We consistently use proven selection techniques such as structured, behavior-based interviews.	Strongly Disagree	Disagree	Somewhat Disagree	Somewhat Agree	Agree	Strongly Agree
6. We keep track of our selectivity and selection success.	Strongly Disagree	Disagree	Somewhat Disagree	Somewhat Agree	Agree	Strongly Agree
Orientation & Training						
7. All new employees (regardless of level) receive orientation that includes issues relative to company strategy, structure, culture, as well as policy orientation.	Strongly Disagree	Disagree	Somewhat Disagree	Somewhat Agree	Agree	Strongly Agree
8. Senior executives are involved in orientation programs.	Strongly Disagree	Disagree	Somewhat Disagree	Somewhat Agree	Agree	Strongly Agree

(Continued)

	1	2	3	4	5	6
9. We have a system of keeping track of who needs what training and whether the training has been completed.	Strongly Disagree	Disagree	Somewhat Disagree	Somewhat Agree	Agree	Strongly Agree
10. We have a system for evaluating the effectiveness of training provided internally or by external vendors.	Strongly Disagree	Disagree	Somewhat Disagree	Somewhat Agree	Agree	Strongly Agree
11. Senior executives are involved in delivering some of our most important training programs.	Strongly Disagree	Disagree	Somewhat Disagree	Somewhat Agree	Agree	Strongly Agree
12. We benchmark our training practices at least every five years.	Strongly Disagree	Disagree	Somewhat Disagree	Somewhat Agree	Agree	Strongly Agree
Performance Management						
13. All employees have SMART (Specific, Measurable, Agreed to, Realistic, Time-bound) goals.	Strongly Disagree	Disagree	Somewhat Disagree	Somewhat Agree	Agree	Strongly Agree
14. We know who the poor performers are and deal with them effectively.	Strongly Disagree	Disagree	Somewhat Disagree	Somewhat Agree	Agree	Strongly Agree
15. We know who the high performers are and reward them proportionately.	Strongly Disagree	Disagree	Somewhat Disagree	Somewhat Agree	Agree	Strongly Agree
16. Individuals can see how their goals are tied to or aligned with company goals.	Strongly Disagree	Disagree	Somewhat Disagree	Somewhat Agree	Agree	Strongly Agree
17. Employees receive effective feedback on their performance at least twice a year.	Strongly Disagree	Disagree	Somewhat Disagree	Somewhat Agree	Agree	Strongly Agree

(Continued)

	1	2	3	4	5	6
18. Employees would say we have a performance oriented culture.	Strongly Disagree	Disagree	Somewhat Disagree	Somewhat Agree	Agree	Strongly Agree
Development & Succession Planning						
19. We systematically gather data on future potential of people through techniques such as 360 assessments.	Strongly Disagree	Disagree	Somewhat Disagree	Somewhat Agree	Agree	Strongly Agree
20. We know who our high potential leaders are at all levels of the company.	Strongly Disagree	Disagree	Somewhat Disagree	Somewhat Agree	Agree	Strongly Agree
21. We have a systematic means of assessing future leadership potential.	Strongly Disagree	Disagree	Somewhat Disagree	Somewhat Agree	Agree	Strongly Agree
22. High potential leaders get systematic feedback on their strengths and weaknesses.	Strongly Disagree	Disagree	Somewhat Disagree	Somewhat Agree	Agree	Strongly Agree
23. We have a strong ratio of potential leaders for every position (at least 2:1).	Strongly Disagree	Disagree	Somewhat Disagree	Somewhat Agree	Agree	Strongly Agree
24. In our organization succession planning is more than position replacement planning.	Strongly Disagree	Disagree	Somewhat Disagree	Somewhat Agree	Agree	Strongly Agree

At the end of the day, all the good work that Chapters 1–9 might inspire can be undone by misalignment of key activities covered here in Chapter 10. It is therefore critical to be thorough and candid in assessing the alignment of what I call the Supporting Five Star Processes.

Notes

1. Joseph H. Boyett and Jimmie T. Boyet, 2001. *The Guru Guide to Entrepreneurship: a Concise Guide to the Best Ideas from the World's Top Entrepreneurs*. Wiley.
2. Angelo S. DeNisi and Ricky W. Griffin, 2014. *HR*, South-Western Cengage Learning.
3. Ibid.
4. Ibid.
5. Ibid.
6. Talya Bauer, 2010. *Onboarding New Employees*, SHRM Foundation, Alexandria, VA.

Conclusion

Let me return to where we began. I started this book by asking seven key questions:

1. Are *people* your firm's most important asset?	Yes	No
2. Does your company seek to be the *employer of choice* in its industry?	Yes	No
3. Is it harder these days than in the past to attract and retain the best talent?	Yes	No
4. Does the quality of talent make a difference to your company's performance?	Yes	No
5. Does your firm have a clear strategy for becoming the employer of choice?	Yes	No
6. Does your firm have good metrics for determining how you're doing as an employer of choice?	Yes	No
7. Do you hold managers and executives accountable for their successes and failures in waging and winning the war for top talent?	Yes	No

If you answered "Yes" to questions #1 and #2, hopefully now you have a much deeper understanding of why people are your most important asset and why you have no choice but to be the employer of choice. If you answered "Yes" to #3, hopefully now you not only understand why it is getting more and more difficult to compete *for* human capital, but you understand how to get the people you want to want you; you know how to construct a compelling employee value proposition. If you answered "Yes" to question #4, you now have a clearer idea of why human capital plays such an important role in firm performance these days and why that role will only grow in the future. Some of you may have answered "Yes" or "No" to question #5. Even if you answered "Yes" to question #5, my hope is that at this point you have a much clearer understanding that having a strategy for how to become an employer of choice first requires a crystal clear business strategy and set of competitive advantages because such is the north star to which an employee of choice strategy must be aligned. If you got to the end of this book, I'm willing to bet that you answered "No" to questions #6 and #7, especially #7. Hopefully, at this point, you can see that holding executives accountable for their successes and failures relative to human capital is not just about establishing metrics or KPIs, or even building a culture of accountability. It is a natural and required outcome of doing all the other things covered in this book. When the business strategy is clear, when the sources of competitive advantage are crystalized, then and only then can you determine the type of human capital you need. Only at that point can you construct an employee value proposition that gets the people you want to want you. Only at that point can you ensure alignment of the Supporting Five Stars Processes. Once you have all this, what you need to hold executives accountable for and why is clear and almost unavoidable. At that point you are well positioned not only to win the contest *for* human capital but also to win your competitive battles *with* human capital. With this you are well positioned for competition in the final frontier.

Index

Taylor & Francis eBooks

www.taylorfrancis.com

A single destination for eBooks from Taylor & Francis
with increased functionality and an improved user
experience to meet the needs of our customers.

90,000+ eBooks of award-winning academic content in
Humanities, Social Science, Science, Technology, Engineering,
and Medical written by a global network of editors and authors.

TAYLOR & FRANCIS EBOOKS OFFERS:

A streamlined
experience for
our library
customers

A single point
of discovery
for all of our
eBook content

Improved
search and
discovery of
content at both
book and
chapter level

REQUEST A FREE TRIAL
support@taylorfrancis.com

 Routledge
Taylor & Francis Group

 CRC Press
Taylor & Francis Group